COLLISION COURSE

The Vatican, the Nuns of America and the Meaning of Obedience

By

CAROL W. GALLIGAN, Ph.D.

Publisher's Cataloging-in-Publication data

Galligan, Carol.
Collision Course: The Vatican, the Nuns of America and the Meaning of Obedience

ISBN-13: 978-1985886902
ISBN-10: 1985886901

1. History 2. Religious Studies 3. Church Institutions and Organizations 4. Churches and Church Leadership

Cover by Jennifer Marmorato
Cover photo credit: Nuns on the Bus/NETWORK Lobby (Jennifer Wong)
Author photograph by Charity Robey

Printed in the United States of America

10 9 8 7 6 5 4 3 2 1

DEDICATION

To the women who raised me - my mother and her sisters - with more gratitude than I can say.

Preface

A word of welcome, apology and advice to non-Catholic readers and many-years-lapsed Catholics about to begin this book; you may well feel like "strangers in a strange land." Church-speak, nun-speak, abbreviations and acronyms can feel confusing and probably at times, daunting. The following may help: until you feel familiar with the players, read with one finger in Appendix A, a glossary of terms and another in Appendix B, a time line of key events, so you can flip back and forth easily. Once you have your sea legs, when you feel you know who's who and where they stand, you won't need to do this, but it might help initially.

Nuns across the United States have been willing, in fact eager, to be interviewed for this book; over and over they have told me that "writing this book is doing God's work." I hope they're right.

Please note several minor authorial conventions:

The terms "nuns" and "sisters," following current usage, will be used here interchangeably.

Popes will be referred to by their given names with their papal names immediately following in parentheses. This is in no way intended as disrespect and hopefully will not be taken as such. It is intended only to remind the reader that before these men were popes, these popes were men; as individuals, they were and are as dramatically different as American presidents. Think Jimmy Carter and John Kennedy or Ronald Reagan and Richard Nixon.

The first name, Joseph, of Joseph Ratzinger (Benedict 16) is often spelled in the European way, as Josef. Since he uses the first spelling on his own stationary, that form will be used here.

In addition, footnotes appear at the end of each section.

TABLE OF CONTENTS

PART ONE

Part One

For the past several decades, thoughtful dissent, especially by a majority of American nuns, has been experienced by the Vatican not as dissent, but defiance. Most recently, and never covered fully in the main stream press, a new Inquisition has been in progress, aimed squarely at those nuns, the eighty percent of American sisters who belong to the Leadership Conference of Women Religious. This group, the LCWR, began in 1956 when the mothers superior of the almost 300 orders of American nuns banded together in a mutual aid organization. As the decades advanced, tensions between the group and the Vatican increased. Finally, a decision was made and action taken – the nuns were to be "reined in." Two divisions of the all-male Roman Curia, the congregations assisting the Pope in governing the Catholic Church, led the assault.

The Congregation for Institutes of Consecrated Life and Societies of Apostolic Life, most frequently referred to as CICLSAL, is charged with the governance of both male and female religious. It began an Apostolic Visitation (or investigation) of the LCWR members in 2008, concluding in December of 2014. The reasons given for the examination were possible "irregularities and/or omissions in American religious life," "a certain 'feminist' spirit," and "a certain secularist mentality."[1]

The Congregation for the Doctrine of the Faith, the CDF, began a Doctrinal Assessment a year later; at its conclusion in 2012, the nuns were accused of "corporate dissent" on issues of abortion, women's ordination, the promotion of "certain radical feminist themes," ministry to the "homosexual community," and an "over-involvement in issues of social justice."[2] In 2012, the sisters were placed for all intents and purposes in receivership, under the mandated authority of an American archbishop, to last for a period of five years, during which time demanded changes were to be completed and all decisions would require that archbishops' approval. The mandate was concluded abruptly and without explanation in April, 2015; a report of eleven hundred words was issued.

The seeds of this present conflict had been sewn and watered many years earlier, in 1950, well before the LCWR came into being, when Eugenio Pacelli (Pius 12) charted a new course for his American nuns. His goal was to elevate the American parochial school system to a position of competitive choice for Catholic parents and for this he needed his nuns educated, actually well-educated.

So he sent his nuns to school. Under the umbrella of the newly formed Sister Formation Conference (SFC), to the dismay of the American bishops who had to fund their replacements in the classroom, these young women, many barely out of their teenage years, were sent out of their strictly regulated convents where they lived according to "The Rule," an elaborate and highly detailed system of schedules and regulations. They were sent into the worlds beyond those walls and to the unforeseen consequences these far-away men had approved for them. The years that followed became, actually, an ongoing saga of unforeseen consequences.

The nuns were sent to Catholic colleges when they were accessible, elsewhere when they were not. They mixed freely with non-Catholics (many for the first time in their lives) and they learned. And learned and learned. They took undergraduate degrees and graduate degrees. And they grew self-confident. Apparently neither Pacelli (Pius 12) nor the men who assisted him in this plan, stopped to ask the now-obvious question: *What would happen on that day when most nuns were better educated than most bishops?* And they soon were.

Then in 1962, Angelo Roncalli (John 23) convened the now famous (or infamous, depending on one's viewpoint) meeting of Catholic prelates, Vatican II. This would be the 21st convocation of Church officials, called in the history of the Roman Catholic Church. It ran for four autumn sessions of eight to ten weeks, opening in October, 1962 and closing in December, 1965, with four corresponding interim "working periods." The previous convocation had been held a century earlier. Vatican II's stated purpose was to examine and finalize internal doctrinal issues, as well as the Church's relationship to the modern world. It was convened by Angelo Roncalli (John 23) who hoped it would be a process of "aggiornamento" or modernization. And it was.

In all, the convocation issued sixteen decrees; among these was the decree Perfectae Caritatis, (See Appendix C) ordering the sisters into the wider world. This decree *specifically* commanded every order of sisters to engage in a process of renewal, to revisit and reassess the aims of their individual founders and to question the degree to which they were still faithful to those original intentions. With these instructions, the sisters were inadvertently set on a course of eventual, actually inevitable, collision with the conservative elements of the Roman power structure.

These nuns had been *living* "feminism," a movement yet to make headlines. They were, along with graduates of the Seven Sisters,[3] among the best educated women in America. They were women CEOs before women CEOs had been imagined, heading Catholic schools and hospitals, founding universities. It is not surprising then that when called "to renew," they moved to warp speed.

But conservative factions within the Curia had been further bolstered after Vatican II's end by the subsequent election of two conservative popes, both committed to restorationist/preconciliar agendas. The liberals of Vatican II, who commanded the renewal process, few of whom were American, had indeed dominated the Council, but the liberals had gone home; in the years that followed, they did not dominate the meeting's aftermath. And there were few American prelates among the liberal bloc.

The nuns contend that what they have done in the recent decades is what Vatican II commanded them to do; the Vatican contends that they have gone well beyond that. And too far. The nuns believe they have simply returned to their roots, "stepped sideways"[4] as one nun put it, out of the hierarchical structure. Each individual order, after literally years of prayerful discernment, has sought to return to its earliest "charism," that is, its own particular animating spirit, its unique reason for being. Their goal was to function again as each of their founders originally intended. They don't see themselves as "the new nuns," but rather as "the original nuns." They believe this is what Vatican II had asked of them.

In earlier periods of American Catholicism, each order had been an independent group. The orders functioned autonomously, within Canon law, but independent of the local clerics. They walked the path determined by their founder, as missionaries, or teachers or ministers to the sick and those in need. Then Vatican II asked them if they were still faithful to their original instruction. Had they changed? And if they had, who or what had they become? Had the needs of the Church, over many decades, with the huge increase in the Catholic population of America, led them far afield? And if the answer was yes, then what should be done?

The nuns of the LCWR began a process of self-examination – of themselves, their priorities, their place within the Catholic faith and their place in the wider world. Decades of that self-examination led to profound redefinitions and it is these redefinitions that have raised even more serious, although unwelcome, questions. How is a religion practiced? How is obedience defined? What role does conscience play? Where does authority lie? To whom does one make a vow? What degree of religious freedom exists within Roman Catholicism?

And perhaps the most important question of all, the underlying issue throughout, how closely does the Catholic Church still walk in the footsteps of Jesus?

The two actions, the Apostolic Visitation, begun in 2008, and the Doctrinal Assessment, begun in 2009, were revelatory; perhaps unwittingly, spot lights had been turned on. Conflicts rarely acknowledged came immediately into sharper focus. A gulf that had gone ignored was now clearly defined, and the depth of that gulf was immeasurable. Whose values are reflected when the Church acts?

Liberal clerics had raised these issues for decades; these were valid questions. But liberal clerics could be ignored or silenced, and they were. No liberal cleric had important, well-organized world-wide groups behind him as the sisters did; nor was any one of them well enough known for the American Catholic population to experience outrage as they did when they perceived their nuns assaulted. But powerful conservatives, including right-to-life groups, the right-wing Catholic press, and certain influential Catholic prelates, continued to raise their voices in anger as the sisters persisted in the path they had defined. The Vatican then made a choice. They chose to listen to those voices. And to act.

To understand what these nuns have become, and why they have taken the road they have, a step back, a visit to the world of the typical sister, living communally in 1950, more than a decade before Vatican II began, would be a useful place to begin to look for an understanding of the situation's complexity.

Before Vatican II:

In the 1950s, the then more than 185,000 sisters had become in fact a Catholic army, to be deployed as troops where needed, by bishops and cardinals in command; although occasional lip service was paid to their value and compliments routinely delivered, in fact, sisters were taken for granted, much as privates and noncommissioned officers are in any other army. They were paid half of what brothers and priests were paid, not enrolled in Social Security as their male counterparts were and had no say in their individual deployment. Yet without them, Catholic schools, Catholic hospitals and Catholic social service agencies could not have functioned. If the sisters were resentful, they never said so.

Most of them, many still in their teens, had only high school diplomas; they taught all grades and subjects in the Church's extensive parochial school system with no training in how to do so. A small percentage of the older sisters had college and graduate degrees, always achieved by what they humorously referred to as "20-year plans," a reference to the credits won in endless summer sessions. No one of them had yet been given the opportunity to attend classes full-time; to want a college degree had the smell of "excessive pride."

Postulancy was the first phase of "formation," the process in which they were "formed" into nuns. During this period the future sister was to become accustomed to the discipline and requirements of her convent and examine her motives for being there. When beginning her novitiate, the next phase, depending on the congregation she had chosen, there would most likely be a "wedding service," in which she would wear a long white gown and become, as watching relatives wept, a "Bride of Christ." She was most likely given a wedding ring as well, and as secular brides did, received a new name, signifying a new life, not in "the real world" but in their own "life in Christ."

It was the task of the Mother Superior, whose words were accepted as absolute and authoritative, to replace any sense of individuality with an unquestioning compliance. Nuns were not to think for themselves; others, more able, would do their thinking for them. "Emphasis was placed on humility, self-forgetfulness, and subservience. Self-promotion and pride were the besetting sins."[5] These, when they appeared, were met with various forms of obligatory penance, not intended as punishment but as an assist on the pathway to sanctification. These included "kneeling during the meal, kissing the feet of other sisters, and lying on the floor of the entryway for sisters to step over on their way in."[6] Mail, both outgoing and incoming was read by the mother superior; there were no radios or television sets. "Silence was the norm … except during meals [when] excerpts from holy books were read aloud."[7]

The system of acceptable behaviors was called The Rule. "Keep the Rule," candidates were told, "and the Rule will keep you."[8] The Rule contained literally hundreds of requirements. "Particular friendships" were not to be allowed to develop; hands were to be kept folded and under the scapular, out of sight. Their walk was to be seemly; they were to "glide." As well, there was a stricture "against immodesty, a 'custody of the eyes' commandment intended to prevent provocative or indulgent gazes."[9]

Families had reason to weep when they relinquished their daughters to the convent; in most congregations family contact was allowed only once a year, and then while home, the sister was to eat alone, lest in the fellowship of family she be reminded of the love she had left behind. Indeed, as little contact with non-religious as possible was the desired course; they were to speak to non-religious only in the course of their assigned work and then only when necessary. One sister of St. Joseph still had vivid memories of those times.

Reminiscing, she recounted how "Every year, because we worked in hospitals, we went to the annual meeting of the regional hospital association," she said. "We would be driven to the meeting in a big chauffeured limousine and hear the speakers and discussion. But at lunch time, instead of eating with the others in the hotel, we filed out of the hotel, climbed into the limo and ate the sandwiches we had brought with us, while the driver kept circling the parking lot so he wouldn't block traffic. That was to help us stay away from talking to strangers."[10]

Eventually, when fully "formed," a sister was sent to work and it was then that she began to lead a double life; from 5 to 9 AM, she prayed and ate and from 9 AM to 5 PM, swathed in a black habit reaching to the ground, and with every single lock of hair hidden within her starched, white wimple, that headdress from the 18th century, she worked "in the real world," most likely in either a school, a hospital or a social service agency.[11] Returning to the convent, from 5 PM to 9 PM she prayed and ate. Then, at an appointed hour, mandated by the mother superior, she slept. According to the Code of Canon Law, this was as it should be.

The Code considered "consecration and apostolate," in other words, prayer and work, to be *unequal* components of the religious life. Rome held that convent-centered prayer defined the sisters' worth; Rome saw their work as secondary. If that view has changed, no doctrine has said so; the sisters, however, whatever they may have believed then, certainly do not believe that now. It may be that at base, it is this differing view, the question of how their worth is defined and *should* be defined, that is one of the issues underlying the current conflict. But this was the hybrid culture that dominated religious life for women from the 1920s through the 1950s.

Among the women who had achieved degrees under various 20-year (or longer) plans were a small number of sisters committed to changing the formation process; coincidently, Eugenio Pacelli (Pius 12) was in complete agreement with their aims. The women were concerned with the development of sisters into better educated and more mature *individuals*; Pacelli (Pius 12) was concerned with his American parochial school system remaining competitive with the public schools, just then beginning to formulate stricter requirements for teachers and principals.

Despite their different motives, it was to mutual advantage that they sought a common goal. The idea of studying and having a degree before stepping into the elementary and high school classroom was counter to the traditional way of educating sisters. Acquiring a degree before entering the classroom would be an almost total renovation of the usual educational plan, and left many bishops irate. Now replacements had to be hired and paid for. But it was an idea whose time had come.

Pacelli (Pius 12) encouraged reforms "aimed at making sisters more effective in their public works."[12] Religious life, he believed, had to adapt if it was to remain relevant. He wanted sisters to "consider modernizing or eliminating outdated customs and to improve the educational level of religious in teaching institutions."[13] He thought the habit was off-putting, introducing an immediate distance into relationships. A sister in full habit, seen anywhere, was hardly inconspicuous, was actually rather an arresting sight. Since they were required always to travel in twos, it might be described as "doubly arresting."

In order to facilitate the implementation of his plans he organized a series of international congresses between 1950 and 1952 and he used his addresses at these meetings to clarify his ideas. And he both inspired and influenced the women attending, more than he may have realized and more than he may have intended.

It was a novel experience at the time for superiors from diverse congregations to meet together, to formulate ideas in each other's company, in fact to cooperate at all, in any way; the women found the process, unsurprisingly, being women, very much to their liking.

As a consequence, "National conferences of sisters that began as obedient responses to papal mandate often developed into vehicles for the particular aspirations of American women religious"[14] and again, unforeseen consequences followed.

Sister Madeleva Wolff, CSC, presented the first paper calling for reform of formation at the 1949 annual meeting of the National Catholic Education Association (NCEA). She had written 19 books and was then president of St. Mary's College in South Bend, Indiana. She had founded the Graduate School of Sacred Theology there in 1944, the first of its kind for women.

In agreement with her, a small group of sisters began to meet and to develop strategies to deal with what they believed to be significant deficiencies in their younger sisters. Then in 1952 the NCEA inaugurated a panel discussion on Pacelli's (Pius 12) ideas. Remarks by Sister Emil Penet, IHM, took center stage. Penet held a Doctor of Philosophy degree from Saint Louis University, awarded in 1951. (The chairman of her dissertation committee had observed that Sister Mary Emil had the mind of a man. It was intended as a compliment.) "Sisters banded together to implement the panel's recommendation that religious collectively create a more coherent and consistent plan for educating and training young sisters. In 1954 this grassroots organization of American women religious named itself the Sister Formation Conference."[15]

"The concept of formation pioneered by the SFC aimed [to replace] the prior emphasis on developing uniformity and obedience in young sisters with a model that sought to nourish and develop the singular and unique potential of each religious as an individual."[16] This may have been a "feminist" idea, although hardly a "radical" one; it certainly was a psychologically sound idea, a rational and logical idea, and it could be said, an idea found in the gospels. Sisters speaking to sisters about sister problems was indeed new, although again more logical than "feminist," and would as the years went on, become the norm.

One of the first moves made by the SFC, perhaps the most important, and one again with many unforeseen consequences, was the monthly publication of the Sister Formation Bulletin; the first issue was published in October 1954. For the first time all congregations were receiving the same information. It was required reading in most convents, often read aloud at meals. A sense of internal isolationism, an integral part of religious life for sisters had finally been challenged. And challenged successfully.[17]

Sister Ritamary Bradley, CHM, was the first editor. She had completed an undergraduate degree in 1938 at Marygrove College, a Masters from St. Ambrose College in 1942 and would be awarded a doctorate from St. Louis University in June 1954. Margot H. Kane, at a tribute to Bradley after her death in 2000, remembered her working as a housekeeper for a local bishop, a congenial and kindly man who allowed his housekeepers to avail themselves of his very good library.

Theological disputes and controversial clerics were covered in the Bulletin and this caused the first stir of uneasiness. Tough minded criticism, theological engagement, had never characterized sisters, in their interactions or their writings. It was not only the seriousness with which the sisters had become engaged that generated concerns among the hierarchy; sisters were moving into positions of leadership. This was new.

Then in 1956 the first formal organization representing women's communities, the Conference of Major Women's Superiors, later to be renamed the Leadership Conference of Women Religious, the LCWR, was founded. Close to 300 major superiors approved and joined, representing their individual orders. By 1957 there was for the first time active and ongoing cooperation and communication among individual sisters and between religious communities.

By 1962 when Vatican II opened, the American sister was a well-educated, self-confident woman, with a responsible position in a world outside the convent. A survey of the women first elected to the U.S. Congress revealed that a majority of them were graduates of small Catholic women's colleges. They had been given examples early in life, of competent and intelligent women, living careers that in "the real world," if that had even been possible, would indeed have marked them as "liberated" or as "feminists." Those colleges had been designed, organized, financed and staffed by nuns, who had yet to hear the word "sisterhood," except of course, insofar as it applied to themselves.

The Congregation for the Doctrine of the Faith, the CDF, began a Doctrinal Assessment a year later; at its conclusion in 2012, the nuns faced extensive accusations, as detailed earlier in this chapter. "Feminist" principles, as well as their ongoing involvement in current affairs appeared to rankle significantly. Unpleasant consequences then followed.

In 2012, the sisters were placed for all intents and purposes in receivership, under the mandated authority of an American archbishop, to last for a period of five years, during which time the demanded changes would be implemented.

The Sister Formation Conference.

The photograph is offered for the benefit of those under the age of fifty, who may never have glimpsed a nun in full habit. Their different headgear represent their different orders.

Vatican II:

Then Angelo Roncalli (John 23), on January 25, 1959, less than 90 days after his election to the papacy, electrified the Catholic world with the announcement of his plans for Vatican II, to open in 1962. The Roman cardinals, taken completely by surprise, were stunned. A sitting Pope had declared the need for change. No one knew what to expect, but everyone, liberals and conservatives alike, knew there would be conflict. Men in high places began to prepare. The nuns of America were more than electrified. They wondered what was to come. They waited; with no role to play they could only watch as battle lines were drawn. With more than two years in which to plan, positions could be taken, sides chosen. And they were.

Leon Cardinal Joseph Suenens, a Belgian, who was to fire one of the opening guns for the liberal bloc in the coming meeting, began writing his book, "The Nun in the World." A graduate of the Pontifical Gregorian University in Rome, with a doctorate in theology and philosophy awarded in 1920, and a later Masters degree in canon law, he had long been an active defender of freedom. During World War II, then a monsignor in Belgium, his name was on a list of 30 hostages who were to be executed by the Nazis; liberated by the Allies in the nick of time, the order was never carried out. "The Nun in the World" was published in 1962 by the Newman Press, American publishers in Westminster, Maryland and as Vatican II opened that fall, it was being read by every nun in America. The book pulled no punches; the Cardinal was a feminist.

"Women," he wrote "live imprisoned in a sort of immutable destiny, in the framework of an idealized archetype set up by men and remaining invariable. She was supposed to be docile, faithful, resigned, hard-working – but all within well-defined limits and sheltered from the draughts and winds of the outside world."[18] He deplored the encouragement of what he called "feminine passivity," and went on to decry a cloister mentality, declaring, "A concept of separation from the world leads... to a kind of psychological isolationism, leading in turn to a failure of dialogue with those in immediate contact with them for lack... of a common language."[19] Women, he pointed out, were adults, not minors. They were capable he thought of thinking for themselves.

Along with Pacelli (Pius 12), he was highly critical of habits and believed that they must seem to the layman "to be ill adapted to current conditions, to have outlived their purpose, to be archaic and inconvenient."[20] Again, agreeing with the Pope, that "The religious of today appears to the faithful to be out of touch with the world as it is, an anachronism. To revalue the religious life of today means, therefore, to bring the religious life into harmony with the evolutionary state of the world and womankind ... to accept the positive contribution of feminism in order to improve the apostolic yield. She [the sister] must be seen to be a contemporary woman."[21] "There is too great a tendency," he believed, "even in parishes," and one might add, *especially* in parishes "to relegate nuns to inferior tasks which could as well be done by others."[22] He didn't specify a cleaning service if the floor of the rectory bathroom needed to be washed, but that is certainly what he meant.

He joined what was to become one aspect of the later and still current disagreement between the sisters and the Vatican – the value of prayer versus the value of the apostolate, that is, the work that sisters did every day. He believed the religious life would be more genuinely religious if a greater emphasis was placed on that work. He went on to point out that time was valuable and must be accounted for, but it was clear that he believed that "time on one's knees" could be more usefully spent at work in the real world. "Too numerous and ill-adapted spiritual exercises tend to make the life of prayer mechanical and to atrophy it; they can become an end in themselves instead of remaining a means."[23] He saw no logic in a monastic life at home and a ministerial life in the world, a conflict still alive and well and often, although unspoken, at the heart of a given disagreement. He believed then, as the majority of sisters do today, that "the true apostolate is prayer in action."[24] Or as one contemporary sister put it, "Mission is all!"[25]

Vatican II basically rewrote the church's constitution, seeking to define it as a fellowship of equals and to end its isolation from the wider world, to abandon defensiveness and the distrust of others. In the final rushed days of the last session, and without further discussion, the decree Perfectae Caritatus was passed. In the previous session, the decree had had a short debate; Francis Cardinal Spellman of New York, as well as the conservative Ernesto Cardinal Ruffini and several additional Italian prelates had spoken against the reforms the decree contained, expressing concern over issues of "obedience." Perfectae Caritatis would be proclaimed a year later by Giovanni Montini (Paul 6), who was proclaimed Pope in 1963, after Roncalli (John 23) succumbed to illness. The subtitle to the decree was "On the Adaptation and Renewal of Religious Life." The decree stipulated that sisters – *not priests and not brothers* – sisters were to follow highly specific instructions, precisely stated. These are reviewed in Part Two.

The Aftermath:

"American sisters had in place a solid infrastructure of reform-oriented collaborative organizations to help them formulate, implement, and ultimately defend their renewal policies"[27] and they moved at warp speed. The conservative prelates outvoted in Rome were, however, supreme at home; the nuns had clearly been set by the convocation on a collision course. Although some congregations lost their struggle to modernize, most notably the IHMs of Los Angeles, (See Part Four, Chapter 1) the majority persevered. Some were even encouraged by local hierarchies.

The sisters answered the question, had the needs of the Church led them far afield from their founders intent, with an unqualified "yes" and a determination to change. Chaos followed, and a degree of outrage. There were nuns asking why, if the founder of their order had tasked them with ministering to the poor, they were now teaching affluent, white 10-year-olds, and then decided to stop doing so. Some wondered why mothers superior *were* superior and why they were appointed. What sort of governance did a given congregation want? Or need? Shouldn't it be *their* decision? Most decided that it should, that superiors would be elected. Why did every member have to live in the same house, why was that relevant? Why not be closer to those they served? Shouldn't the ministries they undertook determine where and how they lived? Their answer was yes. As for "daily identical schedules of group prayer, meals and recreation," why were those considered to be "essential elements of religious life?" What was "essential" about them? Nothing, they decided. As for their habits? They took them off. Many worlds were turning upside down. The nuns, well educated women, were thinking the issues through, thinking for themselves, coming to their own conclusions.

At the same time, there were sisters who wanted nothing to change, who loved the life they had been living and found themselves in the center of a storm not of their making. Some of them discovered the courage, when they found the changes too radical, to leave the familiar and join another more traditional congregation; there can be no doubt that some were indeed less than happy with the changes but "went along to get along." However, the lay writer Ann Carey's formulation,[28] that a handful of radical feminists simply hijacked *thousands* of women religious and *herded* them in directions they didn't wish to go and never would have gone unless *forced* to do so, more than *demeans* those women who stayed. Most were engaged. Change followed change.

Amy L. Koehlinger, in her book, "The New Nuns," begins her work with an anecdote told to her by a sister of St. Joseph. It was 1963, the civil rights movement was in full swing and James Baldwin, the writer, was to speak at the Tabernacle Baptist Church in Selma, Alabama. The nuns' convent was next door and the sisters there were still living the traditional life; it never occurred to them that if they were curious (and they were) and wanted to hear him (and they did) to attend the service. Although if they had asked, they would not have been permitted. But several of them climbed up on the radiator in the room nearest the church, pressed their ears against the glass of the window and tried to listen, to hear whatever they could; how amazed those young women would have been if they had known that only two years later, still in their full habits, they would be with Ralph Abernathy on the march to Montgomery, facing sheriff deputies on "the Selma line," their photographs in every newspaper in America and probably around the world.

It had all happened very quickly. One nun remembered, "All of a sudden we could meet people instead of rejecting them as worldly and dangerous. We could use telephones, watch television, eat in restaurants, go home to visit our families. We could be *with* people. We were encouraged to rethink our vows, entitled to ask why, as though we were grownups. We could even decide for ourselves when to turn off the lights at bedtime. And that idea, the idea of women as adults, would also get us into trouble."[29] And indeed it did. Now, "rather than meditating on … the suffering of Christ while sitting in the convent Chapel, "new nuns" in new and often disorienting locations meditated on the wounds and suffering that was so evident

… in urban ghettos, in "Christ among the poor."[30]

Nuns, it should be noted, do not "refuse" Vatican commands, but in the decades that followed the final meeting, occasions arose when, as one sister put it, they felt on the grounds of individual conscience, deemed sacrosanct in the decrees of the recent assembly, they had to "decline to accept" certain specific instructions and demands. With each of these disagreements, tension grew. Conservative voices were raised; the nuns were "going wild," they needed to be "reined in." Those calls were heard and the "reining in" began.

As described initially at the beginning of this section, two separate congregations of the Curia then chose to examine the nuns of the LCWR. The first of these, the Congregation for Institutes of Consecrated Life and Societies of Apostolic Life, CICLSAL, was, at the inception of their involvement in 2008, led by Cardinal Franc Rodé, well-known for his conservative views and criticisms of the sisters. Following his retirement, his position was taken by Cardinal Joao Braz de Aviz. CICLSAL conducted an Apostolic Visitation, lasting six long years with a final report made public in December, 2014.

During this same time frame, another Curial department, the Congregation for the Doctrine of the Faith, decided to conduct their own examination of the sisters. The CDF was headed then by the conservative cardinal, William Levada, an American who began his ministry in California under the ultra-conservative Cardinal Francis McIntyre (See Part Four, Chapter 1). When Levada retired, he was replaced by the equally conservative Cardinal Gerhard Müller, a German, and considered by many to be "papabile," i.e. an appropriate candidate for the papacy. Both men had been appointed by Joseph Ratzinger (Benedict 16.) The CDF then began what is called a Doctrinal Assessment. With this second examination, the sisters became the target of some of the most powerful and most conservative men of the Roman Catholic hierarchy, men with virtually unlimited power.

It should be noted that following the close of Vatican II, as changes followed changes, a significant number of sisters found these changes unwelcomed and far beyond their comfort level; they found the moves too radical. In 1971, some superiors, roughly twenty percent, wanting to preserve the more traditional models of religious life, unhappy with the greater emphasis on involvement in the outside world, resigned from the conference and began their own group of superiors, the Conference of Major Superiors of Women Religious, the CMSWR.

By 1992, this group had been given canonical standing. America is the only country in the world with two, rather than one, groups of canonically approved sisters. The CMSWR, the traditional group, maintains close ties with the Vatican's hierarchical structure and their members belong to traditional congregations; each congregation lives together in their order's mother house, engaging in daily identical schedules of group prayer, meals and recreation and wearing "modified" habits. The LCWR, the contemporary group, the eighty percent, no longer do any of those things. The CMSWR is looked upon with favor by the Vatican; it is the LCWR that has drawn the Vatican's serious disapproval.

CICLSAL's Apostolic Visitation:

The LCWR rarely comments on the actions of the CMSWR; they have rather adopted a "live and let live" policy. Although the relationship between the two groups could have been described as strained, the disapproval, it seems fair to say, has largely been in one direction; the LCWR remains open to any superior who wishes to join and does not express disapproval of those who have chosen a more traditional lifestyle. Indeed, a few superiors belong to both groups.

However, many of "the movers and shakers" in the CMSWR are more than disapproving of the members of the LCWR. They, or their supporters on their behalf, maintain a continuing drumbeat of criticism and condemnation, and it was a move by champions of and sympathizers with the CMSWR, organizing a religious symposium, that set the apostolic visitation in motion.

The first time the idea of a formal visitation was publicly voiced was in September 2008, at a symposium held at Stonehill College in Easton, Massachusetts. The symposium was sponsored jointly by the college and the Fall River diocese; it was part of the 200th anniversary celebration of the Boston diocese. Cardinal Franc Rodé was among the invited speakers; he was well-known for his disapproval of the directions chosen by the LCWR. Two additional speakers at the meeting were the lay journalist, Ann Carey and Sarah Butler, MSBT, a conservative theologian. Both women were vitriolic critics of the positions taken by the LCWR.

During Butler's presentation, a lengthy critique of the group's views, Butler asked the Cardinal, *actually specifically*, to consider a formal apostolic inquiry. There were sisters who believed that this public condemnation and call for an Apostolic Assessment, i.e. an investigation, of one group of sisters by another was without precedent in religious life and they found it actually shocking. Before three months had passed, however, Rodé, apparently not shocked, did exactly what Butler had suggested; with the approval of the then pope Joseph Ratzinger, Benedict 16, announcing an Apostolic Visitation of the LCWR. His reasons for doing so varied, depending on the date and the setting and perhaps they were all true. Although he claimed that he had been considering an Apostolic Visitation "for months," he had never, prior to Stonehill, publicly said so.

In November of that year, The Catholic News Service reported that the Cardinal hoped that the Apostolic Visitation would "encourage vocations and assure a better future for women religious." In a radio interview the following day, seeking to respond to much negative criticism, he said the investigation was a response to concerns, including by "an important representative of the US church" regarding "some irregularities or omissions in American religious life." He then went on to mention for the first time that part of the problem was "a certain 'feminist' spirit" as well as "a certain secularist mentality."[31]

At other junctures the Cardinal seemed to suggest that his concern was with the decline in numbers of women religious and there was the implication that this was in some way due to the changes brought about by Vatican II, and most particularly the abandonment of the habit. There is little logic here, since there had been an equal decline among male religious, who had no habits to abandon.

The congregations of the LCWR were given literally less than an hour's notice before the press conference announcing the investigation; the sisters were taken completely by surprise. The news of the visitation was met by a storm of criticism in the lay press; this was in large part due to the timing and most especially the style of the announcement. The secrecy of its planning was a guarantee of total shock and was certainly experienced by the sisters as profound and *intended* disrespect.[32] It was as well an invitation to suspect the worst, with or without evidence. Fear and anxiety were immediate and widespread.

It should be noted that an Apostolic Visitation is not some routine checkup; it is not simply an evaluation. It is rather "a juridical process imposed on … an ecclesiastical unit (diocese, order, institution, etc.) which is credibly accused or suspected of or embroiled in serious moral, religious, spiritual, doctrinal, financial, civil, or other types of misconduct or conflict whose solution the unit in question cannot, or will not, undertake on its own." There is an implied accusation and a presumption of guilt. Apostolic Visitations are not "undertaken to showcase the virtues of the accused any more than a grand jury is convened to lift up the sterling quality of life of the defendant."[34]

The visitation was to be conducted in three phases. The visitators would be sisters of the CMSWR, the 20 percent of American nuns belonging to traditional orders and in good standing with the Vatican. The first phase required the superiors of each LCWR order to write a description of their community for their visitator. Many presented their congregation as healthy and stable, suffering more from external factors such as an unfriendly clericalism as well as an experienced disrespect. Their descriptions were filled with not only confidence but pride in the accomplishments of their members; they had used the visitation as an opportunity to make progress, continuing to define the changes, actually the metamorphosis, of religious life that had taken place in the decades following the close of Vatican II.

Phase Two had a different flavor. A very lengthy, highly detailed questionnaire was presented which many sisters believed was "clearly designed to elicit not relevant or useful information for the congregations improvement but self-incriminating evidence of laxity and secularism, disobedience to Church law… and, of course, the hated "feminism," as well as "infidelity to the obligations of Religious Life itself."[35]

Many of the questions also represented an effort to gain detailed financial information; fearing efforts at expropriations, most major superiors, charged to protect the community's assets, "declined" to reply. When pressured to do so, they simply continued their silence. There was an unspoken, never justified fear that their assets would be confiscated to defray the extensive debts owed by most dioceses due to the sexual abuse scandals. Many communities consulted with Canon lawyers; some simply submitted their orders constitution. Finally, in a statement reiterating their right to seek such information, CICLSAL withdrew the hated requests.

Then Phase Three began; there would be on-site visitations of selected congregations. The requirements to serve as a visitator or investigator included an Oath of Loyalty to the Holy See as well as the recently revised "Profession of Faith." The reports written would be kept secret; there would be no opportunity either to correct possible misunderstandings or simply to verify the contents for accuracy.

In January of 2011, Cardinal Rodé, retired. He was replaced by Cardinal Joao Braz de Aviv, an assignment looked upon with disfavor by the conservative Catholic press. When Braz de Aviv was given the post, it was understood by many Vatican watchers as an acknowledgement on Ratzinger's (Benedict 16) part that he had been given inaccurate and misleading reports about the American nuns; these reports had most likely come from the United States Conference of Catholic Bishops, filled by conservative prelates appointed by two consecutive conservative popes. Braz de Aviv had been openly critical of Rodé's decisions.

The "Final Report of the Apostolic Visitation of women (sic) Religious" in the United States" was submitted in January, 2012. A two-year silence followed. This may not have been intended as intimidation, but it could not conceivably have been understood as reassuring. The nuns simply waited… for the other shoe to drop.

In December of 2014, a press conference was held to announce the findings of the Apostolic Visitation; it was noticeably different in style than the announcement of the visitation's beginning. To begin with, those participating in the event had seen the report and had been given time to consider their replies; there was no surprise, no blind siding. Both Cardinal de Aziz and his assistant, Archbishop José Carballo, called for "forgiveness and reconciliation." Although this is not quite an apology, it probably comes as close to one as Vatican politics permit. In short, the sisters were given a clean bill of health; there were no further references to "radical feminism" or "secularism." Nor were the sisters asked to abandon their "over-involvement with issues of social justice."

The planned secrecy was abandoned; publication and release of the entire report at an open press conference as well as the willingness to answer questions as they were asked were contributions to the healing process. Mother Clare Millea, of the CMSWR, testified that the report was an accurate presentation of her findings. In Sr. Sandra Schneiders' commentary on the event,[36] she described Millea as "near tears" and saw that as "her non-verbal recognition of the deep hurt, sorrow and anger" that "acceptance of the task of implementing the investigation had caused."[37]

However, she continued, "Six years of suspicion, threat, judgment, accusations, mutual distrust and justified anger at rank injustice cannot be abolished with a few pages of appreciative acceptance, no matter how sincere."[38] She goes on to acknowledge however that the situation has ended in "a degree of truthfulness and openness that provides some basis for moving forward, perhaps somewhat cautiously, but nevertheless honestly, into a different type of relationship between religious and institutional authority in the church."[39]

Sr. Annmarie Sanders, IHM, Director of Communications for the LCWR issued a statement that read in part "Our members frequently speak of how our experience of the study became the source of profound transformation for our institutes. The process led us to study the heart of our vocation as we engaged one another in significant conversations that explored our spirituality, our mission, our communal life, and our hopes for the future. As we did so, our bonds with one another grew even deeper and our understanding of the potential of this life to serve the needs of the world grew even keener."[40]

The CDF's Doctrinal Assessment:

With the Apostolic Visitation still in its early phases, in February of 2009, the Congregation for the Doctrine of the Faith, the "heaviest" of Rome's "heavy hitters," under the direction of its prefect, Cardinal

William Levada, wrote a letter to the LCWR to inform them that his office had begun a Doctrinal Assessment of the organization and that Bishop Leonard Blair, of Toledo, Ohio had been chosen to carry it out. The letter was received in March, the LCWR membership was informed in April and in that same month, the leadership met with Cardinal Levada in Rome. In May, they met with Blair for the first time. Now the sisters were facing a two- edged sword; the danger had been doubled.

In August of that year, the annual LCWR meeting was held in New Orleans. After it was over, the leadership released a statement requesting from the CDF a more detailed account of the reasons for this second investigation; the sisters believed there had been either misunderstanding or miscommunication. Despite that, they promised to cooperate with the investigation, *engaging in dialogue, however, as equals.* They promised to continue in discussion as long as necessary to resolve what they believed to be misunderstandings; at the same time they made clear they would not compromise "the integrity" of their mission. If it came to that, they would be forced to "reconsider."

Before the year was out, support for the organization poured in; the Asia-Oceania Meeting of Religious, which represents 113 women religious leaders from 17 Asian and Oceania nations, released a statement offering "our solidarity and prayers." The Continental Assembly of Europe, an organization of women religious across Europe, also issued a statement, expressing their "most fervent solidarity." The tea leaves were not hard to read; sisters around the world were now on high alert.

In April of 2010, the LCWR leadership had their yearly meeting with Vatican officials of the CDF. Following the meeting in a letter to their membership, the leaders reported that much of the meeting was devoted to a discussion of the LCWR's support of the U. S. Affordable Care Act, the ACA. The Catholic Health Association, headed by Sister Carol Keehan, whose member hospitals and nursing homes are mostly operated by communities of women religious, had spoken in favor of the bill as well. Cardinal Levada called the sister's support of the legislation, which had been opposed by the United States Conference of Catholic Bishops, the USCCB, "a public display of disunity within the Church."[41] In July, Blair concluded his investigation and submitted his report to the CDF; the report, eight pages long, was not then and has not since been made public.

In April of 2012, again at their yearly meeting with the CDF, after the customary "gratitude" was expressed for the "great contribution" the sisters had made, the criticisms followed. Cardinal Levada informed them that they were to consider themselves formally ordered to revise their organization. The list of complaints was lengthy, with many of the criticisms specific; these included both "positive errors," i.e. errors the sisters themselves had committed and a "second level of the problem," that concerned "the silence and inaction of the LCWR" in the face of errors committed by others. Their silence(s) had been understood, apparently, as agreement and hence dissent.

Among the accusations were:

Addresses at the LCWR Assemblies that "manifest problematic statements and serious theological, even doctrinal errors." These were "a challenge not only to core Catholic beliefs… [but] also a serious source of scandal." *Scandal?* "Since the LCWR leadership has offered no clarification about such statements, some might infer that such positions are endorsed by them."

"Some of the addresses… have scant regard for the role of the Magisterium as the guarantor of the authentic interpretation of the church's faith."

- Policies of Corporate Dissent: LCWR officers protesting the Holy See's actions regarding the question of women's ordination were noted. Referring both to abortion and homosexual ministry, positions have been taken "not in agreement with the Church's teaching on human sexuality."
- Radical Feminism. There was noted "a prevalence of certain radical feminist themes incompatible with the Catholic faith." These included commentaries on "patriarchy" [that] "distort the way" in which sacramental life in the church is structured.

The Systems Thinking Handbook, provided to new Superiors and Formators, was found to be severely lacking. "Confusion about the

Church's authentic doctrine of the Faith is reinforced rather than corrected by the lack of doctrinal content."

Links between LCWR and other organizations, specifically NETWORK (a group that describes itself as "a social justice organization" and sponsors the "Nuns on the Bus" tours) were seen as objectionable.

Consequently, "in order to implement a process of review and conformity to the teachings and discipline of the church, the Holy See, through the Congregation for the Doctrine of the Faith, will appoint an Archbishop Delegate, assisted by two Bishops, for review, guidance and approval, where necessary, of the work of the LCWR." And the Delegate in question was to be Archbishop J. Peter Sartain, Archbishop of Seattle. The revisions would be made under his authority. He would supervise their decisions; they were not to act without his approval. The letter then went on to state *specifically* that speakers/presenters at all major programs, as for example, the annual August meetings, would be subject to and require his approval.

The events of that summer, 2012, did nothing to ease tension. On June 1, the LCWR leadership issued a statement claiming that the criticism from the Vatican was based on "unsubstantiated accusations" and that it had arisen from a "flawed process." On June 12 they traveled to Rome for another meeting with Cardinal Levada; the Cardinal referred to the discussion that followed as a "dialogue of the deaf." In July, Joseph Ratzinger (Benedict 16) appointed Archbishop Gerhard Müller to be Prefect of the Congregation for the Doctrine of the Faith, and the Cardinal announced his retirement.

On July 27, Bishop Leonard P. Blair of Toledo, Ohio, one of the two U. S. bishops assisting Archbishop J. Peter Sartain of Seattle, during an interview on National Public Radio's "Fresh Air" program took an initial hard line, saying, "If by dialogue, they mean that the doctrines of the church are negotiable, and that the bishops represent one position and the LCWR represents another position and somehow we find a middle ground about basic church teaching on faith and morals, then no, I don't think that's the dialogue the Holy See would envision. But if it's a dialogue about how to have the LCWR ... accept church teaching and to implement [them] in their discussions ... that would be the dialogue."[42]

At the annual LCWR Assembly in August, Sandra M. Schneiders, IHM was given the Outstanding Leadership Award. Ann Carey called this "an act of provocation and alienation," because Schneiders had been a vocal critic of the ongoing Apostolic Visitation. It did seem unlikely that her honor had been "approved." But equally, it seemed clear she had been given the award, neither to "provoke" nor to "alienate," but because of her outstanding written contributions to the ongoing "redefinition" process.

And then in March, 2013, a surprised world witnessed the election of a new pope, whose inauguration, yet one more majestic Vatican ceremony, reminded women how far they had not come in the all-male Roman Catholic hierarchy. Jorge Mario Bergoglio was now

Pope Francis. His history as well as many of his opening remarks suggested a personality and style very different from his predecessor's; the sisters held their breath. Would these differences translate into difference in doctrine or into tolerance for perceived differences in doctrine? Would questions or debate be viewed more positively? Would his emphasis on ministering to the poor, since it so clearly mirrored their own apostolates, place them in a more favorable light? Weren't they following exactly in the direction he was advocating? (Some might even say that the sisters had gotten there first.) During the annual April meeting in 2013, these questions were answered; Müller informed the leadership that the new pope had reaffirmed the findings of the assessment and the program for reform.

At the LCWR assembly in August of that year, Sartain addressed the delegates; whether that was by invitation or command was not revealed. In his speech but moreover in his demeanor, it did seem that there was some genuine good feeling between the two contenders, that the Archbishop had developed real respect for if not agreement with the sisters. In a way, this did not seem surprising; they are an unusual group of women and he was spending a great deal of time with them. It seemed unlikely to onlookers however that "permission" had been asked or "approval" given for that year's assembly speaker. Ilia Delio, a Sister of St. Francis of Washington, D.C. spoke at length on the concept of Conscious Evolution, a set of ideas with which the Vatican disagrees; she is also known to be interested in and supportive of the ideas of the Jesuit Fr. Pierre

Teilhard de Chardin, long in disfavor with the Vatican. At the end of her two-hour long address, she was given a standing ovation.

In February of 2014, Bergoglio (Francis) elevated Müller to Cardinal. Whether intended as such or not, the now Cardinal seemed to experience his promotion as confirmation of or agreement with the hard-line he had been willing to take and Sartain had seemed to soften.

At their annual April meeting with the CDF, the sisters were harshly criticized. This time, the gloves were off. Cardinal Müller asserted that the LCWR was engaged in an "open provocation of the Holy See" and demanded that the group evince "more substantive signs of collaboration"[43] with the mandate for reform. In particular he was angered by the group's choice of speaker for their upcoming August assembly, Sister of Saint Joseph Elizabeth Johnson, referring to her as "a theologian criticized by the Bishops of the United States because of the gravity of the doctrinal errors in that theologian's writings."[44] He added that the decision "further alienates the LCWR from the Bishops as well."[45]

He went on to criticize their continued interest in Conscious Evolution, a doctrine he saw as "opposed to Christian Revelation."[46] He pointed out that it was clear to him that no approval of the speaker had been sought or given and warned them *the requirement "is to be considered fully in force."*[47] (Italics the authors.) Referring to the Assembly of 2015, "It will be the expectation of the Holy See that

Archbishop Sartain have an active role in the discussion about invited Speakers." The nuns *will* ask permission. He issued a warning, "At this phase of the implementation of the doctoral assessment, we are looking for … more substantive signs of collaboration."[48] Following the April meeting, LCWR stated that no interviews with the press would be granted.

As 2015 began, nuns everywhere held their collective breath waiting for the annual April meeting between the LCWR and the Vatican. This event was understood by nuns around the world and knowledgeable Catholics in America as an expected flash point in the conflict. Instead, a completely unexpected announcement was made on April 16; the Mandate had come to an end.

An agreement satisfactory to both sides of the conflict had been reached a full two years ahead of schedule. The Vatican issued a brief press release and a report of some eleven hundred words. Only eleven hundred words were needed to bring to a close more than six years of controversy and "investigation." In addition, a thirty day moratorium on statements was announced; silence would prevail for the coming month. Neither side would grant interviews.

The report itself was not only striking for its brevity – it was equally striking for its tone. It was *courteous.* Gone was the "top down," authoritarian instruction; new notes were sounded – "mutuality," "dialogue," "respect." Some snippets: "Substantive dialogue between bishops and religious women," "fruitful dialogue," "extensive conversations," "mutual respect," and finally, "such substantive dialogue between bishops and religious has been a blessing to be appreciated and further encouraged." The "prevalence of certain radical feminist themes incompatible with the Catholic faith" were not mentioned. Neither was "heresy." Neither was there any mention of the speakers chosen for the Assembly in August and how those choices were made or would be made in future.

Another equally striking aspect of the report was its absence of information; no specifics, no details were offered. Generalities were many. Two central points of the initially stated "concerns" were addressed directly, but revealed almost nothing about their solutions.

First, the "manifest problematic statements and serious theological, even doctrinal errors" that were "a challenge not only to core Catholic beliefs…[but] also a serious source of scandal" will, apparently, no longer be "problematic;" "manuscripts will be reviewed by competent theologians,"[49] unspecified. Since almost every order of nuns has at least one sister with a doctorate in theology, will *they* be considered "competent theologians?" Who will say? Who is to decide? As yet unspecified.

Second, Cardinal Müller's profound disapproval of the choices for speakers and rewards recipients at the LCWR's August Assemblies, which he described as examples of "open provocation against the Holy See," that "alienates the LCWR from the Bishops" had also found a solution. "A revised process for the selection of the

Outstanding Leadership Award recipient has been articulated."[50] What was it? Revised how? By whom? No information on the subject was offered.

Various stories in the press suggested that the abrupt end took place to forestall negative publicity during the papal visit to the United States, scheduled for September, 2015. That "public relations" concerns could upend a serious, religious mandate would be so unholy a possibility, any committed Catholic would have to pray that no such thing was true. There is, it would seem to close observers of the scene, another possible explanation, to be found in the role played by Bishop J. Peter Sartain.

To begin with, Sartain is an American, in close contact with the national pulse; he is not contemptuous of American society as many of the Curia are. Vice-President Joseph Biden's comments the previous September, praising Sr. Simone Campbell and the Nuns on the Bus tour, could not have gone unnoticed. His well-publicized remark, "I know no group of people (the nuns) who bring a greater sense of justice and passion to what they do,"[51] may well have been forwarded to Rome.

In addition, Sartain seems to know and appreciate the fact that these are not "rebel nuns." Years now in their company, he would know their commitment to the prophetic stance, their insistence on walking in the footsteps of Jesus, their refusal ever to use power or pressure, their refusal to coerce. Willing only to teach as Jesus did, by parable or example, they would never flex their own muscles, despite their strength.

But if he believed that the sisters had been pushed as far as they were willing to go, that they would never abandon their commitment to social justice, if he understood that they were *beyond intimidation*, that they were never going to "blink," he would probably have lobbied for exactly what has taken place. One superior observed during another struggle, "Powerful men must not be seen to be bested – they must be allowed to 'save face.'" Sartain would understand this as well. If he, well known for his own conservative doctrinal positions, recommended compromise, and recommended it strongly, those recommendations would have to have been taken very seriously. Given his experience, he could not be ignored. This may well be what actually happened, although the full story will surely never be told. But, it would seem, the nuns triumphed.

It is not unreasonable to ask, however, "How deep does the triumph go?" Have the sisters actually been taken seriously? Is their experience of humanity, so different from that of their male counterparts, now, suddenly, seen as valuable? Have they become full partners facing a difficult future? Or, as would seem more likely, has the deep divide been temporarily papered over? Since they will never expand the Imperial Empire or lead a blood-drenched crusade, because power will never be their friend or their weapon, will they ever gain the genuine respect of the most powerful? It seems unlikely.

Then on May 15, the first day after the end of the 30-day silence, Sharon Holland, IHM and president of the LCWR gave a strikingly low-key interview to Joshua McElwee of the National Catholic Reporter. Her presentation of events was such that the reader might easily conclude that the prior seven years of assault had never taken place, that no one had ever mentioned "scandal," "heresy," or anything like "radical feminist themes," that they had never been judged unfit to govern themselves and placed in the control of male authority. Rather, one might conclude from her tone and demeanor, that a group of colleagues had some long and interesting discussions on subjects of mutual concern; then with increased understanding, solutions were found, communion was discovered, and that all of this took place between friends and colleagues, in an atmosphere of good will.

There was nothing surprising, Holland observed, in the mandate ending early; the mandate, she said, "could be five years but it didn't say that there would be five years. We were able to come to this conclusion in three." The language of the interview – nun-speak – was so underplayed, that it has to be read several times before the scope of the sisters victory, and there is no denying that it was a victory, becomes apparent.

McElwee had to sweat for what he could finally report to a grateful readership, the answers to two of the important questions dodged successfully in the formal report. The first of these was the question of exactly who would be the guarantor of the doctrinal soundness of the sisters written work. He proceeds gingerly:

McElwee: **"I wanted to ask about two specifics, and I know that there might be things that you can't talk about. But there are a couple of things that caught us, in reading the final joint report. The one was the mention that LCWR publications "need a sound doctrinal foundation" and that "measures are being taken to promote a scholarly rigor that will ensure theological accuracy and help avoid statements that are ambiguous." To your understanding, what can you say about what those measures will be? Was there some discussion of what those measures would be to promote that rigor or to provide that theological accuracy?"**

Holland: "Actually, some of that language is ours – of desiring the doctrinal and theological rigor and accuracy. Because we want that quality in our publications, for our members and for many people who read our publication. It's mentioned I believe in the report that there is, and there already was, a publications advisory committee that reviews things. And there is the provision for having theological review by theologians whom we will ask to review things, to make sure that there's not unintentional language or things that could cause theological problems.

Our publications are not theological treatises, but we want them to be correct. And we've been working on that and we will continue to work on that."

After she dodged the question, McElwee persisted.

McElwee: **"Is that review of theological accuracy something that will be undertaken by LCWR, or from the outside?"**

Holland: "It's LCWR."

A straight answer. Holland had clearly been channeling the sister who had observed that "powerful men cannot be seen as having been bested." Then McElwee moved to the second unanswered question.

McElwee: **"We also noticed the mention for some sort of revised process regarding the selection of the leadership award each year."**

Holland: "Actually, that revision of the process was already underway. Not because there was a problem with the people who were getting awards…"

Not because there was a problem with the people who were getting awards?

"but we have hundreds of members all over the United States. We come together once a year in assembly, and there's 7-8-900, and we don't know each other that well.

So we've worked out a process that will have a little more potential of getting information out among the membership for the nominees for this so that we can have a more participative and well-informed process.

It's about the quality of the process and our member's participation. It's not about having chosen bad people."

McElwee: **"Again, is that something that was decided or developed by LCWR?"**

Holland: "Yes, that's right. LCWR developed the process."

It was done so quietly that one might easily miss how astonishing some of these assertions, actually flat out denials, really were. Here's another. Holland is discussing what her goals had been.

Holland: "What I have always wanted was the dialogue, the growth in mutual understanding across cultures and experiences and nationalities, that builds up ecclesial communion. My vision for an end was very broad, in terms of mutual understanding and communion, but it didn't have specifics attached."

McElwee: **"Can you expand on the idea of ecclesial communion? What does that mean to you?"**

Holland: "I suppose it means being able to discuss any differences that occur, having the fundamental notion that we all are a part of the church and we work together in the mission of Christ.

And we can discuss difficulties as they may arise, as they do in any organization..."

One must interrupt. *"In any organization?"* The Vatican is a two thousand year-old, absolute monarchy, one of the last few on the face of the planet, and actually an independent city-state. When the LCWR promised to cooperate with the investigation, engaging in dialogue, however, *as equals,* it would seem they meant *exactly that*, one "organization" to another.

It's worth stopping for a moment to consider the egalitarian tone with which this centuries-old monarchy is apparently to be regarded. It is devoid of intimidation. No awe is apparent. Something new has clearly happened. And surely there will be consequences. It is exactly this insistence on equality that will unquestionably kindle rage within the hearts of the ultra-conservative.

There is, of course no way to discover what role Bergoglio (Francis) played in this outcome. Although he speaks frequently about the concerns of secular women around the world, the American nuns never seemed to have received his full attention and it seems unlikely that he intervened directly. His hour-long meeting with the nuns following the April announcement addressed none of the conflict's relevant issues; it seems to have been rather a wide-ranging homily on various concerns of the church and a demonstration of the newly-found courtesy. It did mark the first time a sitting pope had *ever* met with a group of nuns and they were clearly pleased.

It seems unlikely that this particular outcome would have come to pass were Joseph Ratzinger (Benedict 16) still pope; his main thrust was not Bergoglio's (Francis), i.e. evangelization; in fact his inclination was in the opposite direction. He stated many times that a smaller church might be a purer church. It's not hard to imagine his following through in stricter fashion.

There is a wide spectrum of individual opinion within the Catholic hierarchy, ranging from liberal to ultra-conservative. That the world has changed completely and irreversibly since 1950 for everyone, but most especially for women, is never acknowledged by the ultra-conservatives. They have an unquenchable thirst for the pre-conciliar world, when authority was absolute, when obedience was unquestioned, with women in the kitchen and gays in the closet – in other words, order restored. They cannot abandon their dream. What was must always be. They remain determined. Time *will* go backwards.

But one must wonder what these Vatican men make of the fact that their efforts to bring these women to heel seem always to backfire. Not only does the public at large rise to their defense, but the sisters themselves, no matter the truckloads of lemons in which they are buried, continue to hand out pitchers of lemonade. They seem only to grow stronger, their bonds grow closer and their confidence in their positions increases. Their recently published "Power of Sisterhood: Women Religious Tell the Story of the Apostolic Visitation" is clear testimony to just this fact. Is this some unbelievably subtle form of defiance? It might well seem to those men to be just that. They may hear the sisters saying, "We follow our own God, each of us true to her own conscience. No matter what you do, we are not deterred. And we will not *be* deterred."

These men can frighten these women and they surely have. They can worry them, causing them sleepless nights, and they surely have. They can waste their precious time with the need to plan and strategize and engage canon lawyers. They can leave them scarred, they can cause them pain, but it's clear now that they cannot stop them from turning that pain to advantage. They have not deterred them. It is unlikely that they will. They of course maintain the power to try again. It is likely that they will.

It is difficult to read the outcome of this conflict as anything other than a total validation of the path the sisters found, have taken, and continue to take in their quest for renewal; they were wise not to rejoice in their moment of triumph. The leadership of the LCWR came together in August, 2015, for their annual meeting, held in Houston, Texas. It marked the first time the group met since the mandate had been ended. If there was exultation, it was not evident in the symposia open to the press.

The final commentary came from a subsequent editorial in the National Catholic Reporter on August 22nd. "A crisis has been managed.... Francis, however, won't be around forever. But there are lots of men who feel threatened by the changes he is attempting to put in place and who will long remember that the nuns won this round. Those men will be in place for quite some time, grace and the Spirit not withstanding."

These American nuns may yet suffer consequences for their seeming intransigence and subsequent triumph. Enmities smoulder. Powerful men have long memories. When will the flames break out again? In a year? In a decade? There is of course no way of knowing. But nuns around the world share their American sisters commitment to walk in the footsteps of Jesus. They have watched the current conflicts unfold and watched carefully. Many, if not most, have never lived under democratic regimes. But when the fire comes again, they may be ready. And if not then, the next time.

NOTES: PART ONE

1. Congegatio Pro Doctrina https://www.google.com/?gws_rd=ssl#q=congregatio+pro+doctrina+fidei
2. Ibid.
3. The Seven Sisters are liberal arts colleges that are historically women's colleges. They are Barnard, Bryn Mawr, Mount Holyoke, Radcliffe, Smith, Vassar, and Wellesley.
4. "Tasks of Those Who Choose the Prophetic Life Style," By Sandra Schneiders, National Catholic Reporter, January 7, 2010.https://www.ncronline.org/news/women-religious/tasks-those-who-choose-prophetic-life-style
5. Briggs, Kenneth "Double Crossed," Doubleday, 2006. p.28
6. Ibid., p.33
7. Ibid., p.32
8. Ibid., p.31
9. Ibid., p.31
10. Ibid., pp33-34
11. Ibid., p34
12. Koehlinger, Amy, "The New Nuns, Harvard University Press, Cambridge, Massachusetts, 2007. P.26
13. Ibid., p.27
14. Ibid., p.28
15. Ibid., p.31
16. Ibid., p.31
17. Ibid., p.35
18. Suenens, Leon Cardinal Joseph, "The Nun in the World," Newman Press, Maryland, 1961. P13
19. Ibid., p.19
20. Ibid., p.20
21. Ibid., p.35
22. Ibid., p.107
23. Ibid., p.118
24. Ibid., p.116
25. Sr. Simone Campbell in a personal communication to the author
26. Perfectae Caritatus. Appendix C
27. Koehlinger, Op. Cit., p.28

28. Carey, Ann, "Sisters in Crisis," Published by Our Sunday Visitor, Inc., 1997. See Chapter 9.
29. Former Sister Barbara Ferraro, in a personal communication to the author.
30. Koehlinger, Op.Cit., p.61
31. America, The National Catholic Review, Nov. 5, 2009, By James Martin, SJ
32. Schneiders, S. "Prophets in Their Own Country," Orbis Books, New York, 2012. Pp. 2-3
33. Ibid., p.8
34. Ibid., p.10
35. Ibid., p.15
36. National Catholic Reporter, December 18, 2014, "Engage the Future; Reflections on the Apostolic Visitation Report," By Sandra Schneiders.
37. Ibid.
38. Ibid.
39. Ibid.
40. https://lcwr.org/media/report-vaticans-apostolic-visitation-us-women-religious
41. National Catholic Reporter, July 6, 2010, "Vatican Officials, U.S. Women Religious Meet."
42. http://catholicphilly.com/2012/07/us-world-news/national-catholic-news/no-middle-ground-possible-with-lcwr-on-key-issues-bishop-blair-says/
43. http://www.ncregister.com/daily-news/cardinal-mueller-lcwr-stands-in-open-provocation-of-holy-see
44. Ibid.
45. Ibid.
46. Ibid.
47. Ibid.
48. Ibid.
49. See Note 40
50. See Note 40
51. http://www.nytimes.com/2014/09/18/us/politics/biden-drawing-on-his-past-expresses-common-cause-with-activist-nuns.html?_r=0

PART TWO

Vatican II: Setting the nuns on a collision course.

Vatican Two was the four-year long gathering, with twenty-six hundred Roman Catholic prelates attending, that took place from 1962 until 1965, with four autumn sessions in Rome, of eight to ten weeks each, and additional work sessions elsewhere throughout the year. It was not only a saga of epic proportion, but a fascinating, endlessly revelatory story, often providing clear portraits of both the public and the private faces of Roman Catholicism.

For only the second time in their centuries-long history, the leaders of the Catholic hierarchy came together, this time summoned by Angelo Roncalli, (John 23). Their stated purpose? To take stock of themselves, their church and their church's place in the wider world.

Unfortunately for Vatican watchers, popes rarely write memoirs. Consequently, when their behavior is or seems confusing, unless they have spoken to the specific issue concerned, observers are left with only what they can infer. And Roncalli's (John 23) actions, as he planned this monumental enclave, *the* Catholic event of the century, are more than confusing. Indeed, they seem on their face self-defeating.

For example, if change was the direction sought, if "springtime" or "fresh air"[1] was the goal as he claimed, why choose the Curia, the group known by its words, deeds and history to be, almost viscerally, *against* change, to implement his plans *for* change? The motto that Cardinal Alfredo Ottaviani, prefect of the Congregation for the

Doctrine of the Faith, had chosen for his coat of arms was "Semper idem." Translation? "Always the same." Clearly, the Curial position was hardly a carefully guarded secret. But this is what Roncalli (John 23) did. *As if there were no other alternatives*, he chose the Curia.

The Curia is the central governing body, together with the Pope, of the Roman Catholic Church. The nine congregations of the Roman Curia can best be understood by Americans as akin to the departments that report to their president – State, Defense, Treasury and so on. Similarly, the prefects who head the congregations, always with the rank of cardinal, serve at the pleasure of the pope just as secretaries in the United States departments serve at the pleasure of the president and almost all members of the Curia resign their offices immediately after a papal death, just as American secretaries submit their resignations after an election.

These congregations include the Congregation for Divine Worship, the Congregation for the Evangelization of Peoples, the Sacred Congregation for the Clergy, the Congregation for Catholic Education, the Congregation for Bishops and the Congregation for Institutes of Consecrated Life and Societies of Apostolic Life. The congregation most famous and most feared is the Congregation for the Doctrine of the Faith, previously known as the Supreme Sacred Congregation of the Roman and Universal Inquisition. The oldest and the most active of the nine congregations of the Curia, the CDF oversees and enforces Catholic doctrine.

It should be underscored that, although these congregations are comprised of men who consider themselves holy, they are places of politics, that dependable alloy of belief and ambition. The politics practiced there are no more or no less personal, passionate or opinionated than politics practiced elsewhere. They only involve the further complication that each man in the game firmly believes that God is on his side. In this instance, these deeply conservative men were completely committed to the status quo. It was to *these* congregations, that the Pope turned for the implementation of his dream, his "inspiration of the Holy Spirit."[2]

And so, Vatican II opened. And was immediately engulfed in world events. The council was part of the world and the world swirled around the council and that world of the early '60s was one of chaos and upheaval. Events happened. One pope died, another pope was elected. Roncalli (John 23) succumbed to illness in June of 1963; Giovanni Montini (Paul 6) found his way to the papacy. The Cuban missile crisis happened within hours of the council's opening; while cardinals and bishops debated the future of the Catholic Church, Catholics everywhere, with their brethren, wondered if they would live to see that future.

At a later session, two American monsignors went to dinner one evening with several American bishops, to celebrate the passage that day of a document they had supported. While enjoying themselves at the Cavalleri Hilton, just outside Rome, a woman leaned over from a neighboring table and asked them if they weren't Americans. Didn't they know their president had been shot that day? The priests rushed out into that dark Roman night, to find an open church somewhere, anywhere, to celebrate a Requiem Mass for their Catholic president who had died a world away.

But despite the chaos in many quarters, the public ceremonies of Vatican II were calm, as well as gorgeously choreographed, elegant, colorful and inspiring. The assembled prelates on the first day – a "river of white miters flowing steadily … across the square toward the great open portals of the largest basilica in Christendom. At the end was the Pontiff, the incarnation of tradition … sitting on his portable throne, riding above the crowd on the shoulders of the handsome men in rose brocade."[3] Twenty six hundred prelates, clothed in their red and white robes, then took their seats in long rows within the magnificent basilica of Rome's Cathedral of St. Peter's. The scenario was dazzling, the splendor of the centuries-old Imperial Church fully on display.

All appeared calm and controlled. No one reading the 16 documents that emerged from the council, phrased in measured tones, would guess at the passions that had been ignited and burned throughout its length, the flame sometimes on low, sometimes turned up to high. The unrelenting pressure issuing from the glare of the world press and television coverage did nothing to lower the heat. Headlines were generated almost every week. Close to 1,000 reporters were present. Here was breaking news.

In all, sixteen decrees were enacted; only one of these, Perfectae Caritatus, was directly relevant to the lives of American nuns. But it transformed their lives and their relationship to the Roman power structure forever. Although it impacted their lives profoundly, it was passed with almost no discussion and with no input from those most immediately affected and is barely even referred to in the significant literature covering the event.

Should the curious reader enter the index of any of the major works, for example, "What Happened at Vatican II," by John W. O'Malley, in the extensive subject index, they will note that "women" has only one reference point. The word "nuns" or the words "women religious" do not appear at all. Perfectae Caritatus has three reference points, none of which describe content or debate. The following quote, "the council engaged for two days in a basically positive discussion of the schema on religious orders," appears on page 239, but goes no further. What was discussed? Positively? The reader has no way of knowing.

In "History of Vatican II," Volume 5, edited by Giuseppe Alberigo, the volume which covers the fourth and final session, neither the words "women," "nuns" nor "women religious" appear in the subject index. Perfectae Caritatus, voted upon during that session, receives one brief, descriptive paragraph.

In "Vatican II," by Xavier Rynne, the pseudonym for Father Francis Xavier Murphy, there is no subject index. Five of the 581 pages do describe the debate referred to by O'Malley. For that one percent, researchers must be grateful. The negligible degree to which women's lives and more specifically the lives of women religious were considered to be of importance to the men convened at this event seems apparent.

And the men convened at this event leaned significantly towards the liberal position. Every vote taken was lopsided; no vote ever garnered even thirty percent for the conservative factions. Had anyone realized until then how "non-conservative" the majority of these prelates actually was? And a more relevant question: did it matter? Once again the reader is reminded, the Catholic Church is not a democracy; the majority does not rule.

An example of this unevenness, albeit an extreme one, might be the vote on the Sacred Liturgy, Sacrosanctum Concilium, which contained the possible sticking point that Mass was to be said in the vernacular. What was key here was the idea of active participation by all members of the congregation. Francis Cardinal Spellman, from New York, whose comments were seconded by Archbishop Francis McIntyre of Los Angeles disagreed; they wished the Mass to remain as it was.

On November 14, the issue was put to a vote – the outcome surprised everyone. Those in favor: 2,147, those opposed: 46. Among the 46 was the entire American delegation. And it would be to these men that America's nuns would be turning in the months to come.

Among the more than two thousand prelates were two small, but exceedingly significant, clusters of men, numbering probably not much more than 1% of the entire assembly. The men of the left were all men of profound intelligence, with passionate ideals passionately held, who had been gearing up for close to two years for what they expected to be one of the most important battles of their religious lives. They were angry, their heat barely beneath the surface.

The men of the right, of equal intelligence, were at the outset icily calm, accustomed to both power and control, and believing, despite their initial surprise at this unexpected convocation, that they had gained the leverage they needed to avoid what they would experience as disaster. The core membership of this conservative group "had close ties with right wing political parties and ideologies."[4]As events unfolded, what became clear was that both sides were capable of profound and persistent rage.

The remaining 99% of the voting members of the council were, for four years, urged, cajoled, pleaded with and at times threatened by the 1%, as the issues that each cared about ebbed and flowed throughout discussions and decision-making. Some of the voting members were sufficiently doctrinaire that they always voted either with the liberal bloc or its' opposite. Many however, had varied interests and investments; they listened to both sides, and depending upon their particular concerns and/or values, sometimes voted with one bloc and sometimes with another. Again, the degrees of plurality were noteworthy. Very few votes managed to garner even 15% for the conservative viewpoint. In one major disagreement, the conservatives came close to over 30 %, the highest tally of any of the votes. There was never the kind of near-even split one observes in many American elections.

Finally then, in the fourth and last session, with no further discussion, the lives of the more than 100,000 American nuns were significantly altered with the passage of Perfectae Caritatus, the decree which spelled out in precise detail the changes the sisters were *ordered* to make. Let us turn now to Perfectae Caritatus.

The first paragraph states that it (the convocation) " Now … intends to treat of the life and discipline of those institutes whose members make profession of chastity, poverty and obedience (i.e. the sisters) and to provide for their needs in our time."[5]

"The adaptation and renewal of the religious life includes both the constant return to the sources of all Christian life and to *the original spirit of the institutes*[6] and their adaptation to the changed conditions of our time." This sentence is, of course, of the greatest significance, because the sisters had become, over decades, no longer independent functioning entities as their founders envisioned and intended, but a small army for the Church to deploy as it suited their needs; this was now to come to a grinding halt and to great consternation. If the nuns refused, albeit politely, to fill classrooms, for example, then who would do so and who would pay for it?

"This renewal, under the inspiration of the Holy Spirit and the guidance of the Church, must be advanced according to the following principles: It redounds to the good of the Church that institutes (each order of nuns) have their own particular characteristics and work. Therefore let their founders' spirit and special aims they set before them as well as their sound traditions, all of which make up the patrimony of each institute, be faithfully held in honor." In other words, if their founders aim was to minister to the poor, why were they now teaching the children of the well-to-do?

"Institutes should promote among their members an adequate knowledge of the social conditions of the times they live in and of the needs of the Church. In such a way, judging current events wisely in the light of faith and burning with apostolic zeal, they may be able to assist men (sic) more effectively." The current accusation against the nuns, that they were "overly involved in social justice" is clearly not echoed here.

"The manner of living, praying and working should be suitably adapted everywhere, but especially in mission territories, to the modern physical and psychological circumstances of the members and also, as required by the nature of each institute, to the necessities of the apostolate, the demands of culture, and social and economic circumstances." Everything, it would seem, was to be updated.

"According to the same criteria let the manner of governing the institutes also be examined." The manner of governing should be examined? Many prelates must have found this close to heresy; mothers superior had been appointed for centuries. Was this to change as well? The answer was yes. And it did. Soon all convents would elect their leadership and the forms they chose varied. Some, for example, selected governing boards of three.

"Therefore let constitutions, directories, custom books, books of prayers and ceremonies and such like be suitably re-edited and, obsolete laws being suppressed, be adapted to the decrees of this sacred synod." Clearly nothing was to be left unconsidered; no more sweeping change could be imagined. Is it a surprise that consternation and often chaos followed?

"Communities, then, should adjust their rules and customs to fit the demands of the apostolate to which they are dedicated. The fact however that apostolic religious life takes on many forms requires that its adaptation and renewal take account of this diversity and provide that the lives of religious dedicated to the service of Christ in these various communities be sustained by special provisions appropriate to each." So diversity, it seemed, would certainly be both observed and honored.

"Religious should diligently practice and if need be express also in new forms that voluntary poverty which is recognized and highly esteemed especially today as an expression of the following of Christ. By it they share in the poverty of Christ who for our sakes became poor, even though He was rich, so that by His poverty we might become rich (cf. 2 Cor. 8:9; Matt. 8:20).

With regard to religious poverty it is not enough to use goods in a way subject to the superior's will, but members must be poor both in fact and in spirit, their treasures being in heaven (cf. Matt. 6:20).

Religious communities have the right to possess whatever is required for their temporal life and work, unless this is forbidden by their rules and constitutions. Nevertheless, they should avoid every appearance of luxury, excessive wealth and the accumulation of goods." The sisters actually had no need for this particular instruction. They owned no mansions, nor did they reside in any; nor were they driven to appointments in their chauffeured limousines. Nor did they wear embroidered robes or carry crosses made of the purest gold.

"Religious, therefore, in the spirit of faith and love for the divine will should humbly obey their superiors according to their rules and constitutions. Realizing that they are contributing to building up the body of Christ according to God's plan, they should use *both the forces of their intellect and will* (italics the authors) and the gifts of nature and grace to execute the commands and fulfill the duties entrusted to them. In this way religious obedience, far from lessening the dignity of the human person, by extending the freedom of the sons of God, leads it to maturity."

It might be noted that the works of Sr. Sandra Schneiders agrees: "The emergence of religious from the closed and simple context of pre-Vatican II convent life into a complicated involvement in a very complex world has made the traditional theory of obedience inadequate to the present reality of religious life."[7]

"The religious habit, an outward mark of consecration to God, should be simple and modest, poor and at the same becoming. In addition it must meet the requirements of health and be suited to the circumstances of time and place and to the needs of the ministry involved. The habits of both men and women religious which do not conform to these norms must be changed."

This is one of the few instances in which the cries of outrage emanating from the Vatican would seem to have validity; it is difficult to imagine that this instruction, made explicitly to the sisters, ever imagined a nun dressed in a fashion indistinguishable from her lay counterpart.

"Religious communities should continue to maintain and fulfill the ministries proper to them. In addition, after considering the needs of the Universal Church and individual dioceses, they should adapt them to the requirements of time and place, employing appropriate and even new programs and abandoning those works which today are less relevant to the spirit and authentic nature of the community."

It is worth turning to the role of women in the final two sessions of Vatican II, because it was then that the suggestion of Cardinal Suenens, that women be admitted as auditors, silent of course, was implemented. Only one American was among the group invited and as it turned out, she was already on her way to Rome. Sr. Mary Luke Tobin was the mother superior of her order, the Sisters of Loretto, and was as well, president of the LCWR. The major superiors had suggested to Tobin that she travel to Rome for the third session. "During the voyage across the Atlantic, I received a telephone call from a reporter for the New York Times. 'How do you feel about your invitation to attend Vatican II?'"[8] she was asked. When she expressed surprise, the reporter informed her that word had come from the Vatican only just that morning.

The men in charge of planning the sessions anticipated the arrival of the women with concern and apparent trepidation; their presence, it was felt, raised issues that would have to be dealt with and decisions that would need to be made. First among these was the issue of the coffee bars and what should be done about them. These bars were very popular places, usually crowded, actually very crowded. Political arguments were waged at length, as men came together, before and after the daily sessions.

Were there actually to be *women* present? Were these prelates going to be asked, *literally*, to "rub shoulders," *physically*, with women? This was apparently unthinkable. If the underlying emotions were not so serious, the situation might have been considered comical; rather it laid bare what is usually hidden and hidden successfully, and that is the degree to which women are "other" in the view of supposedly holy men. A solution had to be found. The powers to be decreed that a separate coffee bar should be arranged for the women and their presence at the existing coffee bars should be forbidden. And this is what came to pass.

And so the women gathered both morning and evening alone, initially. But as the days went on, and they met more and more of the male clerics in attendance, friendships based on mutual interest of course took place and these men were often invited guests at the women's coffee bar. Actually, at many points, the number of prelates outnumbered the women auditors; apparently they were good company. There is no record of who complained to whom, but on one morning, a Swiss Guard appeared, posted at the entrance to the women's coffee bar; women were to be admitted, men were not. Again, there is no record of how it happened that the following morning, the Swiss Guard had gone back to guarding whomever or whatever Swiss Guards guard.

Although it would be easy to respond to this incident, and the issue of the coffee bars in general, as if these concerns were simply humorous, or perhaps even ludicrous, they beg actually for deeper and more serious consideration. They seem to reflect a surprising level of concern, a concern bordering on actual fear, *a fear both personal, primal and inchoate.* Why were these prelates so unnerved?

In fact, because they lived lives hermetically sealed into worlds of men; residing in the mansions provided them, they took neither crowded subways nor buses to or from work, where they might have encountered the shoulders of – yes, women. Perhaps they might even, eventually, have found this commonplace.

But distance and its' consequent ignorance permit myths, age-old fantasies, and the ideas of St. Thomas Aquinas to continue unchecked; in actual fact, Eve had been too busy for many years, raising her children, getting graduate degrees and making a living, to hang out with serpents or be bothered with apples. But if these prelates were still prisoners of an older, actually an *ancient view of women*, and it seems clear that they were, what were the implications for the future of women in their church? What were the possibilities for any genuine position or experience based on any idea of equality? The bleak answer then continues now as current reality. Even to speak in favor of women's ordination is to invite excommunication.

During the final days there was a change in the council's procedures; there was no further discussion of documents. These sessions now were given over solely to the process of voting; of the 16 documents of Vatican II, 10 were now fact. In early December, the voting on those remaining occurred; the working sessions of the council ended, and the formalities of closure began.

Among these was a Mass, which included an address by the Pope, a "homily." "Perhaps most striking in the talk was the *unidirectional* relationship that the pope depicted between church and world, bypassing the reciprocity that was notable in Gaudium et Spes."[9] One could infer that on the last day of the council, its undoing began.

On the next morning, December 8, over 300,000 people gathered in St. Peter's Square for the final ceremony. The church bells in all of Rome began to ring and the council fathers began the long march out of the papal palace, arriving before the altar set up in the square, where the Pope would say mass. Ceremony ended with the reading of the pope's Apostolic Letter, In Spiritu Sancto, which declared the council at an end. "In the name of our Lord Jesus Christ, go in peace," he intoned. The crowd responded, "Deo gratias" – Thanks be to God.[10]

And so the sisters moved forward, largely unaware although intuited by some, that they had been set by the council on a collision course with conservative prelates, who had been in the minority during the meeting, but at home, continued supreme. And that supremacy would soon make itself felt.

NOTES: PART TWO

1. http://www.thezephyr.com/papabili.htm
2. http://www.thedivinemercy.org/news/Pope-John-XXIII-and-Vatican-II-5670
3. Rynne, Op.Cit., p. 51.
4. *https://www.catholicculture.org/culture/library/view.cfm?recnum=3233*, P.111.
5. The following quotations, unless otherwise specified, are from Perfectae Caritatus. For the full document, see Appendix Three
6. This instruction actually caused more disruption than anyone had foreseen. The church, it would seem, was to be denied the army of sisters previously at their command. Is it any surprise? That both outrage and chaos followed in many quarters?
7. Schneiders, Sr. Sandra. "New Wineskins," Paulist Press, P. 139. NY 1986.
8. Tobin, Sr. Mary Luke. "Hope is an Open Door." Abingdon Press, Nashville, Tennessee, 1981. P. 19.
9. "What Happened at Vatican II," by John W. O'Malley, Harvard University Press, Cambridge, Massachusetts, 2008, P. 287.
10. Ibid., P. 289.

PART THREE

Part Three: Considering the Concept of Obedience

To consider the concept of obedience as conceptualized by Roman Catholicism is a difficult, even daunting, undertaking. Obedience to whom? From whom? Under what circumstances? When? The concept has undergone significant shifts over the timeline of the Church and an in-depth history is beyond the scope of this book.

Three points of concentration, however, might shed some light. First, to consider obedience at a given interval in time seems a useful beginning. The few hundred years after the crucifixion would be the logical choice, since it was then that orthodoxy, i.e. *that to which one must be obedient,* began its torturous path to definition. It was then that the basic structure and the guiding principles of the infant Church emerged, and most of those principles remain unto the present day. Consequently those first three-plus centuries are worthy of attention.

A second focal point which might shed light are the ideas about obedience put forward by American sisters in their recent path to renewal. This would involve an examination of the history and nature of the religious vows. Especially important is the vow of obedience taken by sisters, their understanding of their vows in contrast to the Vatican's, and finally the shift in the concept of obedience following Vatican II. Redefinitions and further redefinitions have continually been put forward by women religious since that time and it is within the context of those redefinitions that much of the current conflict between the Vatican and American sisters has taken place.

Then finally, the Congregation for the Doctrine of the Faith must take center stage; this is the Vatican congregation whose task is both to define and demand obedience and submission, the mandate it has carried out for centuries. Although readers will encounter the CDF in several of the chapters in Part Four, a more formal presentation of their history, as well as a detailed explication of their actual trial procedures is relevant. To proceed step by step with the Congregation for the Doctrine of the Faith as it pursues a case of perceived disobedience should illuminate as well. Consequently, an account of the trial of Father Charles Curran, a controversial professor of theology, will be included.

This section will attempt to follow these three paths, beginning with the "when," the origins of orthodoxy, to which obedience is owed.

The early Christian centuries:

The earliest Church "extended from the first to the sixth century, from Clement of Rome to Gregory the Great, from Ireland to Egypt, and from North Africa to the shores of the Black Sea."[1] But during the life of Jesus, there was no Christian church as it is now understood. Judaism had existed for centuries but at the time was in the throes of its own redefinition; the "rabbinic movement" was in full swing, permitting "the Jewish people to survive the next two millennia."[2] But there was no "Church."

There was only this firebrand charismatic preacher, this "passionate advocate...of justice,"[3] who never wrote anything down and who never used the words "priest" or "bishop"; indeed, the word "Christianity" first appears more than 100 years later. There are no writings from the time of Jesus himself; years pass before the letters of Paul and eventually the gospels themselves are written. Tales of this preacher and his invitations to freedom could only have circulated by word of mouth. "The Gospels as we now have them are not direct or first-hand biographies of Jesus. Nor do they operate under modern conceptions of writing history. Instead, they are early attempts to tell the story of Jesus for a particular audience in a particular context or social location."[4] And for a particular political purpose.

There were many "miracle stories" told in the ancient Mediterranean world, where "wonder working was a conventional way to establish a charismatic leader's qualifications."[5] When charismatic figures claimed miracles, those in power countered with accusations of magic. Mark argues, as Jesus did, that if he is casting out demons, "so he must be from God, since Satan would not consent to overthrow his kingdom."[6]

When Jesus preached, who were his listeners? The answer, of course, is Jews. It was Jews to whom he spoke and it was certain Jews who then followed; they were however considered simply a heretical sect within Judaism, of which there were many others. It was not until decades later, when many more converts were gained, that Roman authorities began to discern that a new religion was emerging and that it should be considered something quite different from Judaism.

Paul of Tarsus was one of the first important Jews to convert to the new religion some forty years after the death of Jesus, and he never considered himself anything but a Jew. His was the role of missionary. Paul is first and foremost, however, a revolutionary, neither impartial nor analytical. "If Luke can be trusted, Paul grew up in Tarsus, a Hellenized city, yet he became a Pharisee. His Jewish past included Pharisaic and Hellenistic components, but no one feature can explain his mode of thinking. And his conversion overturned his past by giving him an entirely new perspective on it"[7] and turned his sights towards the conversion of others.

"Luke reports that each time Paul arrived in a new town, he first turned to the synagogue for lodging and support but then used it as a pulpit from which to advance his mission."[8] Eventually, as it became apparent that although he might consider himself a Jew, he was preaching something quite different from Judaism, his welcome in local synagogues diminished and he turned to the use of private homes, which were eventually recognized as "house churches."

It should be noted that Paul's contribution to missionary work was striking, and his introduction of and concentration on the idea of baptism solidified and simplified the process of conversion for gentiles. He "stands out as the one who really catapulted the movement to a new level by virtue of his mission to non-Jews."[9] But indeed, most missionary work was done by non-missionaries, that is, the early citizens of Judea and the Diaspora, as well as inhabitants of the major cities of Asia Minor, Greece and Rome.

These non-missionaries, "these nameless Christians were merchants, slaves, and others who traveled for various reasons, but whose travel provided the opportunity for the expansion of the Christian message."[10] Countless individuals, these "nameless Christians," brought the news of the gospel down the many roads they traveled, across their rivers and over their mountains to the furthest reaches of the Roman Empire. This constant travel favored the spread of Christianity. Many more Gentiles than Jews found their way to the new religion.

The idea of freedom inherent in Jesus' message had wide appeal. "Freedom in its many forms, including free will, freedom from demonic powers, freedom from social and sexual obligations, freedom from tyrannical government and from fate; and self-mastery as the source of such freedom,"[11] were ideas that resonated, ideas whose time had come. So did the emphasis on persuasion as a means of effecting change rather than the use of power or force.

Seeds of democracy could be found; dissidents argued that "true liberty … involves freedom of speech – that is, the freedom to stand up to unjust rulers."[12] Indeed, it seemed that something new and promising had appeared, and was welcomed, one of those "brief shining moments" when men and women glimpsed a promise that they might not live to realize but in which they could, if only for a little while, believe. Something that they did not yet have still might be possible.

By the end of the first century, James, the brother of Jesus, leader of the Jerusalem church, had been executed. Peter and Paul had been killed. There was "a growing awareness that the old generation had passed on... the age of the "apostles" was gone."[13] New works continued to be written in their name, but "Jewish Christians continued in this tenuous middle ground."[14]

Nonetheless, the shape of things to come was beginning to take form, but "the church needed a fuller and more coherent account of its Gentile mission. ... Luke attempts to synthesize the different interpretations of Jesus' message promulgated by the Jewish Christians and the Gentile Christians. In doing so, he reconciles the ideas of Paul and Peter. He idealizes their thoughts and lives, partly because he views them from a distance of 50 years and partly because he sees Christian destiny more clearly to lie with the Gentile church."[15]

A structure begins then to emerge, a direction sociologists would applaud; definition is required, they believe, for any movement to achieve longevity. By the beginning of the second century, Christian groups were beginning to understand themselves to be different than and apart from conventional Judaism; they were moving towards institutionalization. Formal roles and offices were taking the place of personal charisma. Stricter definitions had come into play; orthodoxy and heresy began to be defined, as part of the growing consolidation of diversity into a more clearly defined movement. "Christians ... began gathering in private houses ... on Sundays for the breaking of the bread, but often more frequently for instruction and for joint support in the increasingly difficult task of living as Christians in a hostile world."[16]

"By the middle of the second century, we find the hierarchical definition of ministry becoming more widespread."[17] In addition, it seems clear that the model for the hierarchical church has become that of the family, with males at the head and women now in clearly subordinate position. "This is a far cry from [the] free flow of charismatic expression and leadership of women as house-church patrons that one sees in the genuine letters of Paul."[18] But that was an earlier time and that time was gone, never to return.

Orthodox Christianity then began to define which elements of its Jewish parentage it wished to maintain and "in order to reaffirm such doctrines, it developed a series of instruments – creeds, the canon of scripture, apostolic succession – that would set limits on orthodoxy and would long remain central themes in Christian life and teaching."[19] In doing so, however, it set the emerging religion on a collision course with the requirements of the Roman Empire's system of government.

All their civil ceremonies, their social events, as well as any activity of the armed forces began with sworn oaths of allegiance that were absolutely required. Those who followed the new faith could not so swear. That would be "tantamount to worshipping false gods."[20] "To be a Christian required a commitment to the sole worship of God, and any deviation from that commitment was a denial of Jesus Christ."[21]

So it came to pass that "Christians were accused of being subversive, for they refused to worship the emperor,"[22] and consequently were seen to be destroying the very fiber of society. If these new religionists believed, as they did, that the worship of the Roman gods had to be rejected, then they were required by their own beliefs to abstain from participation in these civil ceremonies and to avoid service in the armed forces. "Records begin to afford a clearer view of the issues involved in the persecutions, and of the attitudes of Christians toward martyrdom,"[23] a shift from the previous hundred years.

"But what made Christians especially dangerous to the Roman order was their refusal to pay what Romans regarded as ordinary respect to their Roman rulers; and this brought some of them into direct and total opposition to the temporal as well as the divine authorities - to the emperors and to their divine patrons, the gods."[24] The entire basis of Roman Imperial power was being assaulted, and the radical message of Jesus Christ was "spreading rapidly throughout the cities of the Empire. Some Roman officials were dumbfounded by this Christian defiance."[25]

But as the authorities moved against the new faithful, the persecutions that followed seemed only to serve the growing religion; Christian defiance could be interpreted as heroism. By refusing to sacrifice to the gods and the emperors they marked themselves as targets for arrest, torture and execution, while "the boldest among them maintained that, since demons controlled the government and inspired its agents, the believer could gain freedom at their hands only in death."[26] No incense would be offered to the false deities; Christians would stand fast. By the turn of this second century and into the third, Tertullian would observe, "The blood of Christians is seed," and would go on to observe that this new faith was "based upon a new religious ideology and a new vision of human nature. The emperors [rule] by force and violence; but among the Christians, Tertullian said, everything is voluntary."[27]

Before moving ahead to the third century and then the eventual recognition of the new faith by the Emperor Constantine in the fourth century, it would be well to pause and consider another Christian sect, the Gnostics. Gnosticism was a serious competitor with early Christianity for converts. The words "Gnostic" and "Gnosticism" have their root in the Greek work "gnosis," which means "knowledge." The orthodox Christian position of the time "legitimized a hierarchy of persons *through whose authority all others must approach God.* (Italics the authors) Gnostic teaching… was potentially subversive of this order; it claimed to offer to every initiate direct access to God of which the priests and bishops themselves might be ignorant."[28] Despite the looseness of their organization, they were seen by many to pose "a serious threat to Christianity throughout the second century."[29]

Elaine Pagels, the well-known Princeton scholar, author of several books about the early church, describes a particular group of Gnostic Christians "that among themselves … refused to acknowledge … distinctions. Instead of ranking their members into superior and inferior "orders" within a hierarchy, they followed the principle of strict equality. All initiates, men and women alike, participated equally… Anyone might be selected to serve as priest, bishop, or prophet. Furthermore, because they cast lots at each meeting, even the distinctions established by lot could never become permanent "ranks." Finally – most important – they intended, through this practice, to remove the element of human choice.… They believed that since God directs everything in the universe, the way the lots fell expressed his choice."[30] Clearly, the concept of stratification in relation to authority is completely rejected. There is to be no hierarchy; the individual conscience, the private and personal process of discernment is considered paramount. "When Gnostic and Orthodox Christians discuss[ed] the nature of God, they were at the same time debating the issue of spiritual authority,"[31] and the role of power within a given system.

The two groups differed as well over the role of women, who played a significant part in Gnostic ceremonies and among certain Gnostic groups were considered to be the equal of men. In earlier times, "some 10 to 20 years after Jesus' death, certain women [had] held positions of leadership in local Christian groups; women acted as prophets, teachers, and evangelists. [But] from the year 200 we have no evidence for women taking prophetic, priestly, and Episcopal roles among Orthodox churches.

This is an extraordinary development, considering that in its earliest years the Christian movement showed a remarkable openness toward women. Jesus himself violated Jewish convention by talking openly with women, and he included them among his companions."[32] But, "by the end of the second century, women's participation in worship was explicitly condemned: groups in which women continued on to leadership were branded as heretical."[33] So the decisions made by the then emerging Christianity may well have been made *in reaction to* Gnostic beliefs, i.e. the need to differentiate themselves dramatically from this competing faith.

Although much was known about the Gnostics prior to 1945, the discovery then in northern Egypt of what are now called the Nag Hammadi documents, finally translated in 1970 and eventually but slowly available to scholars throughout the world, has shed much more light. The Nag Hammadi find includes the Gnostic Bibles, of which there are many, and these cast the apostles, Jesus and the women who followed him, most notably Mary Magdalene, in a quite different light. These documents were certainly known in their own time, although lost to the world from the sixth through the twentieth century. They will be discussed at length in Part Five when the role of women in the church is discussed and are mentioned here only in counterpoint to the emerging Christianity. Gnostics went on to exemplify certain sociological principles, namely the need for hierarchical structure to ensure longevity. Decrying structure, they disappeared a few centuries later.

As the third century continued, authorities increasingly saw in Christianity "a movement with subversive overtones,"[34] and they increased their efforts to suppress it by whatever means necessary; they saw this as a necessary policy for the defense of the continuation and integrity of the state. "No matter how faithful to the emperor and the empire Christians thought they were, they were in fact subverting the very fiber of society by withdrawing from its main civic and religious functions, and thus acting as if they were not valid. ... These subversive undertones of Christian teaching and practice formed the basis of continued persecution by some of the most able emperors of the second and third centuries, and explain the fact that as Roman officials attained a fuller understanding of Christianity, persecution, rather than declining, became even fiercer."[35]

In the middle of the third century, with the ascent of Decius to the throne, the restoration of the ancient religion, so undermined by the rise of Christianity, was given paramount importance. "What was at stake, as Decius saw it, was the survival of Rome itself. Those who refused to worship the gods were practically guilty of high treason."[36] As a consequence, arrests of Christians increased significantly and then, "through a combination of promises, threats, and torture [he tried] to force them to abandon their faith."[37] But with successive emperors, policies came into existence and then were set aside and Christians continued their policies of resistance. "The superhuman courage they displayed in the amphitheater as they endured … execution, convinced [Tertullian] that they were possessed by an extraordinary power."[38]

"Early in the fourth century, however, the worst persecution broke out."[39] Not only were Christians dismissed from any and all governmental positions they might have held but in addition, it was decreed that all Christian books and buildings were to be destroyed. "Many Christians refused to turn over their sacred writings, and in such cases they were tortured and condemned to death.… The situation grew worse… [Diocletian] then decreed, first, that all the leaders of the churches be arrested and, somewhat later, that all Christians must offer sacrifice to the gods.… The rest were tortured with refined cruelty, and eventually killed in a variety of ways."[40]

Then, in 306 CE, Constantine became emperor of the Western Empire and decreed that Christians, as long as they refrained from direct interference with public order, would once again be allowed to gather in assembly and that their buildings and other properties would be returned to them. Persecution was to come to an end. He wanted the chaos and disharmony to cease.

The origins of Constantine's positive views of Christianity remain obscure; scholars disagree. His mother had become a convert years before, and presumably this event must be considered significant, but his own personal religious convictions remain unclear. He did not himself actually convert to Christianity until he was on his deathbed, and deathbed conversions are usually considered by the faithful, unlike deathbed confessions, to be notoriously unconvincing. However, during his lifetime, regardless of what he may have actually *believed,* he *ruled* as if he were a Christian, from his earliest decrees until his death.

In the autumn of 312 CE, Constantine began a campaign "that would eventually make him master of the empire."[41] He would gather his armies, cross the Alps and march on Rome. One hesitates to report how these events actually unfolded, since basically both reason as well as rationality are defied and the facts sound like a page out of some obscure text written by a madman. But most accounts agree on the salient if extraordinary factors; Constantine had a dream. *A dream?* Yes. A dream.

In this dream, dreamt before the oncoming battle, he saw a vision in the sky and the words "In this you shall conquer." In the dream he was commanded to place upon the shields and standards of his soldiers an emblem, which looked very much like the superimposition of the Greek letters "chi" and "rho," quite obviously the first two letters of the name, "Christ." As inconceivable as it may seem, his plan was to use the name of the "Prince of Peace" *to wage war.* And this is exactly what he did, and did successfully.

With numerically smaller forces, he defeated Maxentius at the battle of Milvian Bridge in 312 CE (Christian Era); retreating across the river, Maxentius drowned, along with the greater part of his army as the bridge he had built out of boats collapsed. Henceforward, the idea that Constantine's forces were favored by God took hold. In battles to come, enemy soldiers were afraid to look directly at those shields emblazoned with their powerful emblem. It is, of course, something of a disadvantage to try to win a battle while not looking directly at the enemy.

Then in February of 313 CE, he engineered, with Licinius, then Emperor of the Eastern Empire, an agreement known as the "Edict of Milan," which officially brought an end to the persecution of Christians. Confiscated church property was to be returned; religious freedom was now the political position of the state. The empire was to be officially neutral with regard to religious worship. All religions were to be tolerated. Constantine favored Christianity for many reasons; most simply, persecution had failed, only resulting in discord and dissension. He became a patron of the new religion.

In 324 CE, he went on to reunite the Roman Empire with the defeat of Licinius, emperor of its' eastern half. Following an uneasy peace after earlier battles with him, Constantine was ready finally to begin the conflict anew. He invaded Thrace in force. Although his forces were smaller in number, they included well-seasoned men, many of whom had fought in previous wars. During the battle, Constantine ordered his men to move his standard, the cross of the chi and the rho, to any of the fields of the battle where his troops may be understood as endangered. This talisman not only strengthened the resolve of his own troops, but undermined the courage of his opposition; *the invocation of Jesus as talisman on the field of war was invaluable.*

Many Christians were appalled. But events had gone on without them and their disapproval was left behind on the dust of the battlefield with 34,000 dead and Constantine sole ruler of the extended Roman world, for the first time in many decades. Christian doctrine finally achieved "a firm hold on the Roman Empire, for it gave to the empire a sense of unity and religious purpose that had been lacking… Christianity gave Rome a universal religion and gave the empire a single philosophical justification."[42]

Success always has consequences and with Constantine's success, the consequences were more than significant. Christianity was led around a hairpin curve. "Becoming a Christian was no longer the heroic choice."[43] Opposition to the emperor ceased. The church was given many forms of financial support, including the endowment of land and other wealth, and the clergy began to receive significant privileges, as well as access to high office, previously unavailable to them.

Bishops, formerly seen as enemies, became principal advisors and were charged with enacting the emperor's will. In return they were given a good deal of power, both religious and judicial. "No longer targets of arrest, torture, and execution, now they received tax exemptions, donations in gold, great prestige, and, in some cases even influence at the Imperial Court."[44] This corruption of the church of Jesus spread rapidly, gaining a solid foothold; there would be no return to pre-Constantine positions, no turning back.

"Incense, which was used as a sign of respect for the emperor, began appearing in Christian churches. Officiating ministers, who until then had worn everyday clothes, began dressing in more luxurious garments – and soon were called 'priests,' in imitation of their pagan counterparts, while the communion table became an 'altar.'"[45] For the first time "the princely panoply of ceremonial that has characterized the Vatican in post-Constantinian times"[46] is on display and continues to be.

There were Christian statesmen, Chrysostom for example, who "deplored what had happened to the church since imperial favor first shone upon Christians: first, the massive influx of nominal converts; and second, the way that a shower of imperial privileges had radically changed the dynamics – and raised the stakes – of ecclesiastical politics."[46] That people were flocking to the church was not a blessing, but rather a significant loss, he thought. They were coming "in such numbers that there was little time to prepare them for baptism, and even less to guide them in the Christian life once they had been baptized. In contrast to earlier times, when there was a far-reaching program of teaching and training for new converts, the church now found itself overwhelmed by the numbers of those requesting baptism, and [was] unable to give them proper training and supervision."[47]

"The new privileges, prestige and power now granted to church leaders soon led to acts of arrogance and even to corruption."[48] And there was a mass exodus of more devout Christians to the deserts of Egypt and Syria where monastic colonies sprang up and flourished.

"Asceticism offered a new path for uncompromising "witness" – a new form of self-chosen martyrdom."[49]

Constantine died, finally baptized a Christian on his deathbed, in 337 AD, and Christianity began a new career as "the Imperial religion of a factionated Roman Empire."[50] Christians are no longer the victims of power; the power is now theirs. Those who had been subject to arrest, torture and execution are now those who have the power to arrest, torture and execute, powers they will soon enact over the many centuries to come. Gone are images of freedom or any idea of democracy; the growth of the eventual Catholic religion is corrupted for all time with the "imperialism" of Constantine. The ideas, the doctrines to which obedience must be paid, are now clear. Orthodoxy has been defined; all else is heresy. Authority is absolute; obedience must be unquestioned. Power, backed by force, is valued above all else.

Jesus is all but forgotten.

The Vows of Women Religious

When nuns make their vows, they are expressing their determination to live "a consecrated life"; they are responding to "a mysterious and personal call to a certain kind of commitment to Jesus Christ to the exclusion of any other primary life commitment."[51] They are making promises, of course, since that is the very definition of a vow, but to whom are they making those promises?

Nuns are not priests; their non-clerical status is extremely important, more than basic, to any understanding of what these religious actually promise. Following ordination, the priest "makes a *promise* of obedience *to his ecclesiastical superior,* which binds him *to obey that superior* (and his successors) in relation to the *exercise of his office* in the church."[52] Women Religious make no such promise. Their vows are made only to God, "not to their superiors or church officials. … [Women] Religious make their vows *according to* the Constitutions of their order (which includes a particular relationship to Church law), in the *presence of* their superiors, but only *to God.*" Nuns, unlike priests, "are *not agents of the institutional Church* as Jesus was not an agent of institutional Judaism."[53] (Italics the authors)

The three traditional vows of both women and men religious are poverty, chastity and obedience. It is this last, of course, which this section addresses, but both poverty and chastity deserve brief consideration. The vow of poverty was "intended to take a person's heart and mind away from the quest for wealth and worldly goods. In practice, it became a vow of sharing."[54] In current parlance, it refers to living simply.

The vow of chastity is actually a vow of celibacy, "a vow to live without an exclusive or sexual love relationship with another human being."[55] The reasoning behind the vow was that a loving or passionate relationship with another person would lessen or distract from the fullness of the individual's love of God. "Human love of any kind was [understood to be] dangerous to the vow of chastity."[56]

There seems to have been a conviction within the hierarchy that without formal and extremely strict constraints, temptation would carry the day, impulse would triumph; external regulation, not personal responsibility, was to provide the necessary backbone for the maintenance of the vow of chastity. It seems in retrospect likely that the men who made these rules for women were reasoning more from their own psychology and experience, an understandable error given their circumstances. But finally, following first the combined influences of Eugenio Pacelli (Pius 12) and the Sister Formation Conference and then the mandates of Vatican II, the convent walls and the rules those walls enforced began to give way, eventually disappearing altogether. Now sisters believe "that embracing human love in the context of their primary relationship with God is the very essence of their vow of chastity."[57]

Vatican II's mandated process of redefinition had profound effects on the vow of obedience as well and it was essentially this process that set the sisters on their collision course with the conservative wing of the hierarchy, placing their very future, at least for a decade, in doubt. That this was unintended, as well as unforeseen, is accepted; the gravity of the consequences, however, was no less real. Historically, obedience had been a relatively uncomplicated concept.

The word "obedience" comes from the Latin ob-audiere, which translates to "listen attentively." The Code of Canon Law (Canon 601) defines obedience as follows: "The evangelical counsel of obedience, undertaken in a spirit of faith and love in the following of Christ who was obedient even unto death requires a submission of the will to legitimate superiors, who stand in the place of God when they command according to the proper constitutions."[58] Obedience was understood as "humble, uncritical submission to the will of an appointed superior, whose commands were received as from God."[59]

Prior to Vatican II, the model was one of domination and subordination. Obedience was understood as "listening to … superiors and to the Rule, and doing what they asked."[60] This vow of obedience had been first instituted in a world "where royalty ruled. It was an age when bishops, abbots and abbesses were generally more educated than their underlings and were assumed to know more about the needs of the larger world."[61] Illiteracy was the rule then, literacy the exception and in most instances those in charge indeed did know more than those for whom they were responsible. "Thus, subjects were supposed to obey them, especially when it came to ministry."[62]

Traditional obedience was to be automatic and unquestioned. Religiously empowered males were given control over religious women "even, and perhaps especially in the minute and personal details of their lives – what they may (and may not) wear, where and with whom and how they must live, what education and employment is permitted them, … and whose permission is required for any modification of their lives. Hierarchical control was absolute."[63] Following Vatican II, "Ruling over subjects as children of God" [was] no longer understood as "a sacred image of responsible decision-making."[64] It was clearly understood to be a system designed to maintain "stratified divisions of class and of power, affirming and continuing the dichotomies implicit in such polarities as domination/subjugation and control/acquiescence."[65]

How well suited this model is for 21st century Catholics, both Religious and lay, is open to debate; where Religious are concerned, most Catholic sisters today live outside the United States, in countries where autocracy may be more familiar or at least not as jarring as it is to those accustomed to a democratic way of life. American Religious are certainly resistant, as the recent collisions with Rome have clearly demonstrated. But the model encounters even further opposition in the American Catholic lay community.

Here many Catholics simply define rules according to their own convictions. The majority of lay Catholics consider the individual rather than the hierarchy as the "proper locus of moral authority" and women in greater proportions than men believe this to be the case; in 2005, more than a decade ago, "66% of women believed this about contraception, 51% about homosexuality, and 51% about extra-marital sex."[66] These percentages are certainly higher now. It should not be surprising that women trust their own judgment when it comes to intimate or sexual issues, and that they honor their own experience before that of celibate men who have never borne children or raised families. "Obedience" as a concept is encountering significant resistance on many fronts.

The orthodox definition of obedience has certainly not been "received," according to the canonical doctrine of "Reception," which, broadly stated, asserts that for a law or rule to be an effective guide for the believing community it must be *accepted* by that community. The hierarchy seems to have forgotten or simply willfully and conveniently overlooked "Reception."

Neither was "obedience" well-received in the late 1940s; in the aftermath of World War II, the trials of Nazi war criminals at Nuremberg placed the question of "obedience" under an unforgiving microscope. One Nazi after another claimed innocence of wrong doing; they were simply "following orders." Could religious men and women continue to accept as an ideal the concept of "total submission to the will of another human being as a good?"[67] The Reverend Bernard Häring, the priest who was Angelo Roncalli's (John 23) confessor and a well-respected Catholic theologian, didn't think so. He said, "After Auschwitz, we can never look at absolute obedience the same way again."[68]

Wasn't a new understanding of "responsible obedience"[69] required? Indeed it was, but was not forthcoming until Vatican II charged the nuns of America to question themselves and the lives they were living. It can't of course be known with any certainty what was in the minds of the men who sent those women on that mission; the fact is, however, that the sisters took them literally. They did exactly what they were told. Once more, unforeseen consequences followed.

What took place in the subsequent decades then, was a complete reversal of many directions: "right relationships ... replaced renunciation; responsibility and collaboration ... replaced submission and protective rules. Most dramatically, the convent walls that protected love from risk … disappeared, an artifact of centuries past."[70] Those changes, taken together over time, constitute what the sisters now refer to as "renewal," a shift "from an ethic of obedience to an ethic of responsibility."[71] They hoped to perceive in Rome "a form of religious authority that inspires by the authenticity of its witness and convinces by the cogency of the reasons given for its positions," rather than "authoritarian edicts and punitive measures."[72] Those hopes have yet to be realized.

Within the renewal process, the concept of obedience was redefined and continues to evolve. Without a book of rules to follow, how are decisions made? Now when sisters strive to practice obedience, they try "to listen attentively and collaboratively, to respond creatively and responsibly, and to embrace generously."[73] Blind obedience is replaced by personal responsibility. Obedience is no longer seen as a specific act, but rather as a process, a process in which *discernment, and discernment in community*, plays the most significant role. To discover God's will is the ultimate goal. This "discernment" is to be achieved by the individual in prayer and then "searching together," coming to "decisions within the bonds of community."[74]

This idea, the concept of "community," has also undergone profound redefinition in the process of renewal; "the community" is no longer understood as the sisters of a given congregation, living side by side in the order's mother house; in some orders, the "mother house" no longer actually exists. In others, it is the place where some sisters choose to live, but others use settings closer to the apostolates they have chosen. The very term “mother house” suggests hierarchy; the “mother,” of course the mother superior, the sisters the docile, well-behaved children, coming and going, two by two, like grade-school children on their way to the lunch room.

This former structure with its implicit, formally mandated physical proximity is no longer the ultimate definition of community. Now members leave their apostolates and come together as community members when necessary, not for hours-long recitation of prayers but for serious consideration of a given issue when required. “They come together when the occasion warrants, and they separate for ministry as the occasion most frequently warrants. … Like the apostles, the sisters have no other family to call their own, no other home to call their own, besides the Community.”[75] This definition of community is not concrete, not physical, as it once was, but it retains the concepts’ actual essence – a shared mission. Members are voluntarily bound together by their common purpose.

These communities are not static but fluid. The community that formed around Jesus in those early years was just that as well. It was “an apostolic community, a community in mission, a community of disciples … Jesus not only gathered the community, he scattered it. He called disciples to come rest with him and then sent them out in mission.”[76] So it is with today’s sisters, many of whom reside with their own apostolate until they come together for a specific purpose. Then, “authority, that is, the right to use power, rests in the members, who, by reason of this responsibility, must discern what is the will of God, the authentic object of [their] vowed obedience."[77] And it is within these newly defined communities that a newly defined obedience is practiced.

American Sisters may be willing to resist hierarchical definitions. They may even insist upon modification of a Church they dearly love, although it is a church "that is not only rigidly hierarchical but functions as a divine right monarchy in which authority is functionally equated with coercive power and is entirely monopolized by men."[78] But, it should be noted, they have gone no further than that. It is indeed acknowledged that sisters are no longer docile, but it should be noted that they do not assert *their own* better judgment; they simply claim *to obey* a superior authority, God's, the authority to whom they have sworn their vows.

If considered in this light, the sisters seem far less *"disobedient"* than the hierarchy has portrayed them to be. Rome's ire is more likely connected to sisters claiming the *audacity to decide anything*, the issue having less to do with obedience, and much more to do with power. Ken Briggs, writing in the National Catholic Reporter, August 9, 2009, recalled the ongoing dispute of 1971, when the then Conference of Major Superiors of Women (CMSW) wished to change its name to the Leadership Conference of Women Religious (LCWR), the name by which it is currently known. When the nuns asked the Vatican for approval of the name change, it was refused. The Vatican denied the request "on grounds that the word "leadership" implied a furthering of autonomy and independence among women's communities.[79] It became then a significant struggle, albeit a symbolic one.

"Friction over giving the upstart CMSW a more commanding title was never resolved by discussion between conference officials and Rome because Vatican officials refused to agree to talks," Briggs went on. In fact, for three years the sisters used their new name when writing to Rome; for the same three years Rome addressed them by their former name when returning the correspondence. Finally, the dispute was settled "the Italian way," i.e. it was no longer discussed; eventually time eclipsed the conflict. But "women Religious claiming even moderate personal and community autonomy from patriarchal control can seem subversive of hierarchy."[80] Some observers have wondered if the sisters' insistence on emphasizing the behavior of Jesus of Nazareth has not pricked some consciences.

Returning to this current concept of obedience, emerging as it does from several decades of the sisters' renewal process, one can observe that it clearly found its roots in the earliest period of the church – not the Church of Constantine but the church of Jesus. The sisters have chosen to take the path that Jesus traveled, particularly in relation to his eschewing power or force as any solution to conflict. They note that Jesus never coerced, never accepted a position of authority. He came rather as a prophet with his only offering his own truth and love.

He never resorted to violence, and he did not ask for loyalty oaths; he never intimidated through shaming or threats of rejection. He never asked anyone "to recant." He taught by asking questions, encouraging others to think, offering parables rather than rules. He was committed to patient persuasion. That is the ministry they wish to renew. They are "deeply committed to the egalitarian, non-authoritarian, collegial exercise of authority and practice of obedience that Jesus inaugurated among his original band."[81]

Jesus warned harshly "against conspicuous religious apparel. Religious professionals are not to ... make themselves stand out in public places so they will be greeted with deference and addressed with religious titles. ... They are not to pray or fast ostentatiously so as to be admired for their fervor. ... Indeed he instructs them to seek inconspicuous places at public events in solidarity with the poor and sinners"[82] and so, obedient to *these* commands, the sisters came out from behind their habits.

"Jesus, in word and work, not in institution maintenance, [became] the model for ministry for women Religious"[83] and for the definition of obedience. The sisters chose "to live their lives like the apostles, by taking Christ at his word, and following in his footsteps."[84] They would practice what Sr. Sandra Schneiders has called "prophetic obedience," using the word "prophetic" not in the sense of foretelling the future as in "prophesy" but as in "of the prophet."

This prophetic obedience is understood as "an explicit commitment to mindful discernment... the prayerful listening for the will of God,

… [and] not about mindless submission [to the will of another]."[85] In this process, the one who prays is seeking to understand what God would want from him or her in that particular time and place and then to live that understanding. It is obedience to an internal vision of God's will, of what God wishes for that person, rather than blind obedience to an external system of rules.

Schneiders goes on to assert that the sisters "by incarnating in their community life an alternative not only to patriarchy but to all forms of coercion-based exercise of power" offer an alternative "ecclesiology of equal discipleship in which no one is called Rabbi or teacher or father because there is only one teacher, Christ, and one Parent, God, and all members of the community are sisters and brothers."[86] And so alternative ideas continue to emerge, and will continue to emerge. Redefinition continues.

Following the close of Vatican II, Giovanni Montini (Paul 6) was succeeded by two conservative popes, Josef Wojtyla (John Paul 2) and Joseph Ratzinger (Benedict 16); during their papacies, the drive to undo the directives of Vatican II began, and continued to receive both significant support and further encouragement from many and various conservative sources and individuals.

It has certainly been clear to Rome that the sisters of the LCWR, who are numerically the most powerful and certainly the best organized supporters of conciliar ideals and values, represent a threat to those powerful conservatives who wish to return to the pre-conciliar church. When nuns around the world come out unequivocally in support of these sisters, and they do, as the recent conflicts have demonstrated, that danger only appears enhanced. Their perceived power may be experienced as unspoken threat. But that's not who they are.

Nor is it how they work. They have called for "honest and courageous approaches"[87] to contemporary issues, but they have not called for rebellion. Neither have they deserved a decade of harassment. Following the commands of Perfectae Caritatus, they have simply redefined themselves and in the process *redefined obedience.* This new definition, which does not require blind or unquestioning adherence, which is not absolute, this "prophetic obedience" is a concept more than worthy of profound consideration.

The Congregation for the Doctrine of the Faith

The oldest of the nine congregations of the Roman Curia, the governing body of the Catholic Church, is the Congregation for the Doctrine of the Faith (CDF). It is the division of the Vatican bureaucracy, "charged with protecting Catholic orthodoxy and examining and judging the theological, spiritual and religious writings and opinions expressed by all Catholics."[88] Its purpose is to safeguard the proper understanding of faith and morals, and to expose and eradicate heresy, a wide dominion indeed; consequently almost any opinion by any Catholic anywhere can be understood and has been understood to fall within its competence. The CDF is assisted by the Pontifical Biblical Commission and the International Theological

Commission. As a division of the Roman Curia, it governs in the name of the Holy See.

Formerly known as the "Supreme Sacred Congregation of the Roman and Universal Inquisition," its' formal beginnings date to 1542, although inquisitions were conducted as early as the 1200s. The CDF, as it is currently known, is housed today near St. Peter's Basilica in the Palazzo del Sain'Ufficio, within the walls of the Vatican, where it has been since the late 1500s.

"Confession, repentance and contrition were the real aim of the whole inquisitorial process"[89] and that goal sounds quite unthreatening; it was the techniques used to obtain the goal that caused the Inquisition to be so feared by so many for centuries. These ranged from death by burning, life imprisonment, imprisonment for shorter terms, house arrest and milder forms of punishment, such as fines, public humiliation and a form of what is called today "community service." Although its' reputation is a bloodthirsty one, well-deserved when its punishment was extreme, the greatest percentage of punishments were among the milder forms. It bore little resemblance to the earlier medieval inquisitions, particularly in Spain, conducted more as state than church policy, when literally thousands of witches, Jews, midwives and dissenters were indeed burned while still alive.

Punishments today consist of excommunication, both "judged" as well as "automatic," suspension from the priesthood, interdiction from the sacraments, and for Catholic faculty teaching in Catholic institutions, the loss of their *missio canonica*, their teaching license as "theologians." Almost all of these punishments are less draconian than their descriptions suggest, are usually reversible, and, can be withdrawn if and when "true repentance" is demonstrated. Those excommunicated are still considered Catholics, since they were baptized, and are actually bound to attend mass, although barred from receiving communion. They are, however, denied burial in consecrated ground.

In most American dioceses, the serving bishop has the power to lift an excommunication; he can and often does delegate this power to his local parish priests, thereby enabling a penitent to confess, be absolved and returned to good standing all in one confessional experience. This is seen as especially advisable when the sin to be confessed, having undergone an abortion for example, is either deeply personal, very emotional or both. The goal in all instances is to reconcile the sinner with the church. Some excommunications, however, are deemed sufficiently serious, so that they require absolution by the Pope himself.

The procedures of the CDF as practiced today have received criticism from around the world, both from without and within Catholicism itself. Its' judicial structure is seen as an unabashed remnant of imperial power, highly secretive, deeply personal, and unknown elsewhere in the western world. Its goal is the submission of the accused. It is not a democracy and has never wished to be one; it seems actually scornful of democratic process. It wields its power unselfconsciously, apparently unworried by the criticism of others and unquestioning in its own convictions of correctness. In conjunction with the pope, it makes its' own rules and seemingly knows no doubts. Its' procedures may scandalize those raised under western democracies; they do not scandalize the Holy See.

The origin of any trial begins with a received accusation; it is unusual for a lay Catholic to be accused, since they are rarely vulnerable to punishment. Priests, theologians, members of religious orders, because they are directly employed by the Church are far more vulnerable, and consequently are far more likely to be chosen. The CDF uses a technical term for accusations; they are called "delations," an unfamiliar word in English. "It is derived from the Latin legal term *delatio*, which in turn is derived from the verb *defero*,"[90] which has a range of meanings; the word can connote "indicting, impeaching, accusing or complaining about someone."[91] If the delation seems serious a file is opened; in the file, all relevant, written materials – books, speeches, articles, newspaper articles – are collected and kept. At this point, the accused is ignorant of the procedure.

Delations usually come from persons residing in the same country as the accused. If the accuser is lay, he, she or they most usually bring their charges to the nearest powerful cleric, a bishop or cardinal. If taken seriously or understood to come from someone powerful their complaint might be forwarded to the papal nuncio and from there, to the CDF. Delations can be sought by political groups as well, and according to the CDF, these would most likely be from either French or American entities. "Delations can also come from reactionary Catholic vigilante groups."[92]

When conflicts break out, as with the nuns, then the other side is heard from. The CDF hears almost entirely from the extremes; Catholics in the center, especially those satisfied with the status quo, are not moved to correspond. A high ranking prelate can of course always complain directly to the CDF, should he choose to do so and this has often been the case, especially when instances of serious differences, perhaps even feuds, have erupted between diocesan participants who are unable to agree.

Delations made against those who teach are taken the most seriously and would follow one of several possible procedures, depending on the gravity of the charges. To summarize, however, the delation moves from one level of conference to the next until a judgment is made by appointed "consultors." Unfortunately these men may be experienced Vatican hands, holding one or more other positions somewhere in the hierarchy, but there is no guarantee, and actually it is unlikely, that they are well-educated or even knowledgeable in the specific area of theology that has sparked the original accusation. The accused is not in attendance nor is he represented by defense counsel as understood in western jurisprudence; rather the Congregation appoints a "relator pro auctore" to defend the position of the one accused; that person's identity however is never known to him. The conferences are conducted in strictest secrecy; the rationale suggested is the protection of the reputation of the accused and the anonymity of the accuser(s).

Eventually the superior of the accused is informed of the charges. The superior is then charged with relaying the details of the situation in writing to the accused, who has known nothing of events until this point, and the accused is instructed to supply a written response and given a time frame, usually several months, in which to do so. From then on, all dialogue passes through the accused persons' superior, conducted completely in writing.

The accused is required "to provide the needed clarifications for submission to the judgment of the congregation; that is they have to explain and justify themselves on the specific points nominated by the CDF consultor. … The accuseds' responses are then judged again. … If at this point the CDF wants to … drop the case, the accused person will be asked to write an article in some theological journal or magazine, either repudiating or "clarifying" their views. In effect this means accepting not only the CDFs' opinion on the matter but often being obliged to quote the CDFs' actual words. The article must be submitted to the CDF for censorship before publication."[93] "Usually there will be long delays, often up to a year or more, between letters from the CDF."[94]

If the accused refuses to write a retraction … the ordinary procedure for examination "is a full-blown trial."[95] A conference is then convened to decide the "gravity" of the situation. At the end of the consultation, the consultors alone vote on the outcome of the examination."[96] It is only at a very late stage in the process that the accused may be involved, if at all.

"The consultors… and the accuseds' superior meet in a kind of closed pre-trial meeting known as a *consulta* (consultation). The accused … is not permitted to attend and may not even know that it is happening. The only person who is acquainted with the accused and who can participate in the consultation is his superior. … But the superior is bound to secrecy … so he or she presumably cannot let the accused know what happened at the consultation. At the end of the consultation the consultors alone vote on the outcome of the examination."[97] The verdict then moves up the line until the Pope is informed. "All of this can happen without the knowledge of the accused. It is only in the second stage that the accused can participate, but even then only at a distance."[98] That is when what the CDF calls "a trial" begins.

Father Charles Edward Curran was a teacher of theology delated to the Vatican, tried and found guilty. Several books, including Curran's own, offer his first-person account. The summary that follows can be found in the book, "From Inquisition to Freedom," by Father Paul Collins, who was himself similarly accused and tried. Their observations are, of course, deeply personal and must be read as such. Further discussion follows Curran's account, which follows.

****

Father Charles Edward Curran was born in Rochester, New York on March 30, 1934, the third of four children. His parents, both second-generation Irish, moved to Rochester in 1926 from New York City, when his father, who was an insurance adjuster, found employment there. He attended Catholic schools, and entered the seminary in 1947, immediately after grammar school; at this seminary, students continued to live at home. He was then sent to Rome where he lived at the North American College for four years and was ordained in 1958, the year that Angelo Roncalli (John 23) was elected.

"I was in St. Peter's Square the night the new Pope was elected and quite frankly I was rather disappointed in him. Pius 12 gave the impression of a saintly ascetic but John appeared to be a roly-poly peasant. How could such a person ever be a good Pope? How wrong I was!"[99]

Still in Rome, in 1959 he began work on a doctorate in Moral Theology at the Gregorian University, where the classes are taught in Latin. His topic was "The Prevention of Conception after Rape." "My thesis was largely a review of the literature, but what helped me immensely later on was that in the process of doing it I came to realize the poor biology upon which our sexual teaching was based."[100] While there, he was significantly influenced by the theological views of the Jesuits as well as the writings of Bernard Häring, particularly Härings' book, "The Law of Christ."

He also became close friends with liberal-leaning priests, including Francis Xavier Murphy, later to become well-known in Catholic circles for his pseudonymous reporting of Vatican II as Xavier Rynne.(See Part Two) He did additional work at the Alfonsiana, the Redemptorist University in Rome and earned a doctorate there as well. His topic was "Ignorance of the Natural Law in St. Alphonsus Liguori." He returned to Rochester to teach at St. Bernard Seminary in Rochester in June 1961.

Friends told him that he wouldn't fit in there, that he was too liberal and they proved to be correct. "Ironically, I never really wanted to teach in the seminary even though I [stayed] there for four years. If I had wanted that I would have become a Jesuit. I really wanted to be a parish priest."[101] Problems started almost immediately. "Eventually there were complaints about some of the things I said and a man named Hugo Maria Kellner got on to me. He was a German refugee with a PhD who worked at Eastman Kodak in Rochester as a chemist. He was very conservative, and he used to mimeograph diatribes which he sent to all the US bishops and to members of the Roman Curia. … He also picked up a couple of things I had written in *Commonweal* – he decided to go after me as a 'heretic.'"[102]

There were also complaints about him from the Bishop of Syracuse who sent his seminarians to St. Bernard's. "It was around this time that I had begun arguing that we needed a change on contraception."[103] In August, 1965, he was told that because of his progressive views he would no longer be teaching in the seminary. He moved to the faculty of Catholic University in Washington, DC. As soon as he was appointed to CU, the same parishioner wrote a letter to every member of the faculty saying, 'You have now accepted this heretic on your staff.'"[104] His contract however was renewed in 1966, but not again the following year.

"At the April 1967 meeting of the Board of Trustees, the trustees voted to fire me. (All of the archbishops of the US were automatically trustees, as well as some bishops and some 'tame' members of the laity.) I was called in by the rector. … [who] told me that the Board of Trustees at their recent meeting had agreed not to renew my contract but that no reason was given. I protested and said that I would fight it and go to the press. He finally got me to agree to think about it for twenty-four hours. A day later some of my friends and colleagues announced that I had been fired and called a meeting. Five hundred students attended. The next day the faculty of theology voted to go on strike. The day after the whole faculty of the university also voted overwhelmingly to go on strike. We closed the whole university down for a week."[105] The story was front-page news in the New York Times for several days. Curran was then 33 years old.

Curran's file in Rome's Holy Office bears the number 48/66, indicating that it was opened in 1966, the year after Vatican II adjourned. The liberals had prevailed at the assembly but the liberals had gone home; the conservatives of the Curia were already at work, their goal a return to the status quo ante. Curran was fired one year later, presumably with Rome's knowledge, and with infuriated and outvoted conservative prelates still riding their wave of outrage and perceived betrayal. "Most of the older US moralists could not make the transition that was implicit in Vatican II. They offered no leadership, so there was a void that pushed me into the position of the public leader of progressive American theologians."[106] Clearly it was not only the American sisters who were inadvertently put on a collision course with the CDF by that famous convocation.

In the following year, 1968, Giovanni Montini (now Paul 6) published his encyclical on birth control. Significant controversy followed immediately. To understand that controversy, a brief review of the encyclical's history follows: When the first oral contraceptives became available to the public in 1960, liberal factions within the Church argued for a reconsideration of Church doctrine on birth control. In 1963, Roncalli (John 23) established the Pontifical Commission on Birth Control, a committee within the Curia, consisting of six European non-theologians to study the relevant issues. What Roncalli (John 23) and Montini (Paul 6) both wished strenuously to avoid was for the issue to be debated by the close to 3,000 men gathered at Vatican II; the subject was declared, with clarity, to be off limits.

After Roncalli (John 23) died, in 1963, Montini (Paul 6) added additional theologians to the commission, which eventually was expanded to 72 members. The participants came from five continents and included sixteen theologians, thirteen physicians and five uncredentialed women. There was in addition an executive committee of sixteen bishops, which included seven cardinals, none of whom were physicians. The report that the Commission wrote in 1966, found that artificial birth control was not intrinsically evil and could be regarded as an extension of the already accepted "rhythm system." It also suggested that Catholic couples should be empowered to decide for themselves which procedures they would choose to use; in other words, freedom and personal choice would not only be tolerated but were the recommendation of the Commission.

A minority report was drafted as well; it was signed by four of the theologians, one cardinal, Cardinal Alfredo Ottaviani (See his record at Vatican II in Part Two) and two bishops. The report insisted that no changes should be made to the teachings of the Church. The report was intended specifically for the Pope, to be relayed in confidence. It expressly charged that should changes be allowed, the Church would be stating publicly that it had been in error, damning acts as sinful that they now declared to be innocent. They would also be agreeing with Protestants.

Unfortunately, the report itself, as well as a rebuttal written by the majority, found their way to the press in 1967; under the most intense pressure possible, brought by the conservatives, Montini (Paul 6) rejected the Commission's report. Perhaps he was convinced, although his rationale that it was not unanimous was strikingly weak, given the lopsided numbers of the vote. The charge that papal authority would be threatened if any changes were allowed was more likely the convincing premise. Uproar followed, leading eventually to the publication of the encyclical, Humanae Vitae. Following the publication of the encyclical, even more uproar ensued.

The encyclical was released on Tuesday, July 29, 1968. Curran was in upstate New York when he was contacted by Time Magazine, and informed that they were in possession of a copy of the report and that contraception had once more been condemned. He found an immediate flight back to Washington, where he and a group of twelve academic theologians from CU, all friends and colleagues, met and began discussion. Phone calls were made; support was immediately forthcoming.

The next morning, the Washington Priests Association scheduled a press conference for 10 AM at the Mayflower Hotel. "We took over their press conference and announced that eighty-eight Catholic scholars had signed a letter of dissent. This was all over the news by the next day. This type of so-called 'organized public dissent' was unheard of; it had never happened in the US Catholic Church before."[107] "Our arguments were that you could dissent from non-infallible papal teachings, which is what the encyclical was."[108] They offered additional theological argument. "We wanted to keep our disagreement very respectful, but also very strong."[109]

The following day he convinced many of the lay members of the Birth Control Commission to come to Washington and another press conference was held. They issued a statement of disagreement, arguing that one could remain a Roman Catholic in good standing and disagree in theory and in practice with papal teaching

The CU Board of Trustees met in September. Cardinal McIntyre of Los Angeles (see Part Four, Chapter 1) was a member and wanted to fire Curran and the others immediately. "But the trustees had learned something from the strike the year before, so they instituted an academic inquiry to see if we had violated our responsibility as Catholic theologians."[110] Through a friend, a fellow academician, he found legal representation for his appearance before the academic inquiry by the Wall Street firm, Cravath, Swaine and Moore on a pro bono basis.

"The first issue that came up at the academic inquiry was the question of dissent. By this stage we had established with the trustees the fact that even in the traditional textbooks of Catholic theology dissent was seen as legitimate. The issue of dissent from non-infallible teaching arose after the definition of papal infallibility."[111] "So because we had already argued that dissent was possible, they changed the charge to 'the manner and mode' of the dissent. They were referring to our public, organized, quick response to the encyclical. There were 20 of us at [the University] involved in this case."[112] In April, 1969 a report was returned, exonerating them.

Although the committee and the academic Senate accepted the report, Curran believes that the trustees never fully embraced it, never forgot what had happened, and that he was now clearly identified as a liberal activist, trouble-maker and target; he believed that the activists of the Catholic right as well as arch-conservative newspapers agreed.

He opted then for a lower profile. "I tried throughout the 1970s to keep much of my writing to a scholarly level and I published most of my books with the more academic Notre Dame University Press. While many of us in this period were disappointed with Pope Paul VI and the latter part of his papacy was not a particularly open period, there were still possibilities and a degree of optimism remained."[113]

Curran continued his specialization in sexual ethics, disagreeing with the theological positions of Thomas Aquinas.

But it was during this time span, that he came to believe that the Congregation for the Doctrine of the Faith was gunning for him. He received a somewhat cryptic letter from his colleague and mentor, the legendary Jesuit moral theologian Joseph Fuchs, who had written: "There were some people in Rome who were 'somewhat interested' in you."[114] Curran eventually learned what those "interests" were. Fuchs had received a phone call from the librarian at Rome's Gregorian University, who asked him to return some books by Curran. The Holy Office, the librarian said, was looking for them. And if Fuchs had anything else by Curran the Holy Office would probably want those too. It was not a good sign.

In 1978, Cardinal Karol Wojtyla (John Paul 2) was elected to the papacy, the first non-Italian pope in more than four hundred years and the most conservative in decades. "Inquisitorial processes increased in intensity. … Curran was the first American tackled publicly by the CDF."[115] In August, 1979, he received a letter from Cardinal William Wakefield Baum of Washington, the Chancellor of the University, forwarding a sixteen page letter from the then-prefect of the CDF, then Cardinal Franjo Šeper.

The letter outlined the concerns of the CDF with his views on dissent, sexuality, specifically contraception, sterilization, homosexuality and divorce. "It was the worst kind of critique: I had never denied that I dissented from non-infallible teaching, but they would cite passages out of context and conclude that my arguments did not add up. However, I took the letter very seriously. I wrote back to them on 26 October 1979 sending twenty-one pages of response dealing with the primary question of dissent from non-infallible teaching."[116]

Correspondence continued; Curran spaced his replies to the time lags of the CDF, often waiting a year to reply. When he did respond, he was told that his responses were inadequate to the objections already raised. Curran admits that he was not, at that point, really alarmed, that he didn't expect "much" would come of it,"[117] since others had made very similar statements. But he was mistaken. Indeed, the situation grew even more serious. Wojtyla (John Paul 2), in the summer of 1984, at a press conference in Rome, cited Curran as one of "four theologians in the world who were responsible for the lack of acceptance of [his encyclical] Humanae Vitae."[118] Curran wrote to Häring, confiding his concerns and Häring agreed with him; the situation was serious.

Cardinal Joseph Ratzinger, later to be elected Benedict 16, succeeded Šeper as prefect of the CDF in 1981. Now the face of the opposition had changed; Curran would have known both his work and his reputation. Ratzinger had been peritus to Cardinal Josef Frings, the most liberal and outspoken German at Vatican II. He and Hans Kung, another German, were then the two "young Turks" of the liberal coalition; after the conclave they taught together at Tubingen University and were thought to be close friends.

But by the 1980s, "the progressive firebrand" had become "the chief inquisitor." This transformation seemed to have less to do with ambition, as some have charged, than with Ratzinger's life experiences. Growing up, he had witnessed the rise of Nazism in Germany and at Tubingen in the late 60's he was a daily witness to the '68 student uprisings across Europe, which were more forceful, more radical than those in the United States and deeply Marxist, where students were chanting, "Accursed be Jesus!" Both these experiences seemed tutorials, leading conclusively to a profound distrust of the relationship between church and culture.

In the fall of 1984, Ratzinger gave an interview, later published in "Jesu," an Italian magazine, entitled "The Crisis of Faith in the World." In it he argued, "Unfortunately the American ethos is so opposed to the Catholic ethos that Catholic ethicists 'across the Atlantic' felt they either had to dissent from Church teaching or from the American ethos, and unfortunately too many of them choose to dissent from the Church."[119]

When Curran read the Ratzinger interview, his concerns deepened. He thought the die had already been cast – and he was probably right. Throughout, Curran believed he was targeted not for the radical nature of his views, since by the theological standards of the time, they were hardly radical, but for political reasons. In part, it was payback for dissent from Humanae Vitae. But it put Catholic moral theology in North America on notice; Rome was in charge.

Correspondence continued. "On September 17, 1985, Ratzinger

wrote 'concluding the inquiry' and asked Curran for a final reply to the finding, that 'one who holds such positions cannot be called a Catholic theologian.'"[120] Curran's argument that dissent from the non-infallible magisterium is legitimate was not accepted.

Curran then began negotiating with now-Cardinal James Hickey of Washington (See Part Four, Chapter 4) and Cardinal Joseph Bernardin of Chicago, Chairman of the Board at CU. He offered to refrain from teaching ethics or sexual morality. "The CDF could declare the errors that it perceived in my works. In return I would maintain my position on the faculty of CU and I would remain a Catholic theologian in good standing. If that offer was satisfactory to Rome, then the problem for Catholic University and the Church in the US would be removed."[121]

Subsequent conversations convinced Curran that actually the offer was never communicated; Hickey informed him, however, that it had simply not been accepted. In its stead Curran was told, Ratzinger had offered the opportunity for an informal meeting. Curran accepted that invitation and went to Rome in March of 1986 to meet with him. Häring accompanied him. Although Curran found Ratzinger "friendly, cordial and courteous in a formal kind of way,"[122] he felt that the two hours spent were never a dialogue. They issued a joint statement to the media.

When Curran returned to the United States he held his own press conference the following day and revealed publicly for the first time the facts of the investigation. He said he had never been defended by counsel or told who his accusers were. Later, Ratzinger replied, "Your own works have been your 'accusers' and they alone."[123]

Curran's final reply to Ratzinger was sent on April 1, 1986. He stood firm in his previously stated positions. On August 18, Hickey relayed Ratzinger's response; Curran was no longer "suitable nor eligible to exercise the function of a professor of Catholic theology."[124]

Unwilling to accept his dismissal, Curran went to court in December 1988; the lawsuit was filed against CU in Washington DC and Curran was again defended pro bono by Cravath, Swaine and Moore. He contended that "the Catholic University had violated his contract because it guaranteed academic freedom. He had been denied this because of the unwarranted intervention of the CDF."[125] The university argued that the Vatican document took precedence over academic freedom. Curran lost.

The judge ruled that no official documents guaranteed academic freedom in a case of conflict with the Vatican. "In other words he found that there was no academic freedom at Catholic University. In the end Curran lost the case because the judge admitted that the University does have a special relationship to the Holy See, and therefore they had to accept the Vatican's decisions. He further said that there was nothing in Curran's contract, nor that of any other faculty member at CU, that guaranteed academic freedom."[126] The judgment was delivered on February 28, 1989. For readers interested in the details of the court case, "Curran v. the Catholic University: a

Study of Authority and Freedom in Conflict," by Larry Witham in recommended.

Curran's statement on the matter reads in part, "I am convinced that the church will eventually have to move in the way that contemporary moral theology suggests. In fact, the large majority of faithful Catholics have already moved that way. They have made up their own minds about a whole range of moral issues.... However in the long run, if the hierarchical church continues to put so great an emphasis on arbitrary authority the Catholic community will simply descend into ever deeper problems."[127]

And finally, "I have hope because of the promise that Jesus made to the community of his disciples to be always with us."[128]

****

In Webster's New 20th Century Dictionary Unabridged Second Edition, several definitions are offered for the word "Inquisition." Words such as inquiry, examination, or investigation are used. At no point does the word "trial" appear and indeed, given the description of the proceedings after an accused enters actively into the processes of the CDF, the proceedings would not be recognized as a "trial" by any citizen of a Western democracy, perhaps even any citizen of a Western government.

That the initial process is secret is not in itself condemnatory. In the process of prosecution, any district attorney consults with other attorneys before deciding to bring charges and does so, hopefully, in relative secrecy, so that indeed should charges not be brought the reputation of the accused has not been damaged. So the Vatican's initial secrecy does not seem to warrant censure. Neither is it condemnatory that there is "a presumption of guilt;" there most likely is in the offices of district attorneys everywhere. If they did not believe the individual guilty, why would they proceed?

However, the situation does not then shift radically, as it would in a democratic procedure, when, if an individual is brought to *trial,* there would be a "presumption of innocence." It does not then shift radically to a procedure in which the rights of the accused are clearly understood and a matter of law. Indeed, before the CDF the accused has no "rights" as such. Nor, as the process continues, is there a "defense counsel," only the unknown and unnamed Relator pro auctore. A witness is never cross-examined or his testimony challenged by or for the accused since the accusers remain anonymous throughout the proceedings. If the accused is found guilty, there is no process of appeal. There is no Supreme Court.

An additional two points, both of which cast an even more negative light on the process must be mentioned. The first of these is the absence of safeguards against accusations brought for other than Christian reasons – personal animosities, competitions, political differences, envy or simple malice. The historical records indicate that accusations have been brought for just those reasons. Prefect Ratzinger would reply that that is irrelevant, that it is their own words that damn the accused, that their own writings are at issue. And that is all that matters. From his point of view, he's quite right. But the word "inquisition" seems more than appropriate standing alone; the word "trial" seems a clear misnomer.

Additionally, another criticism must be leveled; those involved in the decisions to proceed, the consultors, are all of a similar persuasion or point of view. It would not be an unfair analogy to say that it's comparable to rounding up a group of ultra-conservative Republicans in America and asking them if they would like to elect and seat even a moderate liberal. Or vice versa. The answers would be preordained and in the negative. Theoretically, within Catholic doctrine, dissent is allowed. Why not invite a *wider* participation of views? Uninvited, one must assume they would be unwelcome and that raises a fundamental question of fairness which remains unaddressed.

The reputation of the CDF and indeed of the rest of the Church might improve if the proceedings were not billed as "trials." Reputation does matter. Ten percent of the entire population of the United States – that's millions of people – are lapsed Catholics; they're the largest religion, or more accurately, the largest non-religion in America. Many of them believe that the church they can no longer love abandoned the sandals of Jesus for the boots of Empire centuries ago; when observing the CDF's tight-fisted grip, their total insistence on unrestrained power and their relentless willingness to crush any opposition, it is hard to argue with this point of view.

The nuns of America have not argued; they have simply followed a different path. What they have done is to study the life of Jesus, dare to imagine and divine through prayer what his wishes for them might be and then attempt to live that vision; if the men of the CDF have attempted this, or anything remotely like it, if they even consider Jesus, those considerations have gone unrecorded. The Imperial Vatican does not question itself.

If the nuns of America wonder how these men of Rome, who have willingly walled themselves off from a full half of humanity, will ever learn about the nature of women, they have not said so. If they wonder how these men, awash in their willed ignorance, dare to instruct them, neither have they raised that question. They have not drawn attention to the carefully constructed divide in which they live and work. They have not practiced "disobedience." But the CDF chose to accuse them.

In the last section of this book, Part Five, their possible motives for those accusations will be examined. But first a review of some of the "disagreements" of the past decades may be informative; to witness the players in action may instruct.

NOTES: PART THREE

1. Roger Gryson,. *The Ministry of Women in the Early Church.* Liturgical Press, Collegeville, Minnesota, 1980. P.xv.
2. Alan F. Segal,. *Rebecca's Children.* Harvard University Press, Cambridge, Massachusetts 1986. P. 2.
3. *Ibid.*, P. 81.
4. Michael L. White, *From Jesus to Christianity*. Harper, San Francisco, California, 2004. P.116.
5. Segal, *Op.Cit.,* P.143.
6. *Ibid.*, P.14.
7. *Ibid.*, P.105.
8. *Ibid.*, P.98.
9. White, *op. cit.*, P.143.
10. Justo L. Gonzalez, *The Story of Christianity, Volume I,* Harper One, Revised edition, New York, 2010. P. 35.
11. Elaine Pagels, *Adam, Eve and the Serpent.* Random House, New York, 1988. P.xxv.
12. *Ibid.*, P.55.
13. White, *Op. Cit.*, P. 325.
14. *Ibid.*, P. 297.
15. Segal, *op. cit.*, P.163.
16. Gonzalez, *Op. cit.*, P.35.
17. White, *Op. Cit.*, P. 432.
18. Gonzalez, *Op.,Cit.*, P.35
19. *Ibid.,* P. 61.
20. *Ibid.*, P.63.
21. *Ibid.*, P.67.
22. *Ibid.*, P.49.
23. *Ibid.*, P.51.
24. Pagels, *op. cit.*, P.46.
25. *Ibi*d., P.56.
26. *Ibid.*, P.50.
27. *Ibid.*, P.27.
28. Gonzalez, *op. cit.*, P.73.
29. Pagels, *Beyond Belief.*" Random House, New York, 2003. Pp.41-42.
30. *Ibid.*, P.34.

31. *Ibid*., P.61.
32. *Ibid*., P. 63.
33. Gonzalez, *op. cit*., P. 58.
34. *Ibid*., P.67.
35. *Ibid*., P.101.
36. *Ibid*., P.102
37. Pagels, *Adam, Eve and the Serpent.* Random House, New York, 1988. P.36.
38. Gonzalez, *op. cit*., P.119.
39. *Ibid*., P.121.
40. *Ibid*., P.124.
41. Segal, *Op. Cit*., P.177.
42. Pagels, *Op. Cit*., Pp.89-90.
43. *Ibid*., P.90.
44. Gonzalez, *Op. Cit*., Pp.143-44.
45. Pagels, *Op. Cit.*, P.89.
46. *Ibid*., P.119.
47. Gonzalez, *Op. Cit*., 144.
48. *Ibid*., P.143.
49. Pagels, *Op. Cit*., P.150.
50. Segal, *Op. Cit*., Pp.174-75.
51. Sandra Schneiders, *Beyond Patching; Faith and Feminism in the Catholic Church.* Paulist Press, Mahwah, New Jersey. 1991. P.22
52. *Ibid*., P.103.
53. *Ibid.,* Pp.103-4.
54. Phyllis M. Kittel, *Staying in the Fire*. Woven Word Press, Boulder, Colorado, 2009. P.185.
55. *Ibid*., P.185.
56. Catholic Encyclopedia, newadvent.org/cathen/11182a.htm.
57. Sr. Marie Augusta Neal, " *From Nuns to Sisters: An Expanding Vocation."* 23rd Publications, Mystic, Connecticut 1990. P.68.
58. Kittel, *op. cit.,* P.169.
59. Sr. Maureen Fiedler, SL. "*Breaking Through the Stained Glass Ceiling: Women Religious in Their Own Words*." Church Publishing, Inc., New York, 2010. (No page numbers)
60. *Ibid.*, No page numbers.

61. Schneiders, *op. cit.*, 112-13.
62. Neal, *op. cit.*, P.94.
63. *Ibid.*P. 94.
64. Ann Patrick, et al, quoting D'Antonio, "American Catholics Today: New Realities of their Faith and Their Church." in *Conscience and Calling: Ethical Reflections on Catholic Women's Church Vocations.* Bloomsbury, New York. 1998. Pp.97-98.
65. Neal, *op. cit.*, P.85.
66. Amy Koehlinger, *The New Nuns: Racial Justice and Religious Reform in the 1960s,* Harvard University Press,, Cambridge, Massachusetts, 2007. P. 27.
67. Neal, *op.cit.*, P. 86.
68. Kittel, *op cit.*, P.192.
69. Patrick, *op. cit.*, P.154.
70. *Ibid.*, P.13.
71. Kittel, *op. cit.*,P.173.
72. *Ibid.*, P.169.
73. *Ibid.*, P.227.
74. *Ibid.* P.225.
75. Neal, *op. cit.*,P.111.
76. Schneiders, *op. cit.*, P.69.
77. *Ibid.*, No page number.
78. *Ibid.*, P.113.
79. Briggs,. *Doublecrossed; Uncovering the Catholic Church's Betrayal of American Nuns.* Doubleday, New York, 2006. No page number.
80. *Ibid.*, P.69.
81. *Ibid.*, P.92.
82. Kittel, *op. cit.*, P.225.
83. Schneiders, *op. cit.*, P.120.
84. *Ibid.,* P.116.
85. *Ibid.*, P.25.
86. Ibid., No page number.
87. Ibid., P.11.
88. Ibid., P.34.
89. Ibid., P.35.
90. Ibid., P.34.
91. Ibid., P. 35.

92. Ibid., P. 35.
93. Ibid., Pp. 39-40.
94. Ibid., P.40.
95. Ibid., P.40.
96. Ibid., P.41.
97. Ibid., P.41.
98. Ibid., P41.
99. Ibid., P.49.
100. Ibid., P.51.
101. Ibid., P.53.
102. Ibid., Pp.53-54.
103. Ibid., P.54.
104. Ibid., P.55.
105. Ibid., P.55.
106. Ibid., P.56.
107. Ibid., P.58.
108. Ibid., P.58.
109. Ibid., P.58.
110. Ibid., P.58.
111. Ibid., P.59.
112. Ibid., P.60.
113. Ibid., P.62.
114. Ibid., P.67.
115. Ibid., P.64.
116. Ibid., P.65.
117. Ibid., P.67.
118. Ibid., P.68.
119. Ibid., P.68.
120. Ibid., Pp.68-69.
121. Ibid., P.69.
122. Ibid., P.70.
123. Ibid., P.71.
124. Ibid., P.72.
125. Ibid., P.73.
126. Ibid., P.74.
127. Ibid., P.76.
128. Ibid., P.77.

PART FOUR

Chapter 1: The whip lash begins. 1965-1969

And so the unintended consequences began. The nuns were urged by a major conclave to "change," to "renew," to "modernize," to "experiment"; no one, however, told them how. No boundaries were set for them. Perhaps this was a compliment, a nod to their better judgment; or perhaps it represented simply a failure of priestly imagination. The men who set forth these directions seemed to know little about the women they were directing. Many of those men were clearly both surprised and taken aback by what followed. Some were horrified.

The conflict between the Immaculate Heart of Mary sisters, known to the Catholic world as the IHMs, and the then cardinal of Los Angeles, James Francis McIntyre can only be explored or judged meaningfully within the context of its time – what the world has come to refer to as "the 60s," and then of its place – not just "the 60s," but the 60s in California.

The times…

How one dates this period depends; some mark its beginning with the murder of John Kennedy, others with the publication of "The Feminine Mystique," by Betty Friedan. Both events occurred in the same year, 1963. Some would say even earlier, citing Montgomery with Rosa Parks in 1955. Most people who lived through the time would date its end either by America's withdrawal from Vietnam or the resignation of Richard Nixon. The 60s might have begun in the 50s and actually spilled over into the early 70s.

Few under the age of 50 remember those times; many over the age of 50 would like to forget them. Thoughtful Americans, watching the nightly news (CNN was long in the future) did so often close to tears. A nation plunged without warning into both grief and confusion by an event never imagined, never dreamed of, the assassination of their president, went on to experience what seemed to be a never ending procession of events that were the stuff of nightmares.

They watched as Martin Luther King was killed by his enemies and Malcolm X was gunned down by those he thought his friends. They saw four little girls blown to pieces in a Birmingham church. Peaceful marchers were attacked by police on the Pettus Bridge on "Bloody Sunday," marching from Selma to Montgomery. There were riots at the 1968 Democratic Convention in Chicago - and at Stonewall in Greenwich Village. And Watts in Los Angeles. They witnessed another Kennedy murdered, again on television, and the last Kennedy brother lose a future presidency at Chappaquiddick.

Cannon hoses and snapping dogs were unleashed against peacefully protesting teenagers. White women spit on black children, who were committing no crime but attempting to enter classrooms which the Supreme Court had opened for them. Hemlines rose higher than anyone had ever imagined and divorce rates did the same. The raised fist of Black Power made the scene. The Berrigan brothers poured blood on draft notices. Campuses were in a state of rebellion and there were more dead children at Kent State, killed by those who came to keep the peace. This was the world of "the 60s."

Truly it seemed as if some vast unnamed power had seized a celestial spoon, plunged it deep into the center of this country and *stirred*, tearing everything loose, leaving next to nothing as it was. To paraphrase Yeats' "The Second Coming," "Things fell apart; the centre did not hold; Mere anarchy was loosed upon the world." And it was. And it was within these years that the events unfolded that this chapter will try to address. Liberals and conservatives had always clashed but their conflict this time had more the colors of classical literature than the texture of contemporary drama. It was at its base a clash of extremes, lacking in nuance; this is only one of several facts fueling the difficulty of its description.

And the place…

California was… well, California. Its zeitgeist played a significant role in the drama under analysis here. "Hippies" were invented there and any of the experimentations marking "the counterculture" were revved up to high. More than 100,000 came to San Francisco to celebrate the "Summer of Love" in 1967. California gave us "flower children" and "communes." Both spread widely.

As well it gave us a psychology, or to be more accurate, a kind of clinical practice, i.e. a California style psychotherapy, relevant to this story because of the involvement of its two leading practitioners, Dr. Carl Rogers, originator of "non-directive" therapy and his disciple,

Dr. William Coulson. The two men headed the Western Behavioral Sciences Institute and in 1967 began an experiment called the Educational Innovation Project, in which the IHMs took part.

Along with 60 "facilitators," Rogers and Coulson interacted with the nuns in what they called "encounter group" experiences. These sessions were designed to "unmask feelings," sexual and otherwise. Where for centuries, mothers superior had warned against "particular friendships," here "honest" lesbian feelings were encouraged. Therapists engaged with participants in "sex games," deemed "educational." When Rogers objected, the facilitators attributed his disapproval to a "generation gap" and followed their own best judgment.[2]

In considering this behavior, it should be remembered that the young deemed "Far out!" a significant compliment. It seems now certainly extreme, but compared to the treatment offered at Esalen at Big Sur, the nexus of the counterculture, perhaps not. Esalen was founded by Michael Murphy and Richard Price, whose qualifications after graduating from Stanford were a psychotic break and hospitalization for the former and studies with Sri Aurobindo in his Indian ashram for the latter. As well, there was Dr. Arthur Janov's Primal Scream therapy being practiced assiduously at Santa Monica.

By way of a brief comparison, in the doctoral program in clinical psychology at New York University during the same period, the ideas of Carl Rogers were for the most part dismissed; certainly his non-directive treatment techniques were no part of the formal curriculum and practiced by no one. The furthest "out" to which the faculty ever moved was to a consideration of a possible contribution to psychoanalytic theory from Zen Buddhism, not as practiced by Alan Watts but as understood by D. T. Suzuki and pursued by Eric Fromm. What was going on in California was seen as "the lunatic fringe."[2]

Certainly there have always been and will always be therapists who engage with their patients sexually. But main stream clinicians viewed these relationships then and continue to view them now as "boundary violations," not "educational techniques." They are most usually guarded as guilty secrets until uncovered by ambitious biographers or self-confessed in masochistic memoirs. But the events of this chapter took place in the 60s, and in California.

The protagonists…

James Francis Cardinal McIntyre:

The ancestors of the American prelates who attended Vatican II may well have dumped the tea into Boston Harbor and from behind the trees fired "the shot heard round the world,"[3] but there were no revolutionaries in that American delegation. In fact, its leader, Francis Cardinal Spellman of New York, was overheard as his ship left the New York harbor, already envisioning his return, "No change will get past the Statue of Liberty."[4] The Americans were deeply committed to the Roman Catholic status quo and most would vote routinely with the Italian/Curial minority in the coming conclave. They were conventional men more accustomed to action than contemplation and their convictions were strong; McIntyre, then a favored son and former protégé of Spellman's, was very much one of them. They were his cohort.

James Francis McIntyre was born in Manhattan on June 25, 1886 to parents of Gaelic descent who "had the good sense to seek their fortunes in America rather than in France or England."[5] He and his younger brother John grew up on the east side of Manhattan in a deeply religious home. He served mass from the time he was 10 years old and the nightly rosary was a given in the family's life. He went to public school, the expense of a Catholic education well beyond his parent's income. He was a healthy youngster but his parents were not, and his childhood was both sad and eventful.

His mother Molly died quite suddenly when Frank was 10 years old and her niece, Mary Hannon, moved in to keep the household going. In 1903 when she married Robert Conley, an attorney, the couple invited Frank and John to join them in their new home near Manhattanville College. Conley specialized in real estate law and was fairly successful, doing well at the time. Mary remembered Frank as "a serious minded… shy boy."[6] His father had been a New York City mounted policeman but suffered both from injuries sustained in a fall from his horse and later-contracted tuberculosis. Three years after the death of his mother, his father "had become an invalid and remained so for the final decade of his life. Whatever thoughts Frank had about his own future were put aside in order to provide for his father."[7]

Frank's behavior then, for any youngster, was unusual. He left school and with seemingly great energy, this "shy boy" threw himself into earning money by any means possible. He began as an errand boy in a laundry, clerked for a grocery store, and by the age of 13 "with his visored cap, short pants, coat and black leggings found work as an errand boy or "runner" for the New York Curb Exchange."[8]

This was later to become the American Stock Exchange but at the time was simply an unofficial gathering; a hundred or so men traded stocks at Broad Street and Exchange Place in lower Manhattan. "The brokers milled about, trading with each other, signaling manually to men leaning out of the windows, telephones clutched in their hands. The atmosphere was both noisy and frenetic."[9] Transactions were made orally and confirmed then by memorandum between the respective traders. It was an all day affair without interruption, regardless of weather. Frank's job was to roam about among the crowds, watch the changes of prices on the boards, and then report back as fast as possible.

He found a mentor there and was offered a job at a large financial firm. He was hired as a switchboard operator and began classes at Harlem Evening School, studying stenography, mathematics and accounting. By 1915, when his father died, Frank had been promoted to office manager and then to the position of personal secretary to one of the most highly respected partners, a man with substantial financial acumen. He had continued night classes when he could but his focus seems always to have been on the immediate and the practical.

If, during these important sixteen years, he had a relationship of any kind at any time with a member of the opposite sex, it remains unreported.

He was never a man of ideas; he was a man of action and his talent for figures and his financial acumen, born and nurtured early, were to stand him in more than good stead for the rest of his life. Indeed it was his ability in the world of finance, equities, property values and debt management that characterized his entire career and explained early and continuing promotions. Once, turning down a request to speak and suggesting another prelate whom he thought better qualified, he wrote, "He is a man of letters and words, I am a man of ledgers and figures."[10]

Following the death of his father early in 1915, at the age of 29, he left the world of finance to attend first Cathedral College in Manhattan to make up some necessary but as yet unearned credits, and then Saint Joseph's Seminary at Dunwoodie in Yonkers, where he was 11 years older than most of his classmates. Dunwoodie, unlike the pontifical universities in Rome did not teach their courses in Latin; reading English made study substantially less rigorous academically. "The seminary historian… felt that [students] were shortchanged intellectually and spiritually, a sentiment not shared by the two future cardinals … [of] the class of 1921."[11]

He was going to become a priest. About this crucial decision, perhaps the most important of his life, his major biography, "His Eminence of Los Angeles," by Francis J. Weber, tells us next to nothing.

There are difficulties always in writing biography; two factors relevant to this one seem worth noting. The first is access. Weber's book was written in 1997, eighteen years after McIntyre's death. It leaves unclear the question of what the relationship was, if any, between the two men. The book is meticulously researched; where McIntyre worked, who he met, how his promotions came into being - it's all there. What he did, where he was, who he wrote to and what his letters said, as well as the content of his public speeches, is available in detail.

What isn't there or even imagined is what he felt. Msgr. Clement J. Connolly, personal secretary to McIntyre as well as to his successor, Cardinal Timothy Manning, put the necessary criticism well, when he wrote about the biography, "But the man is missing."[11] Was the road to the priesthood a long internal struggle? Or was McIntyre's future course always a foregone conclusion? Did his faith ever present him with questions? The reader is without answers.

Weber tells us that this decision was born in part by McIntyres' lifetime friendship with three priests, perhaps experienced as mentors or father figures. In a footnote, he lists their names, but the reader learns nothing of the men themselves, the relationships, how they might have come about, or what they may have meant to his subject.

Second, in evaluating a biographer, his own background is relevant; his credibility is always subject to possible bias. Presumably, objectivity is desirable. In buying Weber's book on Amazon, no title appears before the author's name, nor does a title appear on the spine of either volume, nor is Weber's position mentioned in his preface. Only on the frontispiece, should the not impatient reader study that page, would he discover that Weber was a monsignor in the Roman Catholic Church. The book, of course then, has to be read within that context. By contrast, in Father Mark S. Massa's books, several of which are quoted here, the initials S.J., identifying him as a Jesuit priest, are always front and center.

The Roman Catholics of New York City refer to St. Patrick's Cathedral, the nearby apartments of the archbishop or cardinal at its head, and the offices that run one of the most powerful dioceses in the world simply as "50th Street." It was to this Chancery Office that Father McIntyre arrived for his first assignment as a priest, soon to be officially named Vice Chancellor, to serve under Patrick Joseph Cardinal Hayes, who had known McIntyre since his student days at Cathedral College.

Hayes knew that the Vatican was disappointed in him, knew of their criticism of his endless preoccupation with the poor. His most important project had been the founding of Catholic Charities in 1920, an organization whose name tells it all, and is still in existence today. He once said of himself that he was guilty of not knowing enough bankers. This was a charge that would never have been brought against his successor, Francis Spellman. The arrival of a young and financially sophisticated priest must have seemed to him a gift. It was a surprise to no one that by January, 1941, McIntyre had become a monsignor, having been promoted by then to Chancellor, the office requiring the title. It was from Spellman, arriving from Boston to become Archbishop of New York in 1939 on Hayes' retirement, that McIntyre received his second honor and advanced to the position of auxiliary Bishop.

It is worthwhile to pause for a moment and consider "the men of 50th Street," led by then Archbishop Francis Spellman, because this was McIntyre's second home and training ground. These men were captains of industry with collars turned backwards; they were *in* the world and *of* the world. Power was theirs and they relished it; they used it well. They had friends in high places, most especially in Rome and in Washington. They built churches, schools and hospitals; they had serious impact on the course of local as well as international events. They knew politics. They were influential and they used their influence. And they amassed wealth for the church. They were characterized by certainty rather than doubt. These were men of power, not to be crossed, much more in the mode of Constantine than Jesus.

During the war years, 1942 to 1945, Spellman was Apostolic Vicar for the Military Forces; this position required long absences from 50th Street, during which McIntyre became ever more competent, ever more experienced and ever more essential. "Spellman once said, "I have never undertaken any important matter without consulting [McIntyre]. In nothing have I gone contrary to his advice."[12]

In February, 1948, McIntyre was appointed Archbishop of Los Angeles in California. Professionally, his financial acumen and expertise had served him well; personally, his fierce and unquestioning loyalty, deeply appreciated, had always been at the service of whatever powers had been in place. Now at last he was his own man; now the power was his. It was rumored in New York City that the railway cars carrying McIntyre to Los Angeles were deemed by the younger priests of Manhattan "the Freedom Train."[13]

"When Cardinal McIntyre arrived in Los Angeles in 1948, he had 366 diocesan priests; by 1962 there were 580. Parishes grew from 221 to 297. The religious orders of women increased from 1,965 to 3,735. The number of seminary students climbed from 312 to 536. The number of high schools grew from 13 to 34. When he arrived, the number of students totaled 5,164. The 1962 total was 23,288. The number of elementary schools grew from 111 to 243. The number of hospitals grew from 12 to 17. In 1948, 86,000 patients were treated. In 1962, 433,223 patients were treated. In McIntyre's first four years alone, 26 new parishes, 64 parochial schools, and 18 high schools were established.[14] "At one point during his tenure, he oversaw the construction of a new church every 66 days and a new school every 26 days."[15]

One of his most significant accomplishments was the successful effort to free parochial schools in California from state taxation. He moved almost immediately and audaciously to lead this struggle, which went on from 1951 to 1957. During those years he operated skillfully, both with legislatures, civic groups and the press, working with both those in favor and the many opposed. It was a substantial triumph.

For the first time, he was without a restraining hand; always authoritative, he moved much more closely to the authoritarian. His politics, no longer shielded by the political sophistication of 50th Street, now appeared front and center. Even while in Manhattan, McIntyre had been seen by some as autocratic; Father George Ford of Corpus Christi parish had resigned rather than deal with what he called McIntyre's "usurpation of messianic authority, a centralized control comparable to the tactics of the Gestapo,"[15] not returning to work until Spellman, under intense criticism, almost literally begged him to do so.

Further negative views began to emerge. Described by others as "mean-spirited" and "vindictive,"[16] as "the rigid, flinty man who confused piety with goodness,"[17] it was said that McIntyre ran the day to day business of the archdiocese of Los Angeles with the same ruthless efficiency that had characterized his tenure in New York City. Terrence W. Halloran, described him as "A deeply secure man, confident of his ability to handle dissent by crushing it."[18] He was described by Harvard historian, Lisa McGirr as "the most extreme right-wing member of the American Catholic hierarchy during his time."[19] "He sent his priests to meetings of the John Birch Society to educate themselves about communism, and recommended subscription to... other Birch publications in his diocesan newspaper."[20] On November 29, 1952 he became a Cardinal.

In 1962, when the American delegation sailed for Rome for the opening ceremonies of Vatican II, Cardinal McIntyre was among them. He was long on record as opposing change of any kind, advocating almost always the familiar, the tried-and-true, the status quo. All Dunwoodie students had sworn the mandated Oath Against Modernity, issued by Guiseppe Sarto (Pius 10) in 1910 and not rescinded until 1967. His reaction to the decisions promulgated by Vatican II is clear and was always without equivocation; he disliked, distrusted, and regretted every change and every new decision.

Most significantly, he was vehemently opposed to mass being said in the vernacular. He spoke against it to his fellow cardinals, in two of the earliest sessions in 1962. On 23 October he argued, "The schema...[advocating mass in the vernacular] proposes confusion and complication. If it is adopted, it would be an immediate scandal for our people. The continuity of the mass must be kept. The tradition of the sacred ceremonies must be preserved."[21]

And then on November 5, "In recent times, even in materialistic North America, the growth of the church was magnificent with the liturgy being in Latin. The attempts of Protestants have failed, and

Protestantism uses the vernacular." And then "Why the change, especially since changes in this matter involve many difficulties and great dangers? All of us here at the Council can recall the fundamental changes in the meaning of words in common use. Thus it follows that if the sacred liturgy were in the vernacular, the immutability of doctrine would be endangered." And then "The Mass must remain as it is. Grave changes in the liturgy introduce grave changes in dogmata."[22]

Sacrosanctum Concilium, the document that would indeed mandate the mass to be said in the vernacular was passed with a vote of 2,147 to 46. McIntyre, one presumes, was one of the 46.

Sister Anita M. Caspary:

On that day that Spellman and his party sailed out of New York Harbor, bound for the coming meeting of which they all disapproved, Anita Caspary, then Sister Mary Humiliata, was happily reading the liberal Joseph Cardinal Suenens' book, "The Nun in the World," written it seems in anticipation of the oncoming events in Rome and possible changes that might follow. It was this book, not Betty Friedan's, that was *her* beginning of the 60s. Although not yet "explicitly conscious of feminism,"[23] she was both pleased and excited about the meeting, anticipating the possibility of the new with interest. She had graduated from college, owned and driven her own car, and dated men before entering the sisterhood. She thought of herself as one of "the California nuns, progressive, liberal, and modern."[24] And she *was* one of the California nuns, a synonym for which might well have been “a thorn in Cardinal McIntyre’s side.”

Anita was the third of eight children born to her parents, Jacob and Murray Caspary of Gregory County, South Dakota. Their first-born son, Maurice, died at birth. Two years later, their first-born daughter, Ruth, died after an illness that lasted only a week. A few months later Anita was born on November 4, 1915, and if her parents were overly protective of her as she claimed they were, their attitude was certainly understandable.

Within two years, the family had moved to Los Angeles, to be near her paternal grandparents, who had settled there in a large Victorian home. She describes herself and the setting in which she grew up as “the product of a German-American Catholic enclave… The descendent of generations of devout and utterly loyal Roman Catholics… I can’t remember any family member or friends ever questioning any official dogma of the church.”[25]

She attended Catholic school, only two blocks from home. She experienced the nuns as they moved through the world of her childhood as “somewhat mysterious beings, quick to disappear into the convent after school hours. Brown-clad, white-quaffed, with black aprons for classroom wear, they never spoke of themselves or ate in our presence.”[26]

She remembered her mother’s elaborate preparation for the first communion and confirmation of each of her children; “the pride she took in our proper clothing for innumerable processions, her insistence on special prayers we said together with her for special feast days – all were affirmations of the atmosphere of school and church. During the month of May she would erect a small altar before which the whole family would pray the rosary every evening."[27]

Caspary felt her relationship with her father was a special one; it's clear that he took her intelligence seriously and at times regarded her almost as an equal. "When I was a little older I was sometimes called in to be a part of family discussions with my mother and father.... I began thinking of myself as an adult long before my years warranted it."[28]

She describes her college years as "growing closer to the Immaculate Heart Sisters," although, as she puts it, "I did not understand fully why I felt attracted to them. Looking back now I can trace how they shared the thrust into the future, the exhilaration and optimism marking the rapidly growing city of Los Angeles."[29] But she found them an interesting group and was intrigued by their history.

Anyone wishing to understand the origins of communities of ordered nuns here in America would do well to watch that old favorite, "Lilies of the Field," made in 1963. Although to the best of anyone's knowledge, no Catholic sister ever met Sidney Poitier, the story itself – a handful of deeply religious women, arriving in America alone, barely speaking the language of their neighbors, without money and without friends, sustained only by their faith, set out to build a chapel, which in the film they mispronounce in their broken English as "shapel," and succeed in doing so – is more fact than fancy.

History tells us that groups of religious women just like the sisters in that film built more than chapels. Arriving in America from Europe, they begged when they had to and borrowed when they could. They worked at any task that paid them money and put that money into building. In the end, through unrelenting effort, often actual physical toil, always sustained by faith, these women built and built and built. Not just "shapels." They built schools and colleges and hospitals, always with their own sweat. The IHM's began in this country much the same way.

The order was founded originally as the Daughters of the Most Holy and the Immaculate Heart of the Blessed Virgin Mary in 1848 in Spain by Father Joachim Masmitja. In 1869, his friend, the Bishop of Monterey, California was visiting; he asked for some of the sisters to come to California. Two years later Mother Raimunda with nine others went to the rough- and-tumble California of Gold Rush days, to the new mission there. She served as the provincial of the California sisters until her death in 1900.

Not speaking English they could only earn money by teaching "music, art, and embroidery to the children of the wealthier Catholic families."[30] Eventually they began schools by employing English-speaking lay teachers. They adapted quickly and a traditional academic curriculum was soon in place. "Their pupils, attracted by these courageous nuns, included children of the first families of

California."[31] "With the entrance of American women into the community, the attitudes of freedom of spirit, rugged individualism, and adaptation to life in California created a distance between the two groups.... More grave was the imposition of Spanish authoritarianism over the sisters of the California province."[32] By 1906 the sisters had built their own motherhouse and began to look for separation from their Spanish parent institute; approval for the two groups formally to separate was granted by the Vatican in 1924.

The Roman document granting the nuns request also declined the then Los Angeles Bishop Cantwell's request to make the Los Angeles IHM's a diocesan foundation (i.e., sisters under his control and that of his successors in Los Angeles). "The Vatican granted the new institute pontifical status ... and [it] was assigned [a] cardinal-protector in Rome to defend the sisters against possible encroachments of their rights by anyone, including the local hierarchy.[33] This canonical status would greatly complicate events in 1967 and 1968.

Caspary joined the order in September, 1937. She found the severing of family ties difficult and was beset with "an unexpected loneliness."[34] She began to reconsider her commitment and wondered if she could remain faithful to the promises she would have to make after her year as a novice "Where were the solitude and silence I had cherished and found even in my home, in the midst of family? Was this really a "more perfect" life," she wondered.[35] She felt no joy of anticipation when she considered the reception of the habit.

At the eventual ceremony, when the religious name chosen for her was called aloud, "Sister Mary Humiliata," "audible gasps were heard in the chapel."[36] Apparently, it might be inferred, someone in a position of authority thought this young woman needed to reflect upon the sin of pride. If the same thought was ever harbored in relation to her future adversary, there is no record of it. Caspary considered it "a reminder of the humility I was encouraged to cultivate. … I soon lectured myself into accepting the name as a part of novitiate asceticism. I was determined to live the life wholeheartedly, and this was the first "humiliating" choice, [the name] to be laid aside only with the changes that the renewal would bring some 30 years later."[37]

After teaching for several years, she entered Stanford, completing her doctoral degree in medieval literature in 1948. She was immediately assigned to the faculty of Immaculate Heart College and appointed chair of the small English department; "Sisters on the faculty worked for room, board, and clothing. Without them the college would not have existed."[38]

But a collision course had already been charted. "As I look back, perhaps the greatest marvel was the cohesiveness and spirit of the college personnel, particularly the sisters, in the face of an endless barrage of criticism and admonition, and even demands for retraction and apology coming relentlessly from the Los Angeles Chancery

Office. … "Do you realize that your college is being criticized in the diocese as "liberal?" the Cardinal asked. This exchange took place in the late 1950s well before the confrontation of 1965. The Cardinal found the courses "too worldly," an attempt "to imitate secular universities."[39] And then "If this keeps up, the college will have to close."[40] "Episodes like this one, denying the academic freedom necessary to effectively operate a college, continued long after this encounter."[41]

In 1963, the IHMs began their efforts to "renew." In the coming 1963 General Chapter meeting, changes were anticipated. Caspary, learning that she might very well be elected mother general, felt almost paralyzed. "The value of personal responsibility and of collegiality and the importance of appreciating the gifts and talents of each person were beginning to grow within me. … The hierarchical model was seen for what it too often easily becomes – a misuse of power that intimidates and cramps the human spirit."[42]

It should be noted that during the 1963 spiritual retreat anonymous letters were distributed almost every day, containing bitter criticism of the previous six-year regime and its progressive spirit. This split within the membership had not healed by 1965. The General Counsel learned that a few members were in continuing contact with McIntyre, alerting him to the events in progress.[43]

On the second ballot Caspary was elected the new mother general. She feared for the community and she feared for herself, understanding she was not the Cardinal's candidate. "Most significant among the decisions of the 1963 General Chapter was the recommendation that a long-range study of all IHM legislative documents – our constitutions, the Book of Customs, and the General Chapter decrees considered every six years – be undertaken, leading to revisions "guided by the spirit and decisions of the second Vatican Council … revisions of canon law… and by the lived reality of the Institute."[44] They began to formulate a five-year plan which would guide the renewal of the order.

Then Vatican II issued Perfectae Caritatis (See Appendix C); this document, more than any other, affected not only the IHMs, but nuns around the world, addressing directly almost every aspect of their daily lives. This was the call for "renewal." Sisters, not priests and not brothers, were to follow the highly specific instructions stipulated in this Vatican II document.

It *mandated*[45] that "The manner of living, praying and working should be suitably adapted everywhere … to the modern physical and psychological circumstances of the members and also, as required by the nature of each institute, to the necessities of the apostolate, the demands of culture, and social and economic circumstances. According to the same criteria let the manner of governing the institutes also be examined. Therefore let constitutions, directories, custom books, books of prayers and ceremonies and such like be suitably re-edited and, obsolete laws being suppressed, be adapted to the decrees of this sacred synod."

Part 17 stated, "The religious habit, an outward mark of consecration to God, should be simple and modest, poor and at the same time becoming. In addition it must meet the requirements of health and be suited to the circumstances of time and place and to the needs of the ministry involved. The habits of … women religious which do not conform to these norms must be changed."

Part 2 required "The adaptation and renewal of the religious life includes both the constant return to the sources of all Christian life and to the original spirit of the institutes and their adaptation to the changed conditions of our time. … Therefore let their founders' spirit and special aims they set before them as well as their sound traditions – all of which make up the patrimony of each institute – be faithfully held in honor."

Massa has pointed out that it was in just this circumstance, i.e. examining their original sources carefully, that they realized, they had been sent out not to be teachers, necessarily, but to be catechists, i.e. to spread "the word," but without specific instructions how to do so. It seemed logical then that staffing the Los Angeles public school system had come about more as an historical accident than as an original instruction; consequently, again logically, if a sister wished to be something other than a teacher, as long as it was as a catechist, why not? They began to find a different identity than the one they had accepted almost routinely for decades. It would seem that "staffing classrooms for affluent white children was, at best, extraneous to the kind of apostolic endeavors they had been founded to undertake. ... They had not been founded (as so many other orders of religious women had been) to be "school sisters," but to be catechists to those who did not have the opportunity to encounter the message of the church in other ways."[47] Accidents of history it seemed had brought them to their present point. They were now "offered the opportunity to right that accident of history and reclaim an identity closer to their original vision."[48]

The conflict is joined...

The first indication that the ongoing conflict had escalated to a new height came while Caspary was in Rome, invited to speak at a meeting convened by Joseph Cardinal Suenens. Delighted to be there, she was both surprised and dismayed when she received a phone call from her vicar-general, Sister Elizabeth Ann Flynn, telling her that the IHMs were to have an official visitation from the priests of the archdiocese and that moreover, theirs were the only religious community to be so graced. Caspary was "overwhelmed by a sense of foreboding."[49] The order had already had a "special canonical visitation" only six months earlier. Now she discovered, the Cardinal had requested an entire team of diocesan priests to act as visitators. She left for Los Angeles, "restless and apprehensive on the long journey."[50] It was now late November, 1965.

Shortly after her return, with the visitation already underway with many of the sisters already questioned, Caspary and Sister Elizabeth Ann were ordered to report to the Chancery office for a meeting with the Cardinal and his staff. Included were Bishop Timothy Manning,

Bishop John J. Ward, and Msgr. Edward Wade, vicar for religious. McIntyre accused the sisters "of disobedience to the Ordinary (the Cardinal himself), failure to cooperate with the archdiocese, and of the adoption of regulations and customs at variance with the views of the archdiocese on what was proper for religious communities."[51] The women were then told they had 60 days in which to respond to the charges, and that at the end of the 60 days they would be expected to indicate whether or not they were ready to conform to "traditional religious life as defined by the Ordinary."[52]

The two sisters replied that they could not agree to the Cardinal's demands. They explained that the decrees voted upon at the 1963 General Chapter meeting of their order had the force of law. In addition they pointed out that the customs the Cardinal objected to were internal to the community and consequently they were not subject to the local ordinary. "Once again, the fact that we were a pontifical Institute was the basis of our argument."[53]

The Cardinal then informed them that if they refused to follow his instructions, "support and help of the archdiocese" would be withdrawn. Caspary found the threat both intimidating and confusing. She wondered what kind of support he was talking about and then if he would withhold the monthly stipend the sisters received, actually their salaries for teaching in the parochial schools.

On the following day they received a letter from McIntyre, reviewing his recommendations for restoring their former way of life. The "fixed rule" was to be resumed. He claimed to base his findings on "unrest, uncertainty and dissatisfaction"[54] among the sisters who had been interrogated by the priest visitators; presumably, these were the sisters in the minority group, led by Sister Eileen MacDonald, who had been in ongoing private communication with the cardinal since the early days of 1963.

He had been informed by them, almost immediately, of the changes the General Chapter wished to make and of which he would have disapproved The group was clearly within their legitimate rights, since all religious are free to approach those in positions of greater authority. But certainly it would have been better, from a moral standpoint, to have approached Caspary straightforwardly. Although it is understandable that these sisters, raised in the traditional rule of the church, had had little training or experience in the expression of disagreement; they simply may not have seen their way clear to such behavior.

Because Caspary had, in prior weeks, consulted with a number of theologians and canon lawyers, anticipating exactly this kind of standoff, she felt that she stood on firm ground but she also believed that she should appeal immediately to the Sacred Congregation for Religious, that body of the Curia delegated to assist religious orders in similar conflicts with local hierarchies. She traveled to Rome and met with Cardinal Hildebrand Antoniutti.[55] He seemed to agree with the positions she had taken. On her return, letters passed back and forth between the two camps; Caspary was trying desperately to indicate good intentions and at the same time, holding fast to what she believed to be their rights as a pontifical institute.

For almost a year, the situation seemed to have reached détente. Then, without warning, in March 1967 another canonical visitation was scheduled, less than two years after the previous one. Two monsignors and a diocesan priest were assigned to conduct the interrogation. In the letter explaining the reason for the visitation, Cardinal McIntyre alluded to the need to "evaluate the truthfulness of … allegations made spontaneously by many persons."[56] He went on to point out that the interrogations would cover discipline, morals, and the regularity and frequency of the reception of the sacraments.

Two important letters followed. On April 2, 1967, 100 of the IHMs, without informing Caspary, wrote to McIntyre in support of the position the order had taken, stating, "We wish to assure you that all experimentation has been undertaken in an effort to discover and to reformulate a manner of life most appropriate to our dedication"[57] and there followed the signatures of each sister. The second letter was from Caspary to McIntyre, pointing out that the Legislation of the Chapter of 1963 that had rescinded earlier rules was the only body that "could reinstate those rules if the members so desired."[58]

This letter also replied to McIntyre's charge that he was unaware of the 1963 changes, with a reminder that copies of the new legislation had immediately been sent to him. Caspary believed that despite the fact that only a small number of sisters disapproved of the changes, it was their disapproval that "was strongly affecting the attitudes of the

Cardinal."[59] But it would seem clear that he was in basic agreement with the smaller group; he would not, one imagines, force such a confrontation unless he himself felt strongly on the issues.

Finally it was decided "that the facts of the Cardinal's strong disapproval of the Immaculate Heart Sisters must be laid before the chapter delegates and a General Chapter Meeting was convened in June of 1967. A decision would be made as to whether to proceed with such complete renewal."[60] After the roll call, Caspary called for a vote; there was unanimous agreement for immediate and complete renewal.

On the following Monday, Caspary were called to the Cardinal's office. The meeting that took place then is difficult to understand; we have only Caspary's account. McIntyre, unlike Spellman, did not keep a diary. It would be much easier to describe what did not happen – it seems clear that the Cardinal had no wish either for compromise or resolution.

It is tempting to believe that McIntyre already knew that his position had been approved by the Vatican. He described himself as "shocked and angered"[61] that the sisters may not be wearing habits when school resumed. Caspary's account is that when she tried to explain, the Cardinal immediately cited compulsory Canon law on the subject of the habit. "He stated firmly and very loudly that he would not have any IHM sisters in archdiocesan schools without religious habits."[62] Weber's statement, "He paid scant if any attention to the "habit issue"[63] would seem clearly to be erroneous.

He then went on, again according to Caspary, as if their proposals were actually an ultimatum. "You want an ultimatum?" he thundered. "Very well, I will accept your threat to withdraw from our schools. The date for your withdrawal is then June 1968." "We were stunned to hear the finality of his announcement."[64] What was clear was that there would be no negotiation.

Since they had never issued an ultimatum, it's hard to discern what may have been in McIntyre's mind. Did he think that they actually had? Or did he simply want the thorn in his side removed. Although this latter seems the most likely explanation if Caspary's description of his demeanor is accurate, it's difficult to imagine this man, so concerned with finances, actually choosing to replace what could only be considered the cheapest possible labor by increasing his own costs by six, seven or eight hundred percent. If this was not his intent, did he believe he was calling their bluff? Did he expect them to cave? If he did, of course, it was a major error.

Caspary's account continues. "His voice, barely controlled now, rose even higher and louder. Again, I can see the dramatic scene and hear his pronouncement: "Very well, you can keep all your experiments and your fine decrees. But I tell you this, you won't be staying in my schools." And with that he turned to Bishop Manning next to him and waved his arm in our direction "See that a committee is appointed right away… so we can see to the orderly withdrawal from our diocese next year." The room was suddenly terribly quiet. The

Cardinal was flushed. No one said a word. … No more explanations were possible now."[65]

At an IHM Chapter session, the delegates were given a full report of the meeting with McIntyre. They voted unanimously to remain steadfast to the decrees already promulgated. They moved that a joint statement be sent to the cardinal. "The essence of the letter made clear that we did not wish to withdraw all our sisters simultaneously from our schools; rather the chapter wished to see a certain small percentage, which was negotiable, have the chance to finish their degrees, etc., but the majority of sisters wished to continue teaching in the schools. Some few who wish to serve in other ministries other than teaching were to have the opportunity to serve God and the church in other ways. Further, members welcome the opportunity to meet with his Eminence to clarify certain points in the decrees that might have been misinterpreted as intransigence."[66]

The Cardinal's response came in a letter, ignoring the sisters offer and including the following: "This ultimatum, with its elements, is not acceptable to the Archdiocese of Los Angeles and its Ordinary. Consequently, there is no other alternative than to accept the threat of the community that they withdraw from the teaching staffs of our parochial schools in the Archdiocese.[67] But in another letter, to the Archbishop of San Francisco, he wrote "Our decision will be that we shall not have them teaching in our schools and living in our convents under the guise of religious women with a quasi-secular rule. Candidly, I feel that the community will compromise and they will not wish to move out of 25 of our schools."[68]

On December 7, another meeting was held presided over by Bishop Ward. When asked if the sisters were still intent on their previously stated decrees, then their withdrawal date from the schools would be set as September, 1968. Msgr. Hawkes, who was also present and thought of as the Cardinal's right-hand man, then stated, "Then you reaffirm your decision. When do you plan to leave our convents?"[69]

To say that the sisters were badly frightened would be an understatement. Many had left the "real world" 30 or 40 years before. They now were "facing a total change of lifestyle, leaving a secure professional situation, a communal structure, and a familiar habitat."[70] The General sent another conciliatory letter, dated December 18. It read in part, "We have never desired the withdrawal from archdiocesan schools and we seek to avoid this eventuality. We respectfully request that the possibility of necessary withdrawals from some schools not be considered to be any form of ultimatum. Our representatives are prepared to meet with Your Eminence or any representatives whom you may wish to delegate for the purpose of negotiations with respect to our Decrees on Education."[71]

The cardinal replied the following day that no negotiations in relation to the schools could be undertaken until it was clear that his position in relation to their ecclesiology had been accepted. This included his setting the rules in relation to times of prayer, their bedtimes, and the wearing of the habit.

Many of the clergy attempted to intervene in this situation, suggesting various forms of negotiation, and those who were especially eager to see an agreement reached were the priests of the dioceses whose schools were staffed by the sisters. One of these was Msgr. Bernard Dolan, pastor in Long Beach. He arranged a meeting with the Cardinal and Caspary for mid-January.

Caspary was in secular clothes, a black tailored suit which she considered to be "very modest and formal."[72] "I do not remember any exchange of greetings as we were ushered by an aide into Cardinal McIntyre's office. The first thing I do remember was the Cardinals very loud and angry voice, shouting "You can no longer call yourself a religious in that clothing! How dare you come to my office this way!" I was shocked into silence. So was the normally genial and talkative pastor of St. Anthony's.

"When I turned to him for support, I was stunned to find that he had fled the room. I had no choice but to listen to a long, condemnatory speech, after which I left with as much dignity as I could muster." Msgr. Dolan telephoned later, "apologizing for his hasty retreat. He gave only one excuse: 'I could not stand to see a woman insulted like that.'"[73] Other attempts were made; none succeeded.

And so it came to pass that another visitation was scheduled by the cardinal for the IHMs, but this time the Vatican was involved. Father Thomas R. Gallagher, O.P. was appointed by Rome and arrived within two weeks. By that time, almost all the sisters had adopted lay attire. Gallagher began his inquiry with a questionnaire that all sisters would fill out in guaranteed confidence.

At the same time, the sisters who disapproved of the proposed changes met as a group and elected Sister Eileen MacDonald as their spokesperson. She, on their behalf, then wrote to Cardinal Antoniutti, Prefect of the Sacred Congregation for Religious, citing their differences and requesting that their rights be clarified. Although Caspary had known of the group's existence, through rumors, it was a relief to her for the disagreement to be out in the open.

What followed from Cardinal Antoniutti, presumably after consultation with Father Gallagher, was a reply that became known as the Four Points Letter. It required the IHMs to 1) adopt a uniform habit, 2) attend mass as a group daily, 3) continue to teach in the Catholic schools and 4) collaborate "with the local Ordinaries in the works of the apostolate in the various dioceses." It went on to state that these prescriptions hold for all Religious, *especially for those of the Pontifical Right.*[74] The letter cited Giovanni Montini (Paul 6) who wrote, "…Even exempt, (i.e. pontifical Institutes) are bound by the laws, decrees and ordinances laid down by the local Ordinary affecting various works." Further it stated "The local ordinary… to prevent scandal to the faithful can prohibit clerics, both secular and religious, even exempt religious, from wearing lay dress in public."[75] Of course, uproar followed.

Some prelates, including the Canon Law Society of America, weighed in on the side of the sisters. Jesuits, both from Loyola University in Los Angeles and Alma College in Los Gatos, the Dominicans of Berkeley Priory and the Christian Brothers of Mont La Salle all rallied behind their California neighbors. A three page open letter was sent by the Jesuits of Loyola University, signed by 30 Jesuit university faculty members, asserting the sisters displayed "A genuine religious vitality which commands our respect as fellow religious."[76] Those Jesuits found themselves in McIntyre's office the following day, to witness a lengthy and furious tirade against the sisters.

Other orders of sisters rallied to their defense as well, while at the same time worrying deeply about their own futures and whatever courses they had planned. Debates raged. The IHMs were grateful for the support of Mother Mary Luke Tobin, Major Superior of the Sisters of Loretto, the only American woman who had "audited" Vatican II.

Although while all of this had been unfolding there had indeed been both newspaper and television coverage, now this increased several fold. The Vatican tried to make clear that nowhere did their instruction grant unrestricted authority for religious to experiment. What they succeeded in doing, which had not been true until this time, was making every sister in the country, whether engaged in renewal programs or not, aware of the details of the conflict between the IHMs and their Ordinary.

Sister Mary Daniel Turner, S.N.D.de N., wrote, "We who serve the church as religious are saddened that however difficult and painful the present moment, the response for this particular Congregation is one so lacking in the Christian qualities of compassion, trust and dignity."[77] And then, "Women religious would hope that the counsel, guidance and sanctions are results of the evaluations *after* experiments have been tried and not pre-judgments made before experiments are undertaken."[78] The noise continued, always ever louder.

"By May 3, 1968 and with considerable media coverage, 25,556 signatures had been gathered, of which 16,401 were lay Catholics, 2,008 were nuns of different religious orders, 1,195 were priests and brothers, 4,146 were members of other religious denominations, and 1,806 gave no religious affiliation. The signatures, along with a petition asking the Pope "to protect and encourage" the nuns in their modernization experiments, were sent to the Holy Father."[79]

At the same time the Conference of Major Superiors of Women, later to become the LCWR, had expressed a willingness to help. In the strictest of confidence, close to a dozen mothers superior decided to travel to Rome together and to place the problem they confronted directly before the Pope. Their plan was to meet in New York City and then fly nonstop to Rome. On the morning of their planned departure, Caspary's telephone rang. It was a prelate that she deemed friendly, suggesting that the sisters cancel their plans because "a new turn of events had taken place."[80] He was not free to divulge the development to which he referred but felt that it would be more helpful than the sisters direct appeal to the Vatican. Caspary managed to reach all the sisters before their departures and waited for further developments.

While she was still telephoning the various mothers superior, she received a special delivery letter, dated March 29, 1968 informing her that the IHM's were to be investigated by a pontifical commission. The commission would consist of three American bishops, James V. Casey, D.D., Archbishop of Denver, consultant to the Pontifical Commission for the Revision of the Code of Canon Law and president of the commission; Most Rev. Thomas A. Donnellen, D.D., Archbishop-designate of Atlanta and chairman of the Bishops' Liaison Committee for the Conference of Major Superiors of Men; and Most Rev. Joseph Breitenbeck, D.D., auxiliary Bishop of Detroit and chairman of the Bishops' Liaison Committee for the Conference of Major Superiors of Women. There would be a fourth member of the group, their previous visitator, Father Thomas R. Gallagher, O. P. "This, then, was the new turn of events!"[81] The men would arrive May 4th and stay through May 7th and they did.

"After their three days of meetings in small groups, the commission members announced that they had not yet reached a conclusion and would return in June to conclude their work, but they hinted that perhaps we had gone too far too fast; they were careful, however, not to condemn us. So we allowed ourselves to hope that all might still turn out favorably."[82] However on June 4, when their follow-up visit was concluded, they issued their judgment in a letter dated June 6, 1968.

"They stated that for practical purposes, and while a final decision from the Holy See was still pending, the commission would officially recognize the internal separation of the two groups of the Immaculate Heart Sisters. Thus they ordered two separate groups, each empowered to act separately. The first and larger group under Caspary's leadership was to be given some time "to experiment, to reflect, and to come to definite decisions concerning their rule of life to be submitted to the Holy See. The second group, temporarily under Sister Eileen MacDonald was to live under the pre-conciliar IHM constitution. Maintaining a pre-1967 lifestyle, they could proceed with their own program of renewal if they wished and could contract agreements regarding the schools with diocesan authorities."[83]

Almost immediately, a poll was taken. Sisters were asked to which group they wish to be assigned. Four hundred and fifty five sisters, clearly the younger ones since their average age was 36, although at least one of them was in her 90s, voted to continue the renewal process. Fifty one members, elected to join Sister MacDonald's group – their average age was 62. Caspary requested separate living quarters for them, since tensions between members had increased significantly, but received no reply to her request.

All of this was covered in detail by both the local and the national media. Although many editorials were in favor of the larger group's conception of renewal, many were not and among the laity, the position taken by the sisters elicited little praise. "To see a sister follow her conscience in stating that obedience to God might supersede obedience to immediate hierarchical authority was scandalizing to some sincere Catholics. The concept of obedience they followed was literal, uncritical, and placed the burden of decision-making on authority not on the individual."[84]

On June 30, 1968, while still waiting for further rulings from Rome, the sisters who had voted to continue the renewal process were "made to withdraw as Cardinal McIntyre had requested as teaching sisters from parochial schools in the Los Angeles archdiocese."[85] Now they were job hunting. With excellent reputations as teachers, many found work immediately. Others ventured further afield into adult religious programs, social work, and hospital administration. However, "a number of the very young sisters, alarmed at the uncertainties of the future, left the community when their schools closed."[86]

In February, 1969, Caspary was elected for a second term. In the same month, they received a request from the hierarchy for information as to the progress on the implementation of the decrees. In the process of the legal separation, a list of the various properties owned by the Immaculate Heart was sent to Archbishop James V. Casey. The financial separation of the two groups went on, to be implemented by the lawyers each group had chosen.

By spring, Caspary's group had still not made a final decision as far as the acceptance of the four points were concerned and so they still were an ecumenical community. McIntyre continued the pressure. He wrote to Caspary in April, suggesting that the chapter decrees be revised. She replied that the Board of Directors was aware of its responsibility and was considering alternatives. In fact, she was still hoping that the Vatican would come to understand their situation and acknowledge their good faith.

Indeed Vatican officials were deeply concerned; the same types of experimentation were now becoming familiar, with other religious communities joining the trend. These included the Sisters of Mercy of Pittsburgh, the School Sisters of St. Francis, the School Sisters of Notre Dame, the Sisters of Notre Dame de Namur, the Institute of the Blessed Virgin Mary, the Sisters of Social Service, the Sisters of Loretto and many others. These orders, with archbishops who were less conservative, were moving ahead full steam. On May 31, 1969, "An immediate vote was urged by the bishops to indicate our decision to remain officially "religious" or to form a lay organization without recognition in the church."[87] The pontifical commission arrived once more.

They met with group after group of sisters, scheduled at intervals. "Endlessly the ultimatum was repeated until it was burned into our memories: follow the four points or accept a dispensation from your vows. Then become any kind of religious association you choose. Just don't call yourselves 'religious.'"[88] Sister Corita Kent asked

Archbishop Casey, "What do you think Jesus would have done if he were given this choice?"[89] The question went unanswered. The priests left.

The sisters continued to delay, still hoping for some sort of reprieve. By fall, no decision had been reached and the pressure began to mount. Caspary decided on one more trip to Rome. She had been told that she might be given a fairer hearing by the Vatican substitute Secretary of State, Archbishop Giovanni Benelli. This man was among the more liberal clergy and although she knew she was grasping at straws, Caspary felt she had to take the chance. She went unaccompanied, met with Benelli and gave him a letter, drawn up by the IHM Board of Directors; in part the letter read "We believe, with good reason, that at least 80% of our Community will withdraw from religious life if the Institute is required to follow the present directive."[90]

She asked that the letter be given to the Pope. The Archbishop "promised to give the matter his most earnest attention and quietly left the room. I was escorted out to the waiting room by an attendant priest. The whole interview had lasted at most about 15 minutes."[91] Although she left the Vatican office with little hope, she did at least believe that she had done what she could.

On December 6, 1969 the community assembled as a group. Caspary announced her own personal decision, to refuse, and then each sister was asked to make her own decision "understanding that belonging to the group in accord with the renewal chapter meant that she had to obtain a dispensation from her vows and would lose her canonical status."[92] She asked each sister to reply in writing by December 15 indicating whether she wished to become a member of a new lay group living according to their decrees or join the more traditionally oriented community.

Before the dreaded day of decision, it should be noted that the major superiors of communities of both men and women in America protested to the Vatican "the threatened interference in the lives of American religious and in particular, the treatment of the Immaculate Heart Sisters renewal program."[93] The Conference of Major Superiors of Men sent a formal protest directly to Antoniutti, approved by 73% of its members. The Conference of Major Superiors of Women, later to become the LCWR, did the same, but to no avail. To Caspary's knowledge, no reply to either of these resolutions was ever received.

Each sister had, of course, been enduring her own personal struggle. These decisions for many, if not all, were wrenching. They varied from individual to individual, but doubts, fears, questions of conscience, the fidelity to vows were common to all of them. Many distrusted their own strengths – would they really be able to do this, to form a new community, to exist and even prosper completely on their own? After all, they never had. What made them think they could now? They spent many hours in prayer.

Some sisters simply left, exhausted by the years of struggle and disappointed in the reactions of the Vatican. And opportunities were opening for women in this new world of the 60s. Other sisters left to join other communities transferring without having to repeat their novitiate. Caspary mourned their departures. When the final figures were tallied, 350 sisters elected to be released from their vows and join the new community; 50 elected to remain with the group headed by Sister Eileen MacDonald.

The first sister who went to Caspary with her signed acceptance was over 70 and dressed in her full habit; Caspary noted that she wore it until the day of her death years later. She had, as it happened, made her vows before Caspary was born.

On January 18, 1970, Archbishop Timothy Manning, who would eventually become McIntyre's successor, arranged for the nuns seeking dispensation from their vows to do so simply by signing a form in his presence. "In the application form was the statement that the petition for dispensation was made freely. Virtually every sister, without consultation with the others, took one final, important step: she crossed out the word "freely.""[94]

The aftermath…

Events, of course, as events tend to do, continued to unfold.

The larger group took the name the Immaculate Heart Community. Caspary had, in anticipation of what she hoped would never come to pass, incorporated the assets of the community under various corporate entities. She understood that a financial settlement with the smaller group would eventually be necessary. She wanted to retain

Immaculate Heart College, Queen of the Valley Hospital, Immaculate Heart High School and La Casa de Maria in exchange for a proportional cash payment representing a value of one sixth of the overall holdings.

The final exchange of documents between Manning and Caspary had as its subject the status of any chapel that might be operated by the Immaculate Heart Community. It was made clear to Caspary that none of the buildings could be considered suitable for the offering of the Mass, nor could they hold the Blessed Sacrament. The aforementioned chapels, heretofore sacred by reason of blessings, were no longer "holy," but were rather reduced to secular status. This was their new reality.

The Community recently celebrated its 40th anniversary. Their mission statement, according to their website, reads in part as follows: "We, the members of the Immaculate Heart Community, rooted in Jesus Christ and united with the people of God commit ourselves to build relations in society which foster access of all persons to truth, dignity, and full human development, and to strategically change practices and situations which impede such access." And then "With reverence for all creation, in our choice of work and living style, and in our use of time, talent, and money, we hold ourselves accountable to God and to one another for effecting this goal and supporting one another in this effort."[95]

Caspary, who lived to be 95, was elected the first president of the new community. Again according to their website, "The growth of the community continued for many years with the accommodations at Montecito being strained at times because of the large numbers wishing to join the community."[96] And "Today the property is the location of a House of Spiritual Renewal. Also located there is a thriving Retreat Center that was established in 1974. Both endeavors are part of the works embraced by the new Immaculate Heart Community."[97] Men and married couples, as well as non-Catholics are accepted as members. However, Immaculate Heart College was forced to close in the first decade due to decreased enrollment.

The smaller group took the name the Immaculate Heart Institute and elected Sister Eileen MacDonald superior general, the post she had held on an interim basis since June, 1968. Because they owned no property, Archbishop Manning was anxious to provide a motherhouse for the Institute, which had received only needed funds in the final settlement. The archdiocese purchased an eight-acre estate for them, which included not only a Gothic chapel but extensive gardens as well. The Cardinal could be generous when he chose.

Those who knew the group, and remained afterwards in touch with MacDonald, describe it as "diverse." It would seem logical that at least some of those members very much wanted to renew, as Caspary wished, but simply could not accept noncanonical status. They may have stayed but may not have been glad to do so. By 1970, MacDonald was unhappy enough to seek an apostolate elsewhere.

She wrote to a number of bishops and was invited by Bishop David

M. Maloney to his diocese in Wichita, Kansas and she and two others of the group, Sr. Giovanni Oliveri and Mother M. Joanne Brummell, joined with her and made the move. They retained their conventional habit and taught in the Wichita school system. Today they are the IHMs of Wichita, living the traditional life. They number 22 vowed sisters, 5 in the process of becoming vowed and were expecting two postulants in September of 2014.[98]

They rise at 4:35, have prayers from 5 to 7, breakfast, teach a full school day, return to early dinners, evening prayers, 45 minutes of "recreation" and a 9:30 bedtime. There is a picture of their "modified habit" on their website. It's an attractive ankle-length navy blue dress with a white collar. With no wimple, their veil is short, simple, a little longer than shoulder length, with a good deal of hair showing. Clearly they have returned to their original charism. But after more than 40 years, there are fewer than 30 of them.

The sisters that they left behind continued to teach until eventually they quite literally "died off." In 2014, three were left, one at age 102, all in assisted living arrangements. The diocese still owns the 8-acre estate.

On the surface, and according to Weber, McIntyre would seem to have emerged from the controversy undiminished. He was still a Cardinal and still the Ordinary of one of the most powerful diocese in America, if not the world. But as events continued to unfold, public opinion seemed to favor the sisters. It was widely believed that the Vatican wished there had been less publicity, as was the case where many orders pursuing renewal did so under the gaze of less conservative prelates. Or, as Ann Carey has hypothesized, under those bishops who "feared a mass exodus of sisters from Catholic schools, hospitals, and social service agencies if the bishops appeared to be interfering with the sisters renewal efforts."[99]

In mid-1966, the Decree on the Bishops' Pastoral Office in the Church had been passed, urging bishops to submit their resignations by the time they reached the age of 75. McIntyre was then 80. It was widely expected that he would be required to give up his diocese before the end of the year, but he declined to comment to the press on any plans he had for retirement. He was then asked (instructed?) by Montini (Paul 6) to consider the appointment of a coadjutor Archbishop; it was a full two years before McIntyre's various objections to suggested candidates were met and on July 11, 1969 it was announced that Bishop Timothy Manning would be the new coadjutor Bishop for Los Angeles. On January 21, 1970 the Vatican announced McIntyre's resignation "because of advanced age."[100] "On the day that McIntyre left the Chancery for the last time, [he] told his staff that he would never return. And he didn't. McIntyre refused to grant interviews, to comment publicly about ecclesial affairs or to attend liturgical events, [unless specifically invited]."[101]

In 2014, Dr. William Coulson is not only alive and well, living and lecturing in California, but has abandoned private practice, and now makes a living lecturing on the dangers of psychotherapy. In a breathtaking example of grandiosity, he claims total credit for the split in the IHM community. This, despite the clear historical record, with the first General Chapter decrees arrived at in 1963, and the second canonical visitation well underway before his arrival.

These events occurred prior to the formal encounter of Coulson and Rogers with the IHM community, which occurred late in April, 1967 when the encounter groups were first introduced and explained to a meeting of the whole community. There had been a prior small "pilot project" and indeed some sisters in that project became involved in lesbian relationships and eventually left the community, writing books about their experience. The larger project had yet to begin. But it was the encounter group experience that was responsible for subsequent events? Were it not for Rogers and Coulson, the IHMs would have put their habits back on and remained canonical?

Clearly events were in their final stages when Coulson entered into the equation; certainly there were sisters who did leave the community because of the pilot study. But among 600 sisters, there must certainly have been some for whom the vocation was not an appropriate choice. However, if one makes one's living by confessing past sins, the more serious the sins the better, and if some lesbian sex can be tossed in for good measure, better yet; more interviews are consequently requested. At least by interviewers who have little concern for the facts.

And so…

The struggle went on, and goes on still, with Caspary providing perhaps a cautionary tale; "going noncanonical" is rarely spoken of now as any kind of solution to conflict. The Vatican has been brought up to date; sisters cannot be relied upon for silence in the face of perceived injustice. Caspary's feminism, shocking to many then, is closer to the mainstream now. A full participant, leading the charge, she was in the 60s way out in front, yes, one of "the California nuns," active not only with her own community but with the LCWR as well, serving there in several leadership positions. When the moment of decision came, Sister Humiliata would not, and perhaps could not, back down.

Remembering, more than 30 years later, Caspary disparaged McIntyre's role, "It was not a single cardinal who forced us to abandon canonical status in the Catholic Church. It was a vast ecclesiastical system that for centuries had used every ploy to keep women beholden to its curiously antiquated rules and regulations. Bishops, Cardinals, priests have inherited the legacy of domination over women, especially over women religious, who by built-in dependencies of their lifestyles were made subservient to male clerics."[102] And then goes on, "The system itself remains intact."[103]

But she always believed "that the spirit of God was with us."[104]

NOTES: PART FOUR, Chapter One

1. http://catholicpsychology.blogspot.com/2007/07/perverting-of-catholic-religious.html.
2. Personal recollection of the author, a doctoral candidate there at the time.
3. "Concord Hymn," by Ralph Waldo Emerson.
4. https://en.wikipedia.org/wiki/Francis_Spellman.
5. Weber, Francis J. *His Eminence of Los Angeles: James Francis McIntyre.* Kimberly Press, Santa Barbara, California, Volume I, P1.
6. Ibid., P.7
7. Ibid., P.7
8. Ibid., P.7
9. Ibid., P.7
10. Ibid., Preface, P.iii
11. http://www.twhalloran.info/page22.html.
12. Weber, op.cit., P.71.
13. https://en.wikipedia.org/wiki/James_Francis_McInyre.
14. https://en.wikipedia.org/wiki/James_Francis_McInyre.
15. Ford., George Barry. 1969. *A Degree of Difference: Memoirs of George Barry Ford.* Farrar, Strauss and Giroux, New York. P.100.
16. http://www.twhalloran.info/page22.html.
17. Weber, Op.Cit., P.39.
18. http://www.twhalloran.info/page22.html.
19. http://www.worldlibrary.org/articles/James_Cardinal_McIntyre.
20. http://www.worldlibrary.org/articles/James_Cardinal_McIntyre.
21. http://www.worldlibrary.org/articles/James_Cardinal_McIntyre.
22. http://www.fisheaters.com/forums/index.php?topic=3456242.20.
23. Caspary, Anita Marie., 2001. *Witness to Integrity: the Crisis of the Immaculate Heart Community.* Liturgical Press, Collegeville, Minnesota. P.xiii.
24. Ibid., P.24.
25. Ibid., P.8.
26. Ibid., P.9.

27. Ibid., P.10.
28. Ibid., P.11.
29. Ibid., P.15.
30. Ibid., P.16.
31. Ibid., P.16.
32. Ibid., P.17.
33. Ibid., P.18.
34. Ibid., P.26.
35. Ibid., P.27.
36. Ibid., P.28.
37. Ibid., P.28.
38. Ibid., P.35.
39. Ibid., P.36.
40. Ibid., P.37.
41. Ibid., P.38.
42. Ibid., P.47.
43. Ibid., Pp. 47-48.
44. Ibid., P.46.
45. Ibid., P.51.
46. See Appendix C, Perfectae Caritatus, for the excerpts in the next three paragraphs.
47. Massa, SJ, Mark J. *The American Catholic Revolution.* Oxford University Press, New York, 2010. P.100.
48. Ibid., P.101.
49. Caspary, Op.Cit., P.68.
50. Ibid., P.69.
51. Ibid., P.71.
52. Ibid., P.71.
53. Ibid., P.71.
54. Ibid., P.73.
55. Ibid., P.76.
56. Ibid., P.79.
57. Ibid., P.82.
58. Ibid., P.83.
59. Ibid., P.83.
60. Ibid., P.62.
61. Ibid., P.120.
62. Ibid., P.120.
63. Weber, Op.Cit., Vol.II, P.436.

64. Caspary, Op.Cit., p.123.
65. Ibid., P.126.
66. Ibid., P.130.
67. Ibid., P.131.
68. Ibid., P.135.
69. Ibid., P.136.
70. Ibid., P.137.
71. Ibid., P.138.
72. Ibid., P.142.
73. Ibid., P.142.
74. Ibid., P.157.
75. Ibid., P.160.
76. Ibid., P.163.
77. Ibid., P.168.
78. Ibid., P.169.
79. Ibid., P.174.
80. Ibid., P.175.
81. Ibid., P.176.
82. Ibid., P.178.
83. Ibid., P.178.
84. Ibid., P.181.
85. Ibid., P.186.
86. Ibid., P.190.
87. Ibid., P.195.
88. Ibid., P.196.
89. Ibid., P.197.
90. Ibid., P.203.
91. Ibid., P.203.
92. Ibid., P.204.
93. Ibid., P.205.
94. Ibid., P.211.
95. https://www.immaculateheartcommunity.org/
96. https://www.immaculateheartcommunity.org/
97. https://www.immaculateheartcommunity.org/
98. Personal communication to the author.
99. Carey, Ann. *Sisters in Crisis.* 1997.Our Sunday Visitor, Inc., Juntingdon, Indiana, P.188.
100. Weber, Op.Cit., Vol.II, P.646.
101. Ibid., P.652.

102. Caspary, Op.Cit. P.220.
103. Ibid., P.220.
104. Ibid., P.219.

Chapter 2: Ordaining women? Roma locuta; causa finita.

Translation? "Rome has spoken; case closed." These are the words that are intended to end Catholic discussion – on any subject – and the papal "No" to women's ordination was stated clearly in 1994. But in the mid- to late 1960s, with the feminist movement in America coming into full flower and the afterglow of Vatican II still bright, the case for the ordination of women was far from closed. Indeed, it was just beginning to find a clear voice and there were women wondering how to make that voice heard effectively.

The 60s…

Catholic feminism should be understood as a branch of, but far from one with, American feminism; Catholic feminists arrived at their position from their own traditions and faith. Some of the most important organizations emerged in the late 60s and early 70s but many had been in existence for years, actually for decades. These included The Grail, the Christian Family Movement, Catholic Action, the Sister Formation Conference and the Conference of Major Superiors of Women, later renamed the LCWR. The first actual protest, an action, not a discussion, took place in 1969, "The Easter Bonnet Rebellion" as it was called, or alternatively, with a touch of humor, "The National Unveiling." Women were asked to come to church with their heads bare. Many did.

The target of the earliest writings was a concept that pervaded all curial doctrine in relation to women, a construct known as the

"Eternal Woman." Echoing centuries-old words and ancient stereotypes, a woman was characterized as "pious, pure, submissive, domestic, and confined to the private sphere."[1] She was as well "gentle, tender, humble, and loving. She was person-oriented, more attuned to the individual, whereas men were immersed in larger societal and intellectual interests."[2] Self-sacrifice was a given, the surrender of self commonplace; "Every woman's duty [is]to sacrifice her body, her will, her work, even her personality for the sake of her family and the kingdom of God."[3]

And then there was anger. "The Eternal Woman not only never expressed anger, she never felt it. In a world of placid submission, sarcasm and irony were unknown. So when feminists in time adopted a tone that revealed how infuriated they had [become] – and what's more, turned their anger on the church itself – they signaled the beginning of the new era."[4] A new, and from Rome's viewpoint, most unwelcome era.

"Over the course of the early 60s, writers systematically exposed every stereotype, myth, falsehood and glorification perpetuated by the Eternal Woman advocates and the hierarchy, while exhorting Catholics to speak of women as they actually were."[5] Major voices came to be heard: Rosemary Radford Ruether began to publish in the mid-60s; Sidney Callahan gave women her "The Illusion of Eve: Modern Woman's Quest for Identity" in 1965; Mary Daley's "The Church and the Second Sex," came out in 1968.

Mary Magdalene had yet to be released from the error made by

Gregorius Anicius (Pope Gregory 1) in 591, who conflated three distinct women of the Bible into one, with the tale of Magdalene as the repentant prostitute emerging; one of the very few independent women in the New Testament became, in his telling, a sad and rueful whore. The Vatican did not correct this characterization until 1967. How useful she might have been to the early feminists, who, with the Gnostic Books of the Bible still in the process of translation, had to make do with what they had.

For the most extensive and detailed review of this early period see the extra-ordinarily well-researched book by Mary J. Henold, "Catholic and Feminist; the Surprising History of the American Catholic Feminist Movement."

1974

Between 1970 and 1973 women's enrollment in seminaries had tripled. In July, 1974, the Episcopal Church electrified the religious world with their ordination of eleven women, and many Catholic women wondered if they might be next. A surprising number of them, both lay and religious, believed they might be, and in their belief were ready to act, perhaps for themselves, perhaps for others.

Among them was a lay woman, Mary Bernadette Lynch, who said of her small group, "We are more of a movement than an organization."[6] She believed, "The task was to befriend, teach, and "convert" the people in power "with great delicacy" because in their hands rested the ability to change the church structures whose design impeded women from full ministry."[7]

Coming together originally in Chicago, Lynch's group formed an initial committee. Their numbers were small, their experience with group meetings nonexistent, and they had no readily identifiable means of support. But joined by a number of women religious, they moved forward with a plan. They would hold a conference, although none of them had ever held a conference. It's title? "Women in Future Priesthood Now: A Call to Action." Scheduled for November 28 through 30, 1975, it would be held in Detroit. A venue was chosen but when applications flooded in, a larger site was required. But the new site was not large enough either and more than 500 women had to be turned away. Fifteen hundred were registered. In addition, 75 credentialed members of the press attended.

1975

Sister Nadine Foley, a member of the Adrian Dominican Congregation, holding a doctorate degree in philosophy from the Catholic University of America and an STM in Scripture from Union Theological Seminary, was president of the LCWR from 1987 to 89. In 1975, she was the titular head of the conference.

Recently, she remembered, "Before we met in Detroit, someone suggested that maybe we ought to go talk to Cardinal Dearden and so we did… because it was going to be in his diocese."[8] He looked at her quizzically, she remembered, his face filled with confusion, and then asked her, "Who *are* these women?" That he didn't know, spoke volumes. "He couldn't figure out where in the world this was coming from. So, so that stayed with me."[9] And the question found its way onstage. In her opening remarks, Foley repeated the Cardinal's question, "genuine in its perplexity,"[10] "Who *are* these women?"

Sister Margaret Farley, RSM, held a masters degree in philosophy and a doctorate in Religious Studies from Yale University and was then Associate Professor of Ethics at the Yale Divinity School. She spoke at the conference on the "Moral Imperatives for the Ordination of Women." When she paraphrased Jesus's response to Philip in the Bible verse, John 14.9, "Have we been so long with you, and you have not known us?" her well-phrased question would have been an excellent reply to the cardinal.

She continued: "The office of priesthood, in fact, offers a particularly potent focus for addressing directly the sources of sexism in Christian thought."[11] She went on to point out that in the past, women have not been considered capable of three required elements for priestly function; these would be leadership, the ability to represent, (God to humans and humans to God) and "the capacity to enter and to stand in the presence of God, in the realm of the sacred."[12]

This element of leadership has been a major stumbling block when the ordination of women has been considered; "Whether it was because Eve was thought to be derivative from Adam, or female infants only misbegotten males, or women subordinated to men as a punishment for Original Sin; or whether it was because women were thought to be essentially passive not active, emotional, not intellectual, destined to contribute to the human community through reproduction, not production; always the conclusion came that women were to be followers not leaders, helpers not primary agents, responders not initiators."[13] She went on to point out that these "facts" were "simply false."[14] Consequently conclusions drawn from them were "simply wrong."[15]

That women could not be leaders was inseparable from the idea that neither could they represent God to humans or humans to God. But Farley pointed out, "That it is a serious distortion to image God in exclusively either masculine or feminine terms. From this it follows, however, that it is false to think that God cannot be represented by women as well as men, and hence equally false to conclude that on such grounds women are to be excluded from the office of priesthood."[16]

Farley asked why men, rather than women, seemed the only appropriate subjects for so sacred a responsibility and answered her own question. "Women... continue to be associated with images of pollution and sin. Ancient myths identifying women with chaos, darkness, ministry, matter, and sin echoed clearly in Christian interpretations of concupiscence, of the body as defiled, as sexuality as contaminating, and thence of woman as temptress, as a symbol of evil."[17] This understanding of women became theoretically entrenched in sophisticated theologies of Original Sin... woman as a special agent of evil."[18]

She then stated the moral imperative for ordaining women. The church "ought to do so because not to do so is to affirm a policy, a system, a structure, whose presuppositions are false."[19] In addition, she felt that women should seek ordination, "for the same reasons that obligate the church to ordain women."[20] And she ended with the question previously cited, "Have we been so long with you, and you have not known us?"

In late 2013, Farley's memories of the event remained vivid. She was "in awe," she said, "in seeing how many women were there and the energy there was in trying to address this question." And she was impressed with their hopefulness. "We were still in the wake of Vatican II and so there was a lot of optimism, tremendous optimism, about many things regarding the Catholic Church. Nobody was thinking this was a hopeless question. Women really did start thinking that [ordination] was a possibility for them, and so it was not just an intellectual exploration.

"But," she believed, "the association of women as evil, keeping them out of the sacred sanctuary" was a powerful force and those ideas needed to be deconstructed. "This was the huge step forward that needed to be taken, that's why I spoke on it." But everyone, she acknowledged, had underestimated the degree of opposition; "It was tremendous." And of course, that opposition soon made itself felt. "In retrospect," she knows now, "the position was overly optimistic."[21]

Additional presenters included Anne Elizabeth Carr, BVM, with a masters degree and doctorate in Christian Theology from the Divinity School of the University of Chicago, at the time their associate Dean. She spoke on "The Church in Process: Engendering the Future," asserting that the exclusion of women from the ordained ministry… had been questioned and refuted logically and theologically."[22]

Elizabeth Schussler Fiorenza, with a doctorate in theology from the University of Munster, was at the time Associate Professor of Theology at the University of Notre Dame. Her address was titled "Women Apostles; The Testament of Scripture." She contended that "the self understanding of the [early] Christian community eliminated all distinctions of religion, race, class and caste, and thereby allowed not only Gentiles and slaves to assume full leadership in the Christian community, but also women."[23]

"According to Paul," she pointed out, "Apostleship is not limited to the 12. All Christians are apostles, he said, who were eyewitnesses to the resurrection and who were commissioned by the resurrected Lord to missionary work (I Cor. 9; 4)."[24] Mary Collins, OSB, Dorothy Donnelly, CSJ, Nancy Lafferty, FSPA, Marie Augusta Neal, SND, and Mary Daniel Turner, SND, most of whom held doctoral degrees in scripture, theology, philosophy, or related fields, also spoke.

As the conference drew to a close, an effort was made to chart a path forward; the hope was for "an experience of reflection in the context of action and action informed by reflection."[25] Fidelity to the traditions of the Church was also stressed.

At one point in the liturgy, women who wished to be ordained, were invited to stand; the press was kept at a careful distance so that the women could not be photographed. But it was unclear to the leadership exactly what percentage of those attending actually wished ordination. A questionnaire was subsequently circulated, and the Cardinal's question, "Who *are* these women?" finally had a more precise answer. "Of the 837 female respondents, 289 (34.5%) responded with an unqualified "Yes" to the question "Do you wish to be ordained?" Of the 142 Roman Catholic lay women respondents, 50 (35.2%) responded with an unqualified "Yes," and of the 676 Roman Catholic religious women respondents, 229 (33.9%) responded with an unqualified "Yes."[26] Additionally, 38.7% of the women had, or were in the process of obtaining, graduate degrees in theology or related fields.[27]

At the conclusion of the 1975 Detroit gathering, the mandate to the conference planning task force was clear: establish an organization to keep this topic alive and still moving forward. "Into the gap leaped Bill Callahan, Maureen Fiedler, SL, and Dolly Pomerleau, who immediately opened the doors of the Quixote Center as an organizational hub for this issue."[28] They named themselves the Women's Ordination Conference and hired a project manager, Ruth Fitzpatrick. By 1983 they were based in Washington DC.

1976 and 77

In the early 1970s, the Vatican's Doctrinal Congregation had directed the Pontifical Biblical Commission (PBC) "to study the scriptural basis for withholding ordination from women."[29] The PBC unanimously declared that the New Testament alone was not sufficient to settle "in a clear way and once and for all" the "problem" of ordaining women.[30] They found the Eucharistic priesthood to be a *post biblical concept.* This was an embarrassment for Montini (Paul 6) who disbanded the commission.

Additionally, the PBC concluded that the only certainty about leadership in the early church was that in conformity with Jewish custom it was exclusively male dominated. This suggested that the male nature of church leadership, was "neither scriptural nor divine, but merely cultural."[31] Despite the fact that Jesus said nothing about maleness or ever used the words "priest" or "priesthood," the hierarchy of the church, without explanation, established maleness as an essential of the sacrament of holy orders.

In January 1977, Montini (Paul 6) issued "Inter Insigniores; On the Question of the Admission of Women to the Ministerial Priesthood." This document intended to supply the reasoning for all future opposition to the ordination of women; it argued that only males can "image Christ," a doctrine known as "in persona Christi." An outcry followed, not only from feminists; every section of "Insigniores" received theological criticism.

Although this was an official statement, further theological investigation of the question was not forbidden. Questions and criticisms came thick and fast. Does the minister of the sacraments represent Christ the Male or Christ the Mediator? Doesn't the question concern the formal element in the representation, not what may be described as the material image in the representation? Didn't the central church teachings of salvation make clear that salvation derived not from Jesus' *maleness*, but from his *humanness?* Supposing, the critics went on, "What if the Vatican said that because Christ was neither African nor American, it followed that African Americans could not act in persona Christi?"[32]

Not only did Inter Insigniores not settle the question, it ignited further and more heated controversy. In the wake of the declaration, "World wide objections to Inter Insigniores prompted the… CDF to issue a commentary."[33] The Vatican then compounded the problem, stating "The tradition was "received from Christ and the apostles" and the church was "bound" to it. This assertion, of course, contradicted a long history of changes in church thinking and practice over the centuries"[34] but reflected Rome's deep concern with the appearance of continuity.

Critics were quick to name just a few of these changes, choosing of course, those that were most embarrassing:

- From the Council of Arles, 1234, "We decree that male Jews from the age of 13 and up, when outside their homes, must wear upon the outer garment… a round badge of three or four fingers in width."[35] From Cum Nimis Absurdam, 1555, It is "sanctioned that all Jews should live solely in one and the same location" [in what would come to be called ghettoes].[36] [Jews] are to be forced under threat of heavy penalties to take on a form of dress by which they can be clearly distinguished from Christians.[37]

- Until the 19th century, church pronouncements often justified the practice of slavery. "As late as 1866, the Holy Office said, "Slavery itself… is not at all contrary to the natural and divine law."[38] Numerous antislavery tracts were placed on the Index of Forbidden Books. "Although the Vatican was officially neutral during the Civil War, Giovanni Mastai-Ferretti, (Pius 9) made no secret of his sympathies for the Confederacy.[39]
- Then, of course, there was Galileo. At first the church unequivocally condemned Copernican theory and Galileo, who espoused it, for a "serious and pernicious" error.[40] He was convicted of heresy, sentenced by seven Cardinals, members of the Roman Inquisition in 1633, and of espousing a doctrine which "is false and contrary to the divine and Holy Scripture."[41] His book, "Dialogue," was banned. He died in 1642, while under house arrest. Some books supporting Copernican theory were subsequently removed from the Index of Forbidden Books, but Galileo's was not until 1835.
- After Charles Darwin put forward the theory of evolution in the 19th century, Mastai-Ferretti, (Pius 9) condemned it

> strongly. In 1950, however, Eugenio Pacelli, (Pius 12) acknowledged that the church "did not forbid" belief in evolution.[42] More than 40 years later, in 1996, Karol Wojtyla, (John Paul 2) recognized its wide acceptance in the scientific world as "more than a hypothesis."[43]

After the publication of Inter Insigniores, almost the entire faculty of the Jesuit School of Theology in Berkeley sent a statement directly to the pope, through the local apostolic delegate, pointing out the historical, scriptural and theological untenability of the document. The letter was firm, direct, and very public: "The priests' letter was particularly concerned with the commentaries claim that what the church had never done, the church could never do in the future. To say that we have never ordained women in the past, and therefore cannot do so now, is to ignore the fact that the issue has never arisen in precisely these contemporary terms and within the new realization of women's place in the world."[44]

James Orgren, a professor of astronomy emeritus at the State University of New York College at Buffalo, further pointed out that the Vatican today may not be able, as it once was, physically to enforce its edicts; nevertheless, it has other means at its disposal. Spiritual and psychological intimidation can be used just as effectively. But silencing dialogue on women's ordination, priestly celibacy, or contraception does not resolve those issues. Rather, such a tactic damages the church and threatens the credibility of the church's leadership. Although it must be noted, credible or not credible, the Vatican continues to hold its grip on power.

1978

In the last years of the 70s, reaction to Inter Insigniores led to increased radicalization; many mainstream Catholic feminists moved closer to their secular counterparts. Many attempted some form of conflict resolution within themselves. Catherine Stewart-Roache spoke for many Catholic women when she identified "the sacraments as the source of her peace, and the institutional church as the source of her pain, yet [she] could not divorce one from the other and so remained caught between the two."[45] What Henold terms the beginning of "a sustained and cultivated ambivalence"[46] was manifest everywhere. Tensions within many organizations were on the rise; ideological disagreements that before could be subsumed in efforts at dialogue now were more and more center stage.

In November 1978, when Catholic feminists met for the second Women's Ordination Conference in Baltimore, Maryland, attendance topped 2,000. But the sense of optimism was gone; signs of discord were apparent. The mood was angry and confrontational. "Participants came to the conference from strikingly divergent positions, ranging from those who still advocated dialogue to advocates of exodus from the institution to rank-and-file members who just wanted ordination, and they were shocked by the mounting tensions in the movement."[47]

The issue of ordination itself was called into question. Under what circumstances, might it be accepted, even if offered? There were journalistic accounts that referred to the meeting as "the anti-ordination conference."[48] In the end, a conference resolution was passed, "asking participants to affirm "the necessity of the differences among us and pledge ourselves to continue the dialogue with all those who have been disenfranchised." The resolution seems to have been an attempt to convince everyone that, indeed, the movement was still unified, when it appeared to be splitting apart."[49]

1979

In 1979, Sister Theresa Kane was 43 years old. Born in New York City, one of seven children from an Irish immigrant family, she was a college graduate with a masters degree in public administration. She was also president of her order, the Sisters of Mercy and president of the LCWR as well. She had been elected to the Provincial of her order when she was 29 years old and became Provincial at the age of 33. She was based in Washington.

Both she and some of the senior membership in the LCWR were aware of a recent speech given by Karol Wojtyla, (John Paul 2) in which he spoke about the religious life of nuns as "very cloistered." Now, on a whirlwind tour of American cities, the Pope was actually in Washington for a meeting with then-president, Jimmy Carter. The very *un-cloistered* members of the LCWR wondered about the possibility of an audience. Was there an opportunity here, through dialogue, for new and increased understanding? Kane had approached a bishop with whom she was friendly and asked him to try to arrange a meeting. Senior members of the LCWR in various cities across the United States were on standby; if the audience was granted they could be in Washington in a matter of hours.

One might well ask when, in the 2000-year history of the Roman Catholic church, had a Pope *ever* sat down and had a conversation with a group of nuns as Kane had suggested.[50] But optimism reigned until eventually, of course, reality intervened. The bishop informed her that the pope's schedule was full. But he told her, perhaps hoping to mitigate disappointment, that he had reserved seats for the sisters in the front row of the Cathedral.

There is no record of the bishop's reaction when Kane informed him that the sisters *knew* what the pope looked like; what they wanted was to *talk* with him.

But a little more than a week before the scheduled event, she received a phone call from a monsignor, who asked for her title. This was how she discovered she was to give the greeting to the Pope. Her recollection? "When I said, "This is the first I've heard of it," he said, "Well, somebody was supposed to call you. Give me your title for the program." I did and then said, "Monsignor, now how long is my greeting?" and he said, "Oh, just a couple of minutes, Sister. They don't want to hear from you, they want to hear from the Pope." Of course, I knew that. I could have said that to him, but I didn't. And that was the only conversation I had. Nobody ever called me, nobody ever said could we have a copy of your script, could you tell us what you are going to say, not a word."[51]

The night before the Pope was scheduled to speak, the Women's Ordination Conference had organized a silent protest; sisters had gone to the Vatican Embassy, holding signs asking for women's ordination and standing in silence. "And the next day, as guests went into the Cathedral, they stood on the steps with a petition they asked people to sign and they offered everyone blue armbands. There were 50 sisters involved in it and they had agreed that when the Pope got up to speak, they would get up wearing their blue armbands and they would stand in silence, which is what they did.

"When I spoke, I think I was being very faithful to what I had learned from LCWR, to what I personally believed at that point. The only concern I had when I gave the greeting… I had talked to the sisters that worked with me on the Executive Committee, but we didn't poll the membership at large, so I *felt* I was being representative of them but I wasn't 100% sure. And there was no way of finding out. So that was my initial concern."[52] But she knew she had a degree of freedom – she could change her mind if she wanted to. "If for some reason when I got up, if it didn't feel like it was going to go well, I could've not said it. But I didn't want to do that at all.

"That next morning I was in the Shrine, we had to be there very early. There was a woman next to me and another woman in a wheelchair and the woman right next to me said, "Are you the one giving the greeting?" I said I was. And she said, "Are you going to say something about women?" and of course, I wasn't really eager to get into a conversation, but I said, "Yes, I am." She said, "Oh, I'm very glad." She turned to her companion and said, "This sister is going to speak about women," and the woman in the wheelchair said, 'Good!'"[53] The "woman in the wheelchair" as it turned out, was not just *any* "woman in a wheelchair." She was the mother of Cardinal Bernard Law, who was not just any cardinal, but the very conservative leader of Boston's Roman Catholics. "So sitting next to her was providential. (Laughing) It was another sign that this was the right thing to do."

"So I had a chance to back away from it, yes, but I would always have regretted it. Because I knew it was important. I knew it was important for the organization and for people to hear this concern that we had for many years, going back to Vatican II. We had gone through the International Woman's Year, the International Woman's Decade. We went through all of that, meetings in the United Nations. It wasn't as if it had popped up just the day before.

"So that's what happened. It was one page and the speech lasted just about three minutes. It took longer to give it because people kept applauding so it might have ended up being seven or eight minutes."[54]

Later, in 2013, Elizabeth Johnson, Distinguished Professor of Theology at Fordham University and a member of the Sisters of Saint Joseph, whose book, "Quest for the Living God" encountered severe criticism from the Committee on Doctrine of the US Bishops Conference, remembered that morning.[55]

"I was there in the Shrine in Washington when Theresa Kane greeted the Pope in the name of the sisters of this country and it was absolutely radicalizing. On our way in, [there were sisters on the steps of the cathedral] handing out blue armbands and a number of us took them. We were just sitting with them. It was two minutes practically in all and she started out, she was very simple and sweet. She went on to say we really did have one question for him and it was so beautifully phrased, asking if he would "listen to the cry of women" for full participation in the ministry of the church. She never said the word "ordination," she didn't say, "do it tomorrow." She said, "Would you listen to our cry?" At which point the place exploded and there was a standing ovation. People were weeping, cheering, stamping their feet on the ground and it wouldn't quit. Everyone was putting on their blue armbands. It was those simple words that she said, "Would you listen to us?" and it just unleashed... It was an iconic moment. And nobody saw it coming."[56]

Johnson wore her blue armband to Kane's 50th Jubilee celebration in Dobbs Ferry.

1983 and 84

Although dismay and dissension characterized much of the early years of the '80s, there were steps forward as well. WATER, the

Women's Alliance for Theology, Ethics, and Ritual was founded. The Women of the Church Coalition, under the leadership of Sr. Donna Quinn, transformed itself into Women-Church Convergence. This was an affiliation of informal Women-Church groups, often small in nature, from across the country. Their purpose was to support women's questioning issues of identity as well as expressions of feminist spirituality through the creation of liturgy.

But the concurrent reigns of the ultra conservative Karol Wojtyla (John Paul 2) and the American president, Ronald Reagan certainly threatened many liberal causes. Wojtyla appeared in every way to be attempting to roll back the changes wrought by Vatican II and often lashed out at women religious. "The Sisters of Mercy, the most visibly feminist order of sisters, bore the brunt of Vatican attempts to control and silence American women religious in the early eighties. First, the Vatican successfully challenged the order's decision to allow tubal ligation in its hospitals by threatening sanctions against the order. Then Vatican officials... forced three Mercy sisters, most notably Agnes Mary Mansour, to choose between their vocations and their positions in public office."[57] All three resigned from their religious communities.

Although the climate was hostile, the WOC, NCAN, the LCWR, WATER and Women-Church continued their efforts. But feelings of distrust, and more significantly, a sense of betrayal, were now evidenced across the spectrum.

1994

As the year began, Wojtyla (John Paul 2) "Having addressed the increasingly prickly issue of women's ordination via pontifical commission, Vatican declaration, canon law, apostolic constitution, apostolic letter, and the universal catechism"[58] was still unable to quell the clamor; advocates for women's ordination would not be silent. The pope was angry; one Jesuit scholar, Father Thomas J. Reese, remembered a papal luncheon where, when the subject arose, the pope "pounded on the table"[59] to emphasize his "No."

On May 30, Wojtyla, John Paul 2 acted. He issued Ordinatio Sacerdotalis, "On Reserving Priestly Ordination to Men Alone." One Vatican observer called the message "clear, peremptory, brutal and decisive."[60] The document offered nothing new, but did signal a change in strategy; the Pope was no longer arguing that the exclusively male priesthood mirrored "in persona Christi." He was simply asserting the monarchical authority of his office. The concept of "collegiality," i.e., bishops sharing authority, was nowhere to be seen; no bishop had been consulted prior to the documents origination. In the document's conclusion, was the statement that this judgment was to be "definitively held" by all Catholics.[61]

The only welcome aspect of the document was its abandonment of the long held argument of Thomas Aquinas, "that women were biologically flawed, irrational, and logically subject to the authority of men hence unqualified to *receive* the sacrament of ordination."[62] By the 1990s, that idea was unlikely to fly. But immediate criticism erupted from theologians everywhere and once again Rome's efforts to silence dissent had the opposite effect.

The widespread criticism of Ordinatio Sacerdotalis was significant; the male-only priesthood might be traditional, but questions were now being raised about its *legal* underpinnings. Were they sound? It should be noted that while all this argument was taking place, American Catholics were living in communities across their nation where Protestant sects of more than one denomination had ordained women clerics almost *two decades* earlier.

A Gallup poll in 1977 tallied support for women's ordination at 36%; by 1993, the year before Ordinatio Sacerdotalis, support was at 64%. Women under the age of 35 were in favor at 80%. The more the Vatican opposed the idea, the less successful they seemed to be. One critic of the church, Peter Hebblethwaite, called the document "an act of the monarchical, or even imperial, papacy, produced without serious consultation on its contents," relying "upon obedience rather than persuasion, disciplinary measures rather than explanation."[63] The only really new aspect to the document and its release was the degree to which Wojtyla (John Paul 2) was willing to rely on authority alone. Unfortunately, from his perspective, "American bishops responded to the papal demand for silence by issuing multiple calls for dialogue."[64]

Despite the fact that the world stood at the threshold of a new century, Wojtyla (John Paul 2) seemed either unwilling or unable to depart from ideas and concepts that many found archaic, even medieval. The women of the world, as Halter so clearly stated, were no longer amenable to limiting their spiritual lives to the Blessed Virgin's triple role of virgin, bride, and mother, the only three functions, sanctified by the Roman Catholic Church for women.

Although popes have never been famous for their personal experience with or knowledge of the actual nature of women, this particular Pope seems to have been monumentally out of touch with their reality. "One graphic example of this lack of understanding can be found in the message Pope John Paul II sent to Bosnian Muslim women who had been raped during the 1993 conflict. The Pope urged them to turn their rape into an act of love and "accept the enemy into them, making him flesh of their own flesh. by carrying their pregnancies to term,"[65] urging them against using the abortifacient pill authorities were making available to them.

1995

In an act that simply poured fuel onto the fire, Joseph Ratzinger, Prefect of the Congregation for the Doctrine of the Faith, and later to become Pope Benedict 16, then issued Responsum Ad Dubium, a response to the criticism of Ordinatio Sacerdotalis. The document averred that the teaching against women priests had been "set forth infallibly by the ordinary and universal magisterium, requiring "definitive assent" from the faithful. This remarkable claim of infallibility had appeared nowhere in Ordinatio Sacerdotalis, opening up a new debate about the boundaries of infallibility itself: could an administrative curial congregation (the CDF) declare a teaching "infallible" *when the Pope had not*?"[66] One week later, the Pope delivered a strongly worded statement supporting the position of the CDF.

In general, the "heart of the Vatican's failure to convince" was the "belief that the word of a teacher must be accepted, simply because of his authority, and not because of his arguments."[67] This unreason most likely stemmed from earlier times when the Vatican made laws for the masses of uneducated men; obedience to the law would have to be paramount in importance. In addition there was little need to consult these masses because they were perceived to have little capacity to contribute to the lawmaking process. But the world had changed; not only were men now educated but women were as well. Reaction against the Responsum was immediate and widespread.

The Responsum, however, finished what Ordinatio Sacerdotalis had set forth. Rome had spoken; the case was closed. "Failing to persuade with its arguments, Rome had used its authority to silence dissenters. ...Two years following the Responsum ... the numbers of theologians investigated, silenced, or removed from office [was] at an all-time high."[68] It was hoped that unbridled power would succeed where reasoned argument had failed. Support, however, for women as clergy continued to grow.

1998

When Karol Wojtyla (John Paul 2) issued Ordinatio Sacerdotalis and described it as "definitive teaching," it remained unclear as to whether this was or was not "infallible doctrine." Although the

CDF's Responsum hoped to define it as such, the authority of this congregation to define any teaching as "infallible" was questioned. So the Pope, determined to silence the controversy, followed through with Ad Tuendam Fidem, "To Defend the Faith," on June 30, 1998. Once again, the letter was issued without consultation with any bishop, but informed these same bishops that "it was their duty to enforce the teaching, and this time he provided for punishment of Catholics who failed to give full assent to "definitively proposed" teaching."[69] He had made changes to canon law to facilitate their punishment.

An additional document, written by Josef Ratzinger, Prefect of the CDF and later Pope Benedict 16, "Commentary of the Profession of Faith's Concluding Paragraphs" accompanied the document, and, more than twice as long, "went far beyond Ad Tuendam Fidem, saying that anyone who denied a definitively proposed doctrine would 'no longer be in full communion with the Catholic Church.'"[70]

The following year, in an address to the bishops of Germany on November 20th, the pope reasserted his position in even stronger terms; he "reminded the bishops that the male priesthood carried "the character of infallibility" and was "to be held definitively and absolutely" by all the faithful, especially the daughters. Then, he leveled a warning: "We should stop at nothing, if necessary, to dispel confusion and correct errors."[71]

2000

The first international Women's Ordination Worldwide (WOW) conference would be held in Dublin in the summer of 2001. Early in that year, Sister Joan Chittister, a well-known Catholic writer and activist, was invited to speak there. Already widely published, her acceptance would add a degree of luster to the event. She was at the time, and continues to be, a member of the Benedictine Order, based in their community in Erie, Pennsylvania. With an extensive monastery on many acres and an adjacent campus complete with lakefront (open to the public on weekends for fishing and swimming), everything about the place speaks to dedicated ministry; a sense of order, care of property and a reverence for the beautiful.

Sister Christine Vladimiroff was the prioress of her order when Chittister received her invitation. Vladimiroff was born in 1940 and grew up in Erie; she not only attended the local Benedictine High School, she also taught there and became its principal. A second generation American, one of three sisters, she was gifted with both nieces, a nephew and grand nieces and grand nephews. She was a past president of the LCWR (2004), and in 2013 continued to work within the Benedictine community, living in one of their houses nearby. She was Executive Director of the Saint Benedict Education Center, administering a "welfare to work" program.

Within days of Chittister's acceptance, Vladimiroff received a communication directly from the Vatican. The letter was from the Congregation for Institutes of Consecrated Life and Societies of

Apostolic Life, CICLSAL, as it is commonly known. This is the congregation of the Roman Curia which has dominion over the "government, discipline, studies, goods, rights, and privileges,"[72] of the religious congregations of both men and women in the world of Roman Catholicism. The communication ordered her to give a Precept of Obedience; she was *commanded* to "forbid and prohibit" Chittister, under her vow of obedience, to speak at the conference.

Nuns do not "refuse" Vatican commands; Vladimiroff, however, "declined to accept the invitation."[73] Had the Vatican instructed the prioress of an order other than the Benedictines, events may have unfolded quite differently. But they addressed their precept to an order with a history spanning 15 centuries, in which concepts of obedience had been defined with both reverence and piety. Benedict had set forth The Rule; authority and obedience in authentic Benedictine monastic life would be no automatic event. It would be rather a process of discernment and this process would necessarily involve three major concepts intimately interwoven, each with the next; these involve "listening with the ear of the heart, the labor of obedience and the search for God."[74]

Although Vladimiroff was the prioress, and as such, headed the community, she understood immediately and implicitly that the decision process would have to involve the entire community. "The labor of obedience will be undertaken in the company of others."[75] Although no future decision would be subject to any sort of vote, her decision would have to come through "listening," a fundamental value of Benedictine spirituality. The community would have to be involved in every difficult step of the difficult path forward.

Vladimiroff knew as well that both she personally and the community at large were now, without warning, standing directly in harm's way; every religious was familiar with one or more events in which a community, in disagreement with the Vatican, had been taken over and their duly elected "superiors" replaced by the Vatican with choices of their own. After a period of similar tension with the Vatican in 1981, the Jesuits were informed ... that the Pope had appointed a "personal delegate of the Holy Father" to oversee the Jesuits, instead of allowing a normal, internal election to be held for their next father general.[76] CICLSAL could, if it chose, disband, resettle or dismiss any community, and/or any member of any community. *Their power was absolute.* No sister in residence at that moment had any way of knowing where she might be living one year in the future; for the oldest of the nuns, the burden of anxiety was significant.

For Vladimiroff, the burden of responsibility was equally so. She had more than a single obligation, and they were perhaps contradictory; she needed to protect Chittister's rights, protect her community at large and behave in a way consistent with her understanding of her own beliefs and vows. The challenge would be to find a solution which "allowed the Vatican to dialog and enter into negotiations"[77] since nothing would be won she thought by an effort to "best" them. Powerful men need to save face.

Her first thoughts, as the tectonic plates of her universe shifted in place, were of canon law. She knew it existed, she knew it offered rights as well as strictures, but she had no idea what if anything it might offer her in this new and unfamiliar situation; she contacted and engaged canon lawyers immediately. They were Sr. Patricia McGreevey, a member of the Erie Benedictines and Father Daniel Ward, from the broader Benedictine community. They were instantly of invaluable assistance. She would request a hearing and plead her case.

After educating herself to the degree possible, and continuing to meet with the community, if not hourly, almost certainly daily, she then telephoned the Vatican and asked for a hearing. She was ready to leave for Rome, but she was told it probably would not be necessary, that she might simply write a letter. "Have you seen what I was sent?" she asked, and faxed a copy. The reply was immediate; yes, a hearing would be scheduled and was, for the end of May.

Over the days since the precept had been received, the community had continued in what must have seemed endless discussion and interaction. Vladimiroff's term as prioress also came to an end; when she suggested postponing any election until the situation was resolved, the community resisted the idea. Their processes, they believed, should not be dictated by events others had set in motion. The election was held; Vladimiroff was reelected. And the "listening" and the discussions continued in search of "discernment."

For Benedictines, discernment must be a way of life. It is about "making choices at the soul level, it is a stance, an attitude of humble and *ready obedience to what we hear in the silence of our being.*"[78] And the community continued to listen. They were, of course, a diverse group and as such not necessarily in complete agreement; but because of the Benedictine commitments, each member was equally important.

There was a group that wished to enter into some form of protest; Vladimiroff was not averse to protest per se, but had difficulty finding the logic in any way forward that the group suggested. What point would there be in having a protest in front of some church in Erie, Pennsylvania, when no church in Erie, Pennsylvania had anything to do with the recent action of the Vatican? She also felt keenly that issues of integrity and honesty had to have primary place; "How could I in conscience have conversations with the Vatican, in an honest search for discernment, if there were sisters in the basement making placards?" Her integrity had to be above question.

"There's no question," she remembered recently, "that scars were left. Some wounds still probably haven't healed." It was such a special and unusual kind of event, the kind that breeds emotions of every sort, not least of which were fear and anger, deep and pervasive. But, Vladimiroff pointed out, "The community put their trust in God, searching for God's will."[79]

And the situation placed the person primarily responsible completely alone; the community could discuss and debate but in the end only one person would plead the case and make the decision. It's difficult to grasp fully the degree and kind of strength required to carry that burden successfully through many a long, dark night – and there must have been many – but it's not difficult to know that it's extraordinary.

Vladimiroff received a hearing date; she was to appear in Rome the last week of May with the conference and Chittister's speech then three weeks away. With her two canon lawyers, she made the trip. In Rome, she met with the head of all the Benedictines, the Abbot Primate, Father Notker Wolfe at San Anselmo for consultation and advice. In fact, in his position, he had the power to assume the decision-making role; he could have simply relieved her of obligation in the case and proceeded himself. He did not do so. She understood his decision as an indication of his faith in her and in the integrity of the community to make the decision within the precepts of The Rule.

The hearing was held on May 28th, with an official interpreter; the proceedings took place in Italian. The Vatican presented their case, which Vladimiroff had not seen prior to the hearing. She had been given no advance notice of their position. Now she replied to them. She pointed out that the citations attributed to Chittister in the file they produced were all from books and/or speeches made before 1994, when the definitive papal instruction forbidding ordination was made; consequently, she maintained, Chittister was not in defiance of any Vatican command.

If there was consternation that their case was ill-founded, it was not voiced. Without any decision, Vladimiroff was sent home. She returned to Erie and waited; no communication arrived. When the conference was then a week away, she acted. Each of the sisters in the community, both those who were on site and those whose work took them far afield had been notified. It was understood that Vladimiroff would write a letter, outlining her decision; the letter would then be sent to CICLSAL. Each member would have the option, after hearing the letter, of adding her signature or electing not to do so. In addition, absent members working elsewhere or on vacation, would have the opportunity to name a proxy, i.e. another sister who would be informed of her wishes and given instructions to sign or not to sign.

Finally, with the conference only days away, she acted; her letter was read to the community at vespers one evening. Chittister would not be forbidden to attend. Of the 128 sisters, 127 added their names to her letter; reading accounts of this event, one might easily conclude that a single nun disagreed and had the strength of character to stand alone within her community. As it happened, the most elderly of the nuns when telephoned had misunderstood the situation completely.

Her "no" to a proxy was duly recorded; when she finally returned to Erie weeks later and discovered that she had completely misunderstood the instructions and that she was the only sister not to have added her name to the letter she was, as it's easy to imagine, more than dismayed.

Chittister attended the conference and spoke. Over time, Vladimiroff came to understand how events had actually unfolded; the Dublin hierarchy had been appalled that the conference was to be held on their turf and wanted it either scotched altogether or moved elsewhere. If Chittister was disallowed, they believed, the situation might well unravel. This would be neither the first nor the last time Catholic prelates in positions of authority have moved, either on their own behalf or that of favorite or wealthy or powerful members of their diocese, to influence events.

There was reprisal, or so the sisters believed. The order was informed within months that they would be subject to an Apostolic Visitation; a Vatican "oversight" committee would be arriving to assess them. The group would have unlimited power – to require changes if they deemed changes necessary.

Once again, these women faced the sword and once again found the necessary strength in each other and The Rule. A Benedictine precept is "to accept all visitors as if they were the Christ."[80] They responded quietly, carefully, welcoming the visitators. "Of course, they had to find *something*," Vladimiroff said. "You can't do an inspection and find *nothin*g wrong."[81] But the suggestions for change were very minor and easily implemented. So the months, literally *years*, of unease, stress and conflict came finally, finally, to an end.

Vladimiroff died in September, 2014 from cancer. She had scheduled the interviews for this book, in November 2013, between chemotherapy appointments. Perhaps without the stress of the years long conflict, she might have contracted cancer all the same. The cost of those years in human stress and suffering? Enormous. The quiet triumph of integrity over power for those who lived through the struggle? Priceless.

2008

During the previous decade, several groups within the United States and others in Europe had been actively ordaining women priests, despite the decree, Ordination Sacerdotalis, published in 1994. One of these groups, Womenpriests, described its members as “loyal members of the church who stand in the prophetic tradition of holy disobedience to an unjust law.”[82] Rome, of course, did not agree.

On May 28, the Congregation for the Doctrine of the Faith (CDF) issued and caused to be published in the Vatican newspaper, L’Osservatore Romano, yet one more decree, written by Cardinal William Levada, who has since retired. The decree referenced the existing ban on women priests, stating that women who had been “ordained” and the bishops who had participated in their “ordinations” would be excommunicated “lata sentencia,” i.e. automatically. More than one priest was excommunicated.

2012

On November 20, the National Catholic Reporter, (NCR) a well-respected Catholic weekly, reported that Fr. Roy Bourgeois, a Maryknoll priest for 45 years, had been told that “the Vatican "dispenses" him "from his “sacred bonds." The order’s hierarchy, “caught in the culture that finds advocating for women's ordination such a grievous and unpardonable offense, "warmly thanked” Roy "for his service to mission." It was, the Vatican stated, "a clear case." The priest attended a woman's ordination ceremony and, as the release noted, his "disobedience and preaching against the teaching of the Catholic Church about women's ordination led to his excommunication, dismissal and laicization."[83]

This action and other similar excommunications took place under Joseph Ratzinger's (Benedict 16) reign.

2013

On September 24, NCR reported that an Australian priest who had supported women's ordination had been excommunicated.

"Fr. Greg Reynolds of Melbourne, Australia, told NCR by email late Monday night his initial reaction was "shock" upon learning of his separation from the church. Australian media have reported he is the first member of the Melbourne archdiocese excommunicated and the first priest from the area laicized for reasons other than pedophilia."[84]

"The letter, a copy of which NCR obtained and translated [from the original Latin], accuses Reynolds of heresy (Canon 751) and determined he incurred latae sententiae."[85]

The document, dated May 31 – which was actually Reynolds' 60th birthday – did not given a reason for his dismissal. However, in another, later letter sent Friday from Archbishop Denis Hart to his archdiocesan priests, Reynolds clearly suggested that his support of women's ordination was the basis for the action.

This action took place under Jorge Mario Bergoglio's (Francis) reign.

In conclusion:

On September 16, 2013, reporters covering Bergoglio (Francis) asked about women's ordination; his reported response? "The church has spoken and says no ... That door is closed."[86] Almost unbelievably, there are feminists asking "But is it locked?" demonstrating what can only be considered a degree of unparalleled optimism. The answer seems simple. Yes. It is. The ordination of women, despite the clamor for it, will not take place; given the events of the last decade, however, it might seem surprising to some that it is still even considered desirable. Bergoglio's (Francis) style is assuredly different than Ratzinger's (Benedict 16); style, however, is not doctrine. And doctrine is what counts.

NOTES: PART FOUR, Chapter Two

1. Henold, Mary J. *Catholic and Feminist.* University of North Carolina Press, Chapel Hill. 2008. P.25.
2. Ibid. P.28.
3. Ibid. P.26.
4. Ibid. P.43.
5. Ibid. P.43.
6. Daigler, Mary Jeremy. *Incompatible with God's Design.* Scarecrow Press, Toronto, Canada. 2012. P.37.
7. Ibid. P.50.
8. Personal communication to the author.
9. Personal communication to the author.
10. Personal communication to the author.
11. Gardiner, SSND, Anne Marie, Ed. *Women and Catholic Priesthood: An Expanded Vision.* Paulist Press, New York, 1976. P.36.
12. Ibid. P.37.
13. Ibid. Pp.39-40.
14. Ibid. P.42.
15. Ibid. P.42.
16. Ibid. P.44.
17. Ibid. P.41.
18. Ibid. P.42.
19. Ibid. Pp.48-49.
20. Ibid. P.49.
21. Personal communication to the author.
22. Gardiner, Op.Cit., P.67.
23. Ibid. P.95.
24. Ibid. P.96.
25. Ibid. P.172.
26. Ibid. Pp.174-75.
27. Ibid. P.175.
28. Daigler, Op.Cit., P.83.
29. Ibid. P.119.
30. Halter, Deborah. *The Papal "No."* Crossroad Publishing, New York, 2004. P.37.
31. Ibid. P.38.
32. Ibid. P.52.
33. Ibid. P.59.

34. Ibid. P.60.
35. Fiedler, Maureen and Rabben, Linda, Eds. *Rome Has Spoken.* Crossroads Publishing, New York, 1998. P.69.
36. Ibid. P.71.
37. Ibid. P.70.
38. Ibid. P.81.
39. Ibid. P.85.
40. Ibid. P.169.
41. Ibid. P.170.
42. Ibid. P.178.
43. Ibid. P.180
44. Halter, Op.Cit., Pp.61-62.
45. Henold, Op.Cit., P.198.
46. Ibid. P.199.
47. Ibid. P.204.
48. Ibid. P.206.
49. Ibid. P.208.
50. None ever had. But in April, 2015, at the conclusion of the LCWR investigation, Mario Bergoglio (Pope Francis) did exactly that, for an hour.
51. Personal communication to the author.
52. Personal communication to the author.
53. Personal communication to the author.
54. Personal communication to the author.
55. Personal communication to the author.
56. Personal communication to the author.
57. Henold, Op.Cit., P.238.
58. Halter, Op.Cit., P.94.
59. Ibid. P.94.
60. Ibid. P.94.
61. Ibid. P.98.
62. Ibid. P.99.
63. Ibid. P.106.
64. Ibid. P.108.
65. https://www.ncbi.nlm.nih.gov/pubmed/12178901.
66. Halter, Op.Cit., P.120.
67. Ibid. P.121.
68. Ibid. P.124.
69. Ibid. P.131.

70. Ibid. P.133.
71. Ibid. P.139.
72. http//www.vatican.va/roman_curia/congregations/ccsa.
73. Personal communication to the author.
74. http//www.osb.org/rb/text/rbejms1.html.
75. " "
76. "Church and State," By Martin A. Lee, July/August 1983 issue, "Mother Jones."
77. Personal communication to the author.
78. "The Rule of St. Benedict," by St. Benedict. Vintage Spiritual Classics, Random House, 1998. No page number.
79. " "
80. " "
81. Personal communication to the author.
82. http://www.women priests.org/
83. https://ncronline.org/blogs/ncr-today/roy-bourgeois-they-finally-got-him.
84. https://ncronline.org/...australian-priest-advocate-women's-ordination-excommunicated.
85. Excommunication.
86. https://www.ncronline.org/blogs/francis-chronicles/pope-francis-and-womens-ordination

Chapter 3: 1984: The abortion Ad. Dissent or Defiance?

When the Democratic National Convention met in San Francisco, in July of 1984, the Democratic nominee, Walter "Fritz" Mondale, running then against President Ronald Reagan, made major headlines when he named Geraldine Ferraro to be his running mate. Whatever his hopes or expectations may have been, what followed was controversy.

Almost immediately, there was a negative response from the Catholic hierarchy and one must wonder why, since Ferraro's political position, that she herself was anti-abortion but she would not seek legislation that would curtail the freedom of others, was very little different from the positions held by Edward Kennedy and Mario Cuomo. Then-Archbishop John O'Connor of New York, and then-Archbishop Bernard Law of Boston began increasingly to characterize Ferraro as a politician for whom Catholics, in good conscience, could not vote.

That October, Ferraro was scheduled to march in the Columbus Day Parade in Philadelphia. At the last minute she was forced to cancel her participation by John Cardinal Krol, a conservative (who had delivered the invocation when Ronald Reagan was renominated). He threatened to forbid any Catholic school children, as well as their school bands, to participate in the parade if Ferraro appeared, calling her "a disgrace to the Italian and Catholic communities."[1]

Two years prior to all of these events, in 1982, Frances Kissling, a scholar and activist, had become president of Catholics for a Free Choice, a position she held until her retirement in 2007. Kissling had co-authored a position paper, "A Catholic Statement on Abortion," with Catholic ethicist, Daniel C. Maguire and his wife, Marjorie Reiley Maguire, a theologian and a member of the Catholic Theological Society of America; the paper outlined the possibility of nuanced positions on abortion within the Catholic Church.

When Archbishops O'Connor and Law opened their attacks on Ferraro, CFFC fought back, intending to defend her. They turned the position paper, already written, into a letter and called theologians for their signatures. Then, without any notice or consultation with those who had signed, the position paper was converted into an ad in the New York Times. This led to dismay on the part of some signers, who were willing to agree with a position paper but may not have wished to see their names in public print.

But so it came to pass that on Sunday, October 7, 1984, a full page ad appeared there, headlined "A DIVERSITY OF OPINIONS REGARDING ABORTION EXISTS AMONG COMMITTED CATHOLICS" with the subheading, "A Catholic Statement on Pluralism and Abortion."

The first paragraph of the ad stated "Continued confusion and polarization within the Catholic community on the subject of abortion prompt us to issue this statement. Statements of recent Popes and of the Catholic hierarchy have condemned the direct termination of prenatal life as morally wrong in all instances. There is the mistaken belief in American society that this is the only legitimate Catholic position. In fact, a diversity of opinions regarding abortion exists among committed Catholics."[2]

Prominent Catholics, including theologians, nuns, priests and laity, 97 in all, signed. The ad concluded with a statement asserting that the list of signers was only partial, that 75 priests, members of religious orders, and theologians had written in support of the ad's content, but did not sign, fearing reprisals. Among the 97 signers were two Catholic priests, two Catholic brothers and 26 Catholic nuns from 14 different orders. Reaction was swift. On November 14, 1984, little more than a week after Mondale lost the election, the Conference of Catholic Bishops issued a statement denying the legitimacy of the position taken in the ad, asserting in fact the contrary, that it was well known and unequivocal that the Church had consistently held that abortion under any circumstances was objectively immoral.

The Congregation for the Doctrine of the Faith, then headed by Joseph Cardinal Ratzinger, later to become Pope Benedict 16, directed Archbishop Jean Jerome Hamer, a Belgian whose name is pronounced "Ha – mare," with the accent on the second syllable, who was prefect of CICLSAL, to head the Vatican's response. CICLSAL has the authority to approve or disapprove of a congregation's mission and goals as stated in their Constitution. By extension, they claim the authority to approve or disapprove of a congregation's *members*, whatever any particular congregation may think of them. In other words, they wield significant power.

Archbishop Hamer then, in a letter to each order's superior pointing out that "the signers of the ad are … seriously lacking in religious submission of will and mind to the magisterium," "requested" those signers subject to church authority to issue immediate public retractions of their statements or face dismissal from their respective communities.[3] The Vatican, it was clear, was playing hardball.

The four male clerics swiftly complied, actually within weeks. Two of the 26 nuns were not under Archbishop Hamer's authority and their cases were dropped. Now only 13 communities were involved. The 24 remaining nuns, "the Vatican 24" as they were referred to in the press, would not retract on grounds of conscience. They were relying on "Dignitatis Humanae," the Declaration on Religious Liberty, published by Vatican II. That declaration said that, "It is through his conscience that man (sic) sees and recognizes the demands of the divine law. He is bound to follow this conscience faithfully in all his activity, so that he may come to God, who is his last end. Therefore he must not be forced to act contrary to his conscience. Nor must he be prevented from acting according to his conscience, especially in religious matters."[4]

Reprisals against the lay signers began almost immediately. Daniel Maguire, then a professor at Marquette University, began to receive cancellations of long-standing teaching and speaking engagements; the cancellations came from other Catholic colleges, including St.

Martins College in Washington, St. Scholastica in Duluth, Minnesota, Villanova University in Pennsylvania and Boston College. Speaking or teaching engagements as well as contracts came to an end. Many signers simply experienced the "drying up" of assignments from Catholic sources.

Then, early in December 1984, the superiors of each of the 13 orders heard from Rome; they were instructed to seek a retraction from each individual nun and to verify that nun's compliance with Catholic teaching on abortion. Should a nun refuse to recant, the superior was instructed to begin the appropriate procedures to insure her expulsion from the community. *No superior obeyed that instruction.* When the nuns who had signed indicated that they would not retract and their superiors did not threaten them with dismissal, for a short time there was silence from the Vatican. Some of the nuns wondered if a standoff had occurred, but the Vatican was only gearing up for the actions that would later come.

On December 19, 35 of the signers, including 18 of "the 24," met in Washington in an effort to decide how to respond. Marjorie Tuite, a Dominican sister and an activist, among the key organizers of the first international Women's Ordination Conference, was there. So was Donna Quinn, another Dominican, with the National Coalition of American Nuns, Ann Patrick Ware, a sister of Loretto, with the National Council of Churches in New York City, and Margaret Farley, a sister of Mercy and a tenured professor of ethics at the Yale School of Divinity, who had addressed the first Women's Ordination

Conference. So was Anne Carr, a Sister of Charity, a theologian and a professor of systematic theology at the University of Chicago Divinity School, Barbara Ferraro and Patricia Hussey, codirectors of Covenant House in West Virginia, sisters of Notre Dame and Maureen Fiedler, another Loretto, who was then codirector of the Quixote Center, a social justice organization in Washington DC.

From the beginning of that December meeting, a number of the sisters and many of the lay signers were both upset and suspicious; they wondered why the group was not meeting as a whole, why nuns, superiors, and laity were each meeting separately and who had decided on that procedure. They wondered why the superiors were meeting alone, why they had met alone the day before as well, and when the nuns would know what decisions were being made about them and for them; from the outset, it was clear that a strategy had been decided upon, but with no input from the 24. They had yet to learn what the strategy was.

Then the superiors asked the nun signers not to attend the meetings with the lay signers. If they attended, the superiors believed, according to Sister Patricia Hussey, "There wasn't much chance that we would pour oil on troubled waters, and that was exactly what the leadership group hoped to do by being quiet, avoiding publicity, and playing for time."[5] Hussey also pointed out that at the time almost every order of nuns involved in the controversy was in the middle of having their new constitutions approved by CICLSAL. Indeed, she thought it was "brave" of their governing groups to be replying to the Vatican that they found no cause for any dismissal, that no one was being asked by their governing group to retract.[6]

Some nun signers sincerely believed that because the Vatican had interfered with the autonomy of their communities and denied their freedom of conscience, that the most appropriate response should be no response at all. But they were in the minority and in the end, stood in solidarity with the larger group.

Among the nun signers, several commented recently on their memories of the experience. The two sisters of Notre Dame, Patricia Hussey and Barbara Ferraro thought little of signing at the time, it didn't seem "like a very big deal."[7] They had spoken out in the community in which they lived and worked – they were jointly in charge of Covenant House, a community center/ homeless shelter/social service agency in West Virginia – against several issues in which the local hierarchy had had a stake and had never suffered any negative consequences.

Margaret Farley thought she was signing a position paper calling for open exploration regarding the views on abortion in the Catholic community; she has stated that she would not have signed an "advertisement."[8] Maureen Fiedler, then director of the Quixote Center, remembered that she "wanted to support Geraldine Ferraro. Many of us were thrilled with the idea that a woman was a candidate for vice president of the United States and we thought had a chance to win."[9]

Then, after a time, the hierarchy's silence ended and the situation became clearer; there would be no backing off. Noncompliance was unacceptable. By March, 1985, two months before Archbishops O'Connor and Law were created Cardinals, it was clear that no more ground would be given; if the course the Vatican chose required a collision with these American nuns, so be it. The 24 must affirm the church's teaching authority on abortion or face the consequences. Archbishop Hamer stated publicly that conscience cannot be proposed as a principal to legitimize contradiction of the church's clear and authoritative teaching. If these nuns were to leave the church, that might not be such an unhappy eventuality.

Many of the nuns believed the real issue for the Vatican had less to do with abortion than with obedience, and the "obedience" that the Vatican required was one of "total submission to ecclesial authority."[10] In fact, the sisters had steadfastly resisted the blunt sledge hammer of absolutism demanded by the hierarchy. They had chosen in their own lives and remained committed to the same "egalitarian, non-authoritarian, collegial exercise of authority and practice of obedience that Jesus inaugurated among his original band."[11] They were prepared to resist a "Church that [was] not only rigidly hierarchical but [functioning] as a divine right monarchy in which authority is functionally equated with coercive power."[12]

The ad asked for "dialogue" on abortion. The nuns were indeed "pro-life," but they were not, as the hierarchy was, automatically and necessarily in every situation, pro-fetus. Where there was a fetus, they knew, there was also a woman. They believed her life must be respected as well and equally. The ad asked for discussion of the many complexities involved, *automatically,* they believed, in any consideration of abortion.

In an earlier conversation with Ferraro and Hussey, a priest who was also their friend, said to them, "Very soon, nuns like you will face having to decide between your principles and the commands of the Vatican. This new Pope John Paul is deaf to women. Your movement is beyond his comprehension. And as for the Curia, every time they hear of a nun standing up and asking to be ordained, they cross themselves." Hussey remembered being shaken by what he had said, "about the possibility that some time in the future our conscience might no longer allow us to remain as nuns." She had believed she went on, "that after all these years of renewal, the church would keep moving forward," and then had to wonder if "I had been fooling myself."[13]

One aspect of what deeply disturbed these consecrated women was what they saw as the profound distance between the men of the Vatican and the women caught in unwanted pregnancies. How many of those privileged clerics, they wondered, had held the hand of a sobbing woman, perhaps in impoverished circumstances, as the nuns on the front line of poverty often had. It was *their* experience they believed, that gave them expertise – not as nuns but as *women* in close proximity to the emotional and complex reality *of other women.* And they further believed that their experience was not only judged to be irrelevant and disregarded, but scorned. Who knew more about abortion, some of them wondered. Who among the Vatican hierarchy had ever had any contact, real contact, human contact with the experience? Was it only an abstraction to them? Was it more than a moral principle? How close was Rome's position to the life that Jesus lived? And they had no way, no forum, to express these concerns, except among themselves. For some, the ad must have been very welcome.

Years later, in the winter of 2013, looking back on that time, many of the nuns had not changed their minds. Margaret Farley, a Mercy sister, professor now emerita, at the Yale University School of Divinity, believed her behavior and beliefs had been and continued to be well within Catholic ethical and moral bounds.[14]

Following that initial meeting, the 24 issued a statement decrying the Vatican's reaction, asserting that it did not conform to the guidelines set down by Vatican II, and they reaffirmed their view that they were within their rights to dissent respectfully on an issue where there was no infallible teaching. Two more meetings followed; very little changed. The nuns continued to believe that they had acted within their rights and that "to recant," as they were being instructed to do, would be simply to lie. It was not possible to believe something one day and not to believe it the next. They were, they believed, being asked, *actually pressured*, to lie. And they found this immoral.

Eventually an agreement was reached that each nun would make her own decision as to how to proceed. She would retain full autonomy in relation to the other signing members. No one individual would or could make binding commitments on behalf of anyone else.

To understand these events and those that followed in the rest of 1985, one must see them in the context of those highly political and politicized times. In the preceding decade, at the beginning of the 70s, the backlash against Vatican II was, for Rome, in full swing. As Briggs put it, "It seemed that Rome had changed its mind… The sisters had been double-crossed,"[15] a fact they were just beginning to come to terms with. The Curia may have been in full retreat from Vatican II; the nuns were not. Quite the contrary. They had actually left the starting gate at a full gallop and were still moving forward. And American feminism had flowered. The word "sisterhood," a concept which the nuns had actually lived for many decades, continued for them to acquire deeper meaning.

The pressing issue for most of them then, certainly for the activists, had been women's ordination. The Women's Ordination Conference was in full swing and their actions may well have been the flashpoint for the Vatican. It was bad enough that these nuns had taken off their habits, had become politically active, were espousing liberation theology in South America, marching in the American South for civil rights and had banded together under the banner of the LCWR. But now these women were actually proposing that they should be *priests*?

The second important factor, which many of the 24 failed to recognize at the time, was the actual experience of each of the superiors of their orders. Some of the 13 communities were governed by groups of three, some had individual superiors; some orders were international, some were diocesan. But each superior had more than one obligation; she had to protect her entire group and she had obligations to each individual nun. Superiors, unlike the individual nuns, were in close proximity to the absolute power of the Vatican.

Although they, like the nuns, were American, they had a deeper understanding of what it meant to struggle with the Vatican, that the individual struggling had none of the rights that Americans expected and actually took for granted. The Vatican's power was as absolute as the power of Henry VIII; exile or beheading, or the current day equivalent, was only one nod, one communication or, actually, excommunication away. Yet, they were obligated, and their obligations were profoundly contradictory, if not impossible. They had to follow their own individual consciences, protect the existence of their order and its leadership, and assure justice to their individual members.

Certainly each of the superiors knew of instances in which, if superiors continue to dissent, Rome simply dismissed them. Their orders may have *elected* them but Rome could and did replace them with individuals of *their* choosing. And it is impossible to discover a single instance of a dispute between a member of the hierarchy and an individual lower down in the hierarchical order, where the dispute was not resolved in favor of the religious in the superior position, regardless of any relevant facts.

None of the superiors have, since that time, gone on record in regard to their experiences during those months that eventually became years. But certainly fear and worry must have been genuine and profound. Some, when contacted recently for comment on this period simply did not answer or replied with regret that they did not wish to remember "such painful times."[16] When Hussey observed that she thought it was "brave" of their governing groups to be replying to the Vatican that they found no cause for any dismissal, that was probably a masterpiece of understatement.[17]

And if the superiors were afraid, what of each individual nun? What did they stand to lose? Not only their security, both financial and emotional, their sense of community, their vocations, but perhaps most importantly their self-identification as nuns. Many of them had joined their orders as teenagers; they had never lived any life but that of a nun. Just as many women remain in profoundly unhappy marriages, not only because they cannot face the insecurity of life as a single woman, but more basically because "married" is a deep and irreplaceable aspect of their personal identity, so was "nun" meaningful to the 24, perhaps even intrinsic. One of them referred to the possibility of life after nundom as "winter at the bottom of a wall."

Sr. Margaret Cafferty, PBVM, was then LCWR president. She and the membership shared with the 24, the belief in the primacy of individual conscience and the thesis that personal and collective moral choices are made within the context of particular social traditions and cultures, not simply in relation to abstract sets of laws and norms. Dissent, she pointed out, could be understood differently, within the American tradition, than was understood by Rome, but the distinction never carried weight.

In the many months that followed, as 1985 bled into 1986 and beyond, it could be difficult, sometimes impossible, to ascertain the truth or the details of what actions were actually occurring. Often, the Vatican declared a sister "cleared," when that sister steadfastly insisted that she had not, *and would not*, "recant."

The Dominican sister, Margery Tuite read in the newspapers that her case had been cleared and that the Vatican was satisfied that she basically supported the church's teaching. She had signed nothing. She had never agreed to let the superiors of her Dominican order settle her case. When she demanded from them to know why she was included in the list of nuns who had been cleared, her order refused to tell her.

The Vatican also repeatedly claimed that Margaret Farley had "recanted" although she consistently denied this. Rather, she said, she had simply "clarified" her views to the superior of her religious order.[18]

Ferraro and Hussey observed, "We were American nuns, educated and professional, and they had vastly underestimated us."[19] But one might conclude that the underestimation worked in both directions; it seems unlikely that many of the 24 really understood the possible eventual consequences. Looking back, Loretto sister, Maureen Fiedler, remembered those months as "sheer hell." She went on, "No matter what I was doing in other parts of my life, this controversy never left the back of my mind. They were asking us to do something, this business of recantation, to me this was being asked to violate your conscience."[20]

By the winter of 1986, the solidarity of the 24 had begun to crumble. Some of the 24 signed as their superiors requested simply because they wanted to remain nuns, feared the future or wanted to get on with their lives. Statements and promises were frequently either misunderstood or broken. One of the superiors of Notre Dame told no longer Archbishop but now Cardinal Hamer that some of the nuns were having difficulty with the word "retraction," and suggested that if the word "clarification" were used, negotiations might go more smoothly. Hamer agreed. This "concession" was hailed in the Catholic press as a tremendous compromise. In fact, the Vatican continued to release statements that never used the word "clarification."

By spring, the nuns who had not yet been "cleared" numbered 11. Among these were two sisters of the Humility of Mary, Sisters Kathryn Bissell and Caridad Inda and one sister of St. Joseph of Carondelet, Judith Vaughn. The uncleared nuns were in constant communication with each other, planning and reporting, as each of them were scheduled for meetings at the Vatican Embassy. Bissell's case was resolved after she signed a statement, that "she agrees in principle that abortion is always wrong" and that she "accepts the church's position on the issue." Inda's case was closed without a meeting, since her work kept her in Mexico and she simply never appeared. Vaughn, after her meeting, stated that she wished time to reflect before she put anything in writing. She never signed anything, but within days her order designated her case as closed. No details were released.

When on July 21, 1986 the Vatican issued a press communication claiming that the 25 (sic) nuns, priests and brothers whose cases had been settled had recanted, eleven of the nuns who signed the original ad immediately issued a press release which categorically denied the Vatican's statement. They said they believed that the demand for such declarations constituted a dangerous precedent in the life of their Church and deplored the continuing threats leveled against the Notre Dame community and their sisters, Barbara Ferraro, SND and Patricia Hussey, SND. As well, they objected to the misuse of the settlements in their cases to pressure and isolate them. They stood with them in solidarity.

Then two meetings were arranged to deal with the eight cases remaining to be cleared. One meeting was with the six sisters of Loretto, the second with the two sisters of Notre Dame. Both meetings would be with Archbishop Vincenzo Fagiolo, the second in command at CICLSAL. At first, this seemed to be auspicious - until the nuns discovered that it was pressure from pro-life groups that was bringing the situation to its conclusion. The New York Times had reported that anti-choice leaders met with Vatican officials, including the Pope, and asked for action against the nun signers whose cases remained open. They claimed that the remaining "ambiguity" damaged the political efforts of the United States' right-to-life movement.

Archbishop Fagiolo, second in command at CICLSAL, accompanied by Sister Mary Linscott, the highest ranking woman in the Vatican, traveled to Denver to meet with the Lorettos: Sisters Maureen Fiedler, Ann Patrick Ware, Patricia Kenoyer, Mary Louise Denny, Virginia Williams, and Mary Ann Cunningham. The six drafted their own statement, consisting of four sentences, each one of which, they believed, clarified their position without denying their dissent. Three decades later, Fiedler's recollections were still clear.

"Our first sentence was, "We had no intention of making a pro-abortion statement." We thought, since the ad had asked only for dialogue and discussion of alternate views, that this was simply true. Further we reasoned, no one could be "pro-abortion," only pro-choice. The second sentence read, "We regret that this statement was misconstrued by some who read it in that way." This sentence too, we felt was simply accurate, and not a recantation."[21] It was, after all, the Vatican that had misconstrued their statement and they did assuredly regret it. Their third sentence was "We hold, as we have in the past, that human life is sacred and inviolable." Although they had indeed used the language of the Vatican, they had carefully avoided the words "fetal human life." "The fourth sentence said, "We acknowledge this as teaching of the Church," again only an obvious point. They had done their best not to compromise themselves; from their vantage point, they had not recanted. Rather, they had walked the tightrope successfully.

Looking back, after three decades, Sister Maureen Fiedler recently said, "To ask somebody to recant what is a conscience statement struck me as contrary to the teachings of the church itself. The church always taught, and certainly Vatican II did, that conscience was extremely significant and important. You had to follow your conscience. I learned that in Catholic grade school. No matter what, you were to follow your conscience. The request for recantation struck me as a violation of person, a violation of conscience, a violation of what it meant to be a Christian or a Catholic. After our statement was made public, I worried very much about whether I had violated my own conscience." It took her many months, she remembered, to find peace within herself. [22]

Then, on March 22, 1986, the two sisters of Notre Dame, Sisters Barbara Ferraro and Patricia Hussey, traveled to Washington to Trinity College for their meeting with the hierarchy. Their superiors were there, as was Sister Mary Linscott and Archbishop Fagiolo, who did not speak English and for whom Linscott would again translate.

They were joined by Archbishop Pio Laghi, the Vatican's ambassador to the United States.

Laghi opened the meeting with a prayer and the following statement, "This meeting is meant to be a dialogue with signers who have not yet clarified their position. This is a pastoral meeting, not a juridical visit nor an Inquisition. … But I must insist that before this meeting is over, you put in writing that you support and adhere to the Roman Catholic Church's official teaching on abortion."

Both nuns introduced themselves, recited their educational credentials and described the place where they worked, and then Hussey, according to the notes she took at the time, said, "Archbishop, I find it very interesting that you say we are here for a dialogue, and yet, to use your words you insist that after our time together we must put in writing that we support and adhere to the Roman Catholic teaching on abortion. That does not sound like dialogue to me."[23]

The discussion went on and the atmosphere in the room grew tense. When Laghi mentioned his Ph.D., Ferraro mentioned hers. When the nuns insisted on their right to dissent, they were reminded of their option to become noncanonical, i.e. to leave their order. After some time, Laghi left the meeting, stating that he didn't feel his presence was helping. Then Archbishop Fagiolo, speaking in Italian, which Ferraro understood, spoke of doctrinal teaching. Linscott translated: "Make a statement in line with the doctrine of the church so that your parents won't see this as a sign of contradiction for their daughter who is a nun." Ferraro realized that Linscott had upgraded his comment in her translation. What he had actually said was "What would your mommies and daddies think if you were no longer nuns?"

Hussey remembers a lull in the conversation and then Archbishop Fagiolo getting up out of his seat and moving into the chair next to her. She was writing notes on the pad in her lap. He "reached over and picked up a hand I was writing with, and held onto my thumb. At the same time, he began to stroke my arm."

Eventually the nuns asked, "What is your expectation of us to resolve this?" "A statement that you accept the teaching of Vatican II and the church on abortion" was the answer. "And if in conscience, we can't?" Ferraro asked. She was told "A member of the church can hardly have a conscience that will not accept it." After hours of discussion, they were at an impasse. What bothered the two nuns the most was knowing that, if they had finally signed the required statement, the Vatican would have been pleased, "even though we would obviously have been lying." They were given until April 4 to make a written statement.

In the days that followed, in the discussions between the two Notre Dame sisters and their order, the unity and support that had characterized the prior relationship was no longer so apparent. The order requested that the nuns remain silent and this request was one they could not accept. To complicate the matter further, during the year they had spent in limbo, they had used their time to study in depth the history of the church's position on abortion. The more they learned, the more their position began to shift; by mid-1986, they were no longer the sisters who had simply asked for dialogue. They were now ready to support abortion activists wholeheartedly. They could not honor their orders request for their silence. They resigned as sisters of Notre Dame.

In 2013, looking back, they had no regrets and in fact expressed surprise that it had taken them so long to change their minds and to act. It should be noted however that in contrast to the other signers, Hussey and Ferraro worked in a totally ecumenical setting. Covenant House was a free standing institution. They wore blue jeans to work and many of their clients had no idea they were actually nuns. Their "nundom" was within themselves, not visible to the outside world; it was within that being a nun was valued. Looking back, Ferraro said, "If I had been working in a Catholic enclave, if Covenant House had been in Boston or even New York, instead of in West Virginia, I don't think I could've done it." But it wasn't. And she did.

And so, with neither bells nor whistles, with no bangs or whimpers, a chapter that in retrospect seems only sad, came to a close. What was won? What was lost? Were any hearts or minds changed? What was revealed?

A small group of serious women, armed only with the depth of their convictions, tried, unsuccessfully, for a short space of time, and with courage, to make themselves heard by equally serious but so much more powerful men. The new Pope may have pastoral concerns; the men of the CDF have one focus only.

The name of this division of the Curia, the Congregation for the Doctrine of the Faith, should be understood with the utmost seriousness. Their only reason for being is to discover heresy and heretics, *non-doctrinal ideas*, and to purify the church by their subsequent actions. The souls of the 24 were never their concern. What mattered was the nuns absolute and immediate *submission*, and *submission without question*, to doctrine as defined by an all-male hierarchy.

If persuasion would not work, then threat would become the weapon of choice. There would be threat of loss and threat of punishment. If the invocation of guilt would work, then guilt would be used. "What will your mommies and daddies think if you are no longer nuns?," the final appeal from a prince of the church. If, in submitting, they were lying, that apparently would have been found to be both irrelevant and acceptable. It is difficult to discover where, when or how morality entered in or if, in fact, it ever had any relevance.

Several decades later, one can ask what was learned and by whom. The answer may well be – very little. But one must imagine that the stereotypes held by each side of the controversy were simply reinforced. Certainly from the Vatican's viewpoint, the "intransigence" of the sisters was only further documented; although the nuns continue to keep their own counsel, this was probably for almost every one of the 12 orders, their closest experience of the ultimate power of the hierarchy. If they had ever questioned the need for solidarity and mutual reinforcement among themselves, it seems unlikely they would ever question it again. What had been demonstrated was that the only strength they had, the only hope they could look to, was in each other and the teachings of Jesus. They might well have wondered if the hierarchy even remembered that Jesus had once actually existed.

And so, the years marched onward.

NOTES, PART FOUR, Chapter Three

1. https://books.google.com/books?isbn=1466891084.
2. https://marianronan.wordpress.com/2014/07/28/the-new-york-times-ad/
3. http://www.religion-online.org/showarticle.asp?title=1926.
4. See Appendix G.
5. Personal communication to the author.
6. Personal communication to the author.
7. Personal communication to the author.
8. Personal communication to the author.
9. Personal communication to the author.
10. Schneiders, Sr. Sandra. *Prophets in Their Own Country*. Orbis, New York. 2011. P.24
11. Ibid., P.69.
12. Ibid., P.69.
13. Personal communication to the author.
14. Personal communication to the author.
15. Briggs, Kenneth. *Doublecrossed; Uncovering the Catholic Church's Betrayal of American Nuns*. 2006. Doubleday, New York. P.7.
16. Personal communication to the author.
17. Personal communication to the author.
18. Personal communication to the author.
19. Personal communication to the author.
20. Personal communication to the author.
21. Personal communication to the author.
22. Personal communication to the author.
23. The following quotes are from the notes taken by Barbara Ferraro at the time.

Chapter Four: A gay ministry is condemned, 1999.

In 1971, with Father Robert Nugent, a Salvatorian priest, Sister Jeannine Gramick, then a member of the School Sisters of Notre Dame, founded New Ways Ministry, a group ministering to homosexuals and their families. The group describes itself, then and now, as "a social justice organization working for the reconciliation of lesbian and gay people with the institutional Catholic Church."[1] It began and continues as a 501©, a nonprofit organization, supported largely by small contributions and grants, mostly from religious communities.

Within a decade, the church hierarchy objected to their ministry. Gramick and Nugent first met with James Cardinal Hickey, Archbishop of Washington, DC, in 1981, when "We were still naïve enough to think that we could begin a dialogue. About two weeks later, Hickey sent a letter to every Bishop in the country telling them he had met with us and that he was not satisfied that we were presenting the authentic teaching of the Church. That charge originated with him and has hung over us like a cloud for over 30 years. He also wrote a letter to all the religious communities that supported the symposium [they were planning], asking them to withdraw their sponsorship and participation, but none of them did. We went ahead with the symposium and about 200 people attended.[2]

"From then on our reputation was tainted. Some bishops would say to us, 'Didn't you have some trouble with Hickey?' He pursued us in any way he could. If we were giving workshops in a diocese and he found out about it, he would write to the local Bishop and say that he had examined us and that he had difficulty with our 'lack of adherence' to Church teaching and that we should not be allowed to speak in a Catholic location. Some of them barred us, but most of them just ignored his interference. And several of them with whom we met personally asked us why Hickey was so obsessed with us and the issue of homosexuality. It is hard to understand, given that he is Archbishop of the capital of the country, with an immense range of national and international issues facing society and government. He just wanted us out of this ministry and out of Washington."

In 1984, Hickey informed them that they could no longer undertake their activities in his archdiocese. They continued their ministry. In that same year, they came to the attention of the Congregation for Religious and Secular Institutes, a Vatican department, which instructed both of them not to engage in any program that did not clearly state that "homosexual acts are intrinsically and objectively evil." They made no changes in their presentations.

Gramick grew up in Philadelphia, a very conservative Catholic city, born in 1942, an only child of first-generation Polish-Americans. "More than 50% of the population of Philadelphia was Catholic," she remembered. "I did go to Catholic school, and looking back now, I will say I was in my little Catholic ghetto." She was very happy there, taught by sisters, and felt called to be a nun by the time she was seven years old. Her teacher in first and second grade was "a wonderful nun, very kind," and clearly inspirational. "I was a pious child. I went to mass every day and I was really in love with God and I hope I still am. And my great desire was to show other people God's love, to bring them closer to God."

When she told her mother she was going to be a nun when she grew up, her mother was kind enough not to say some version of, "Yes, all little Catholic girls think that but you'll grow out of it." When she didn't grow out of it, "I think they tried to bribe me, to 'stay in the world.' They gave me a car for my 16th birthday, and for graduation I got a trip to Europe, you know, all those things. I took the goodies (laughing)" and then she went into the convent. Her mother wept for the lost grandchildren.

Gramick had been very popular in high school and at the top of her class academically, with lots of friends. "I was translating that on a human level into, 'If people like me and I am a nun, it will speak to them of God's love for them.' That was the way I looked at it. And you know, at 18, in those days you made your choice for life. You went into the convent or got married or went on to study to be a teacher or a nurse, those were the only two professions open to women." She went into the convent.

She entered the School Sisters of Notre Dame, in 1960 at the age of 17, under the old form of "The Rule," i.e. traditional habits, silence after 9 o'clock at night until after breakfast the next morning, hands in sleeves, eyes cast downward, no "special friendships." "There was the old Rule of kneeling down and humbly acknowledging your faults, begging forgiveness. You begged for toothpaste, you begged for a bar of soap, all designed to help you understand that you own nothing, that it's all given to you. The principles were admirable because I don't believe we *do* own anything. It *is* all given to us, it *is* a gift from God through others."

She was sent to college, to the College of Notre Dame in Maryland, which was operated by the SSND, through Sister Formation and went on to study for a masters degree in mathematics at the University of Notre Dame through a grant from the National Science Foundation. In 1971, she received additional grant money and entered the University of Pennsylvania as a doctoral candidate in mathematics.

She lived there rent free in an attic room in the household of the associate pastor at St. Mary's, the campus Episcopal Church, in exchange for child care and thought it was an excellent arrangement; nuns were of necessity on strict budgets. That church had begun an outreach program to the gay and lesbian community, who were allowed to have meetings and dances in the parish hall. "I remember my initial reaction when I heard that there was going to be a *dance*," she said. "I didn't know anything about homosexuality and I had all these stereotypes, and I thought, "Oh, my gosh! This is like having a party with alcohol drinks for a group of alcoholics, like feeding what shouldn't be fed." That was my feeling."

Then the pastor told her that he could use some help at the dance, that she should "come on over and you can serve Cokes or something;" feeling like a voyeur, she said, "I'd love to." That was her first introduction to the gay community. "At the dance, I'm serving Cokes and just observing, with my eyes wide open. I couldn't believe all this!" And then she had a conversation with a gay man, named Dominic Bash.

"He said he had lots of gay friends who were Catholic but hadn't set foot in a church in years, they felt that the church rejected them. So I said, 'Why don't we have a mass, but just for your gay friends?' I said, 'I'll get a Roman Catholic priest," she knew a number, "and you invite your Roman Catholic friends who haven't been to church for years. We had a mass at his apartment. It was a life changing event for me and I think for the people who came, too. There were a lot of tears, a lot of joy. They never thought there would be a priest and a nun who would welcome them. It was very moving." And remembering, even after all these years, her voice breaks slightly.

Then Bash, who was an activist, arranged an interview for her with one of the daily newspapers and as a result of that newspaper article, she received a couple of dozen letters, mostly favorable. "I was very surprised. In conservative Philadelphia, in 1971, that these Catholics would be writing to me? Two to one in favor of an outreach community? That was a surprise."

As time went on, her attitudes changed. "I initially thought I had great compassion for these people, but I thought they were sick, that there was something psychologically wrong with them. But I was told that by society. But I started to meet … like a lesbian woman who worked with the ACLU and she was smart, she was savvy, and I'm not a psychologist but she was not psychologically sick. She was more well-adjusted than some heterosexuals that I knew. Two and two don't add up to five here, I thought. It's four. So my attitudes changed." And so did the course of the rest of her life.

Among the letters that she received, after the interview that Bash arranged, were a number from priests. One of those priests was Father Robert Nugent, who closed his letter with "If there's anything I can do, let me know." Gramick thought there was a great deal he could do and he became involved with the group. He stayed with that group, which eventually became a Dignity chapter, and although Gramick finished her degree and moved to Baltimore for some months, they cofounded New Ways Ministry and worked together over the next decades.

During that time, there were several successive superiors of the SSND and four or five provincials. Three times the order received instructions from the Vatican to investigate Gramick. Three times the order replied, praising the good work they believed she was doing and not recommending sanctions. Eventually, the Vatican appointed the Congregation for Religious and Secular Institutes, a Vatican Office to do the investigation and she was called to examination.

In 1988, the Congregation formed a commission, whose mission was to study and evaluate the public statements of Gramick and Nugent and to determine whether these were faithful to Catholic teaching on homosexuality. The group was headed by Adam Cardinal Maida, then the Bishop of Green Bay, Wisconsin with Msgr. James Mulligan, a moral theologian from Allentown, Pennsylvania and Sister Sharon Holland, IHM, who was later replaced by Dr. Janet Smith.

Maida was both a canon and civil lawyer, who had played significant roles in some major ecclesiastical cases. He was certainly within an inner circle trusted by Rome.[3] Smith was an associate professor of philosophy at the University of Dallas, not a theologian, but a classical scholar. She had published a book defending the encyclical Humanae Vitae and criticizing all dissenting theologians. She often spoke at conferences of right-wing Catholic fundamentalist groups. When the communities to which Gramick and Nugent belonged requested that they be able to nominate two additional judges to join the commission as members, they were allowed to submit a list of names; the list was submitted in May 1989. No change in the commission was made.

Gramick said, "They wrote and told me what they wanted me to say, that I made errors and that I beg forgiveness." She would not say any of those things. When there was little response to the submitted request for additional members to be added to the commission, it seemed for a time that the matter had been dropped. But in 1994, their case was transferred to the Congregation for the Doctrine of the Faith (CDF) with Joseph Cardinal Ratzinger (to become Benedict 16) then at the helm.

After a period of study, the commission met with Gramick and Nugent three times, along with their respective superiors and theological consultants, in March, May, and July of 1994. Although there were many favorable comments in support of their work and the degree to which they had clearly been helpful to gay Catholics struggling with their commitment to the church, the focus of the commission was *doctrinal*, specifically with their published work. A major point of departure was their book, "Building Bridges: Gay and Lesbian Reality and the Catholic Church," published in 1992. Prior works, beginning in 1983 when "Homosexuality and the Catholic Church" was published, were also at issue.

The Commission submitted a series of questions for the two, referring to specific selected passages from the book, asking for written responses which were provided. Significantly, the commission recognized "the great difficulties involved in this endeavor and its controversial nature" and acknowledged that the language of Orthodox doctrine "can sometimes sound insensitive and even offensive if not properly understood." They were referring here to the use of such terms as "objectively disordered," "intrinsically evil," "unnatural," "dangerous and insidious," "grave depravity" and the like.

The Commission believed that one of the major issues to be addressed was that neither Gramick nor Nugent considered the question of the *morality* of homogenital acts *as in any way central to their ministry.* Although this matter was secondary to their primary purpose, the hierarchy considered it relevant if not central.

When an explanation was requested of several given passages that seemed critical of the hierarchy and the teaching of the church in general, Gramick stated that she was presenting the views of homosexuals rather than her own. But the Commission held that nothing in these passages made that clear. "The Commission believes it would be a reasonable interpretation of these passages to conclude that the author thinks the Church should change its teachings."[4]

Another objectionable passage from "Building Bridges" read as follows: "Instead of condemning the perpetrators of violence against lesbian women and gay men, the Vatican [statement] claimed that increasing violence is understandable. In a classic example of blaming the victim, the Congregation erroneously asserted that lesbian and gay people have no 'civil rights' to any civil legislation that protects their behavior. Society, the Congregation said, should not be 'surprised' when 'violent reactions increase.'"[5]

Although Gramick stated that in many instances the passages cited represented an expression of the anger of the homosexual community rather than her own, as in this instance, that view was questioned. The commission went on, citing its belief, "that a reader would reasonably understand [these passages] to be the expression of the views of the author."[6] It would seem difficult to quarrel with that opinion.

One major focus of the inquiry was the issue of the church's teaching that homosexuality is "unnatural," and that the writers had failed to clarify the actual teaching itself. The Commission went on to object to the use of the term "natural" in reference to homosexuality in "such a way that one could reasonably conclude that homosexual

sexual acts should be considered morally permissible."[7] When Gramick responded that she was using the term "natural" in the "popular" sense, the commission objected that this distinction was never made clear; consequently their discussions of homosexuality as "natural" seemed to contradict church teaching.

Specifically, they cite the passage from Gramick's "Building Bridges," "I am now convinced that homosexual and bisexual feelings and behaviors are just as natural as heterosexual ones." And further, that theological discourse has "failed to keep abreast of scientific developments or have willfully ignored current findings in order to legitimize a preconceived notion of divine intent for the human order."[8]

They went on to object that although both Gramick and Nugent state the church's teaching clearly, "they merely *present* the church's teaching, but give no evidence of personal advocacy of it." "It would be a reasonable judgment… to conclude that they are lobbying for a change in the church's teaching." "They are careful not to state explicitly that they are lobbying for a change in church teaching, and deny (when asked) that such is their intent. The manner in which their thoughts are expressed however is not consistent with that denial."[9]

"They were again asked to respond unequivocally to certain questions regarding their position on the morality of homosexual acts and on the homosexual inclination."[10] When their responses, dated February 22, 1996, were received, the commission found them still to be ambiguous. In addition, it was believed that although their understanding of the church's teaching on homosexuality was clear and correct, neither Gramick nor Nugent professed adherence to that teaching. Further it was stated, that the publication of their latest book in 1995, "Voices of Hope: A Collection of Positive Catholic Writings on Gay and Lesbian Issues," made it clear that there was "no change in their opposition to fundamental elements of the church's teaching." It was then decided on October 8, 1997 that their statements were in fact, "erroneous and dangerous."[11]

This finding was then sent to their respective Superiors General and in February, 1998 their responses were returned to the Commission, to be evaluated the following May. The Commission was unanimous in finding their responses "unacceptable." Neither Sister Gramick nor Father Nugent had expressed "personal adherence to the church's teaching on homosexuality in sufficiently unequivocal terms."[12]

"On June 27, 1998, I was informed that my response was unsatisfactory because I did not reveal my personal assent to the church's teaching on homosexuality. I was asked to make a public declaration." The declaration would express *interior assent* (italics added) to the church's position on homosexuality and acknowledge that their published works contained doctrinal errors. On July 29, 1998, she responded personally to the CDF. "In freedom, I choose not to publicly reveal my personal beliefs regarding any doctrinal positions on homogenital behavior and homosexual orientation. The approach I have taken in my pastoral ministry requires this reticence."[13] She also "accepted responsibility for the contents" of her books.

Gramick's provincial became increasingly worried that Gramick was going to be excommunicated and believed a pilgrimage to Munich, to pray at the grave of the founding member of their order, might provide the miracle she believed would be required for this frightening event to be avoided. Gramick acquiesced. So it came to pass that the two women found themselves on a Lufthansa flight from Rome's DaVinci Airport to Munich on July 30, 1998, looking for their miracle. Coincidentally, Joseph Cardinal Ratzinger, then prefect of the CDF, was on his way to Germany for an August vacation and was seated on the same plane.

Ratzinger, sitting by the window in a row of three seats, with the two adjacent unoccupied, was reading his breviary. The provincial recognized him immediately and pointed him out to Gramick, who disagreed. "I had seen pictures of Ratzinger and I said, 'Oh, it's just somebody that looks like him because this man looked old and haggard, and I thought of Ratzinger as bright-eyed and alert. He was just wearing a black suit, without a collar on." Her superiors had requested a personal interview for Gramick but had been told that that was not the way CDF conducted business, that meetings were not arranged face-to-face. Consequently this opportunity seemed too good to miss.

After some hesitation, Gramick took the seat next to Ratzinger and introduced herself, beginning with the phrase, "You don't know me, Father, but my name is…" And when she said her name, he smiled and replied, "Oh, I've *known* you… for 20 years," and indeed, that's how long the CDF had been maintaining her file. "He had been reading from his breviary," she remembered, "and he closed his book and talked to me. He murmured, in a sort of aside, three times during our conversation, 'Providence.' I knew what he meant, that it was providential that we would meet."

He asked how she had gotten into ministry and she told him about Dominic Bash and the mass for gays and lesbians. He had no problem with that because it had been private but pointed out, "But when you become public," that was a different matter. He asked about her workshops and whether the bishops in those dioceses had invited her. She answered truthfully, although technically, "Some do, some don't. If I had been perfectly truthful I would have said, 'Most don't and some do.' Because most of the workshops we have given have been in mother houses of nuns. Or institutions run by nuns."

They discussed her having taught mathematics and he asked her if she would like to teach mathematics again and she replied, "No, not really," and wondered, laughing as she recalled the exchange, if he was planning a career for her after he saw to the dissolution of her ministry.

Her provincial had subsequently come and joined them. Praising Gramick and her work, she confided her concerns about her possible excommunication. And Ratzinger reassured her, saying, 'Oh, no, no, no. It's not that level of doctrine. You only get excommunicated for certain things,' and then cited the urging of the ordination of women as an example. With her concerns put to rest and her miracle perhaps achieved, the provincial relaxed to enjoy the rest of the journey.

"As we were landing, he said, 'Pray for me and I will pray for you.' I believe that the real miracle for me was the opportunity to put a human face to the Vatican bureaucracy. I sensed in Cardinal Ratzinger an intelligent, gentle and prayerful man, filled with the love of God, who had devoted a lifetime of service to the church, even in the face of enormous unpopularity among the people of the Vatican II church. Of course, we disagreed but he was gracious." Looking back, she added, "I think basically he's a very good man. We are branches of the same tree. My branch is to the left and his is to the right, but it is the same tree."

Providence may or may not have played a part on that airplane and the hoped-for miracle may or may not have happened; what *was* clear was that no change was evident in the behavior of the commissioners or the content of the questions that they asked when meetings resumed.

Gramick and Nugent had returned their declarations to the Commission that August and once again they were judged insufficient. Although Nugent was found to be more responsive, his statement of interior assent was found not to be unequivocal and Gramick simply would not express any agreement to the teaching of the church on homosexuality. "We said as much as we could of what they wanted to hear. And it didn't work." They couldn't bring themselves to call homosexuality "intrinsically evil."

After the February, 1998 finding, Gramick had replied to the CDF again, attempting to explain and clarify her writings in an effort to have the Vatican decree "reversed." Her reply was lengthy. It included the following statement, explaining she hoped, the absence of reiteration of the church's position on homosexuality: "I have learned that lesbian and gay people are already familiar with the Church's teaching about homogenital behavior, and that the constant reiteration of it has driven many of them from the church."[14]

"As we honestly told the commission in the July meeting, we do not overemphasize the Church's well-known teaching. Rather, we place it in a wider moral context. To require that ministers to gay and lesbian persons concentrate on an emphatic proclamation of the objective immorality of homogenital acts makes the pastoral task more difficult. When Jesus was confronted with a pastoral situation involving a woman about to be stoned for adultery, he did not take the occasion to deliver a sermon on the evils of extramarital sex."[15]

And then, "Those who minister today to the divorced and remarried do not constantly proclaim the immorality of divorce and remarriage. Those in prison ministry do not constantly proclaim the immorality of criminal acts. Military chaplains do not constantly proclaim the immorality of war. I have assumed that the pastoral expectation of those in lesbian and gay ministry are similar." "This pastoral need, and not the desire for a change in the church's teaching on homogenital acts, was my motivation in publishing "Voices of Hope."[16]

She ended then with the following paragraph, "It is my intent to present the truth of the church's teachings in its integrity in such a way that will enable lesbian and gay persons to live an authentically Christian life and to convey more effectively my loyalty to the Church in my future ministry to them."[17] She hoped someday or somehow to have the decision "overturned." One must wonder exactly by whom.

And so, after the months that had become years, a final conclusion was reached and an official Notification issued: "The Congregation for the Doctrine of the Faith is obliged to declare for the good of the Catholic faithful that the positions advanced by Sister Jeannine Gramick and Father Robert Nugent regarding the intrinsic evil of homosexual acts and the objective disorder of the homosexual inclination doctrinally unacceptable because they do not faithfully convey the clear and constant teaching of the Catholic Church."[18] They were then permanently silenced and forbidden further ministry. The finding was dated May 31, 1999 and was signed, "Cardinal Joseph Ratzinger, Prefect."

When asked in 2013 what it had been like to participate in this lengthy ongoing process, Gramick replied, "At first, I did not want to participate at all. Actually throughout the process I didn't want to participate." Could she have refused? "Of course, you could refuse. You could choose to do anything, as long as you took the consequences. That's one thing I learned through all of this and I learned this from the superior general of the SSNDs, that you *choose*. Even though we are in this very horrible situation, oppressed, and I felt oppressed, I can make choices. So in the end I said 'I choose not to cooperate in my own oppression.' And I would not have used that language without learning it from her. 'Now what do you choose to do?' she would ask me and I kept saying, 'What do you mean *choose*, I don't have any choice.' But I did, I had a choice. I could choose to do what they wanted or I could choose to follow my conscience, so I chose to follow my conscience. That's one thing I've learned, that you do have choices. Even when we are hemmed in, we can make choices."

About the Commission, "They knew what they wanted; the SSNDs examined me three times but had not given the answer they wanted, to have me removed from the ministry. We had letters, that the main complainant was the Archbishop of Washington. The problems with him started in 1980. He went to my community then, asking them to reassign me and they would not do it. At a meeting with my provincial at the time, she was meeting with him as a courtesy, he spent one hour of the hour and 15 minutes talking about me. 'Why is she doing this ministry? I did not assign her to this ministry.' And the provincial replied, 'Yes, but we assigned her. I assigned her to this ministry.' Well, he didn't like that." Gramick believes that the eventual decision had been decided at the "outset."

"But getting back to the Commission, these SSND superiors had been courageous, doing battle for me, standing up to bishops. They were all wonderful. In the beginning, my superior then said, 'Well, let's just show good faith. Let's just go to the Commission hearing'. So I wrote, 'Under duress, I will meet with the Commission.' And during that first hearing, she stood up to the chair, this Vatican investigator, Cardinal Maida. In the first meeting, he wanted to put on the agenda that, according to the National Catholic Reporter, I had urged people not to contribute to Peter's Pence (the yearly collection taken up for the Pope) and that I was urging people to put their money into Mary's Pence or a group that works for women in the church. So he wanted this on the agenda. And my provincial said, 'Why should this be on the agenda? It has nothing to do with homosexuality.' And the Cardinal said, 'Well, this is an insult to the Holy Father.' And the superior said something to the effect that in this country, we have freedom of speech."

Ideas such as freedom of speech, the presumption of innocence, double jeopardy, the right to face one's accuser, the right of appeal, all these building blocks of democracy, come as naturally to these sisters as the air they breathe. They may have been baptized with holy water, as Catholics are around the globe, but reading their words leaves little doubt that *their* holy water was drawn from an American well. It must be noted once again, however, that American concepts have no relevance within orthodox Roman Catholicism; they are concepts of American justice, guaranteed in the American Constitution, buttressed by the American Supreme Court. American nuns seem slow to realize that the Vatican *is* the Supreme Court, at least, *their* Supreme Court, their *very* Supreme Court.

The autocracy of Roman Catholicism does not sit well with these sisters; indeed, it seems to rub them raw. What is surprising is that the majority of their male counterparts appear at ease; American males within the hierarchy seem to have joined a different city state. Or perhaps, the conservatism of Ratzinger's CDF has simply quieted any and all theological dissent.

"Well, I think we're trying to change that totalitarian state," Gramick said recently. "In 1989, when we saw the totalitarian structures in Eastern Europe crumbling, we facetiously said that the church is really the last bastion of totalitarianism, and I think it is true." As I look back over the whole affair I feel the church authorities followed rigid and totalitarian procedures. While I knew that in theory before, I now know it experientially. I guess it has made me more convinced than ever that we need governmental changes in our church."

She went on, "Like the LCWR now refusing to let these representatives of the Vatican just come in [and take over], saying, 'Look, we need to dialogue.' Sartain, who is the chair of that committee, is going to give a talk at the end of the LCWR meeting. [August, 2014] I don't know if he asked to give that talk or if he was invited. He's very conservative but he's very polite and he's not autocratic. He may not agree with LCWR's position but I think he would be respectful. He's a good guy to be in charge."

She went on, "New Ways Ministry has always been present at the meeting. We're not members of the LCWR obviously, but we always have a booth with our materials and so on. I thought maybe we wouldn't be invited [this year], but no, we are still invited. So we will be there." New Ways Ministry continues.

On September 23, 1999, Gramick released a public statement, "Regarding Discernment on the Notification of the Congregation for the Doctrine of the Faith." (It might be noted here that Webster defines the verb "discern" in several different ways. One of these, and it seems to be the usage that many sisters have adopted, is "to see the difference between two or more things; to discriminate; to understand the difference, as, to discern between good and evil." The first section of her statement is entitled "Obedience in Response to God's Call." The last paragraph of this section reads as follows, "Obedience to God is not reducible to blind acceptance of Church injunctions. Thus, I needed to undertake prayerful discernment in light of the CDF decision."[19]

She goes on to speak of "authoritarian methods," including "the dismissal of the objections raised by the Superiors General" of her order as well as Nugents, and "the composition of the Vatican Commission which resulted in imbalance and bias; the shift from the mandate [which was] to investigate my public presentations on homosexuality to an intrusion into my private beliefs."

She then states her inability to "acquiesce in a decision I considered unjust and harmful to lesbian and gay Catholics and still be faithful to our mission." She reiterates her hope that working within the Church structures she might have the CDF decision reconsidered, "and … ultimately reversed.[20]

"I have no trouble articulating the Vatican's position, and in our workshops I have done that. The problem is that the Vatican has demanded to know if I actually believe that. My view is that as a baptized Catholic, and as a public minister in the church, I have an obligation to present what the church teaches and to explain why the church teaches it. However, I do not have an obligation to give my personal viewpoint. Church authorities have a right to ask me if I assent to the essential beliefs of the Catholic Church, to what it means to be a Catholic. But what the Church teaches about homosexuality is not one of the core beliefs of being Christian or Catholic. My status as a vowed religious and a public minister in the Church should not deprive me of the right which every believer has to maintain the privacy of her or his internal conscience in matters which are not central to our faith. To intrude, uninvited, into the sanctuary of another's conscience is both disrespectful and wrong."[21]

It should be noted that according to at least certain understandings of Canon Law, the question should never have been asked. It's not *simply* "disrespectful and wrong." It is rather, "an utterly unjustifiable invasion of what had traditionally been held by the Church to be completely inviolable. … To demand any form of revelation of individual conscience is an invasion of both personal dignity and integrity. It is a misuse of power."[22]

"Traditionally, Catholic moral theology has always recognized the complexity of making a conscientious decision, yet this very element seems to be completely missing from the CDF's analysis of the Gramick-Nugent approach to talking about the morality of homosexual acts,"[23] despite the fact that it is in just such a morally and psychologically freighted situation as theirs, that it is the most relevant. And *Gaudium et Spes,* Vatican II's pastoral constitution on the Church in the modern world, states clearly that conscience is "the sanctuary of man, where he is alone with God, whose voice echoes within him."[24]

On the following day, newspapers across America announced the Vatican's order to Gramick and Nugent to end their thirty-year ministry to gays and lesbians and their conclusion that they failed to comply with the Roman Catholic Church's teaching on homosexual acts. The Vatican then placed a "gag order" on both Gramick and Nugent, thereby ending their careers. Or trying to.

Nugent was given another chance to express unqualified acceptance; once again his reply, dated January 25, 1999, was found unsatisfactory. The following July, after another finding, Nugent issued a signed, public statement, accepting the Vatican's May 23, 2000, Silencing Order. He left New Ways Ministry and began pastoral work in a Harrisburg, Pennsylvania diocese. In 2013, he had retired in Florida, with a member of his community who had a parish there. He entered a hospice in Milwaukee later that year and died in January, 2014; Gramick was at his side.

In 2000, in an effort to avoid further conflict with the Vatican, her then community, the School Sisters of Notre Dame, having resisted pressure for close to two decades, commanded her silence and reassigned her to "a period of prolonged study." She was unwilling to remain silent, and "as a matter of conscience," resigned from her community; in 2001 she made her vows with the Sisters of Loretto and continued her ministry.

When asked how and why the Loretto community seemed immune to the kind of pressure brought to bear against the SSNDs, she explained that they were not immune. "Well, they *are* pressuring the Loretto's in the same way. They say, 'Well, this document is in effect and you must enforce it,' and the Loretto's are simply not enforcing it. And each time, yes, they do write back and point out that [the community] is not enforcing it.

"I have been a Loretto now for about a dozen years, and we have gotten nine letters. In the beginning, it was almost a letter a year but for the last two or maybe two and a half years, we haven't gotten any. We think it's because of the Vatican investigation of the LCWR. One little person is not enough on their radar screen - are they going to go after *all* the nuns? That's my analysis, but I don't know. But they haven't issued another document from the Congregation for the Doctrine of the Faith, which is what the SSNDs were confronted with. These letters come from the Congregation for Religious, not from the CDF. I think the CDF gets people more frightened. But really, both are involved because the letter is on their letterhead but a copy goes to the CDF." But Gramick is not discouraged.

"I meet younger gay people now who *are* so discouraged with what's happening in the church, and I want to say to them, 'Listen, I have been in this ministry for over 40 years and there's been progress. When I was at University, and in the Catholic Church, you would never *hear* the word "gay." They weren't even using the word "homosexual." You would not see it in any Catholic newspaper and my story, which had all this confrontation with church officials, put the issue on the agenda. It got people starting to talk about it. And now, I'm so happy to say that, of all the Christian denominations in the United States, from polling, Catholics are more pro-gay than any other Christian denomination. Three fourths of Catholics favor some civil legislation to protect gay couples. That's higher than any other Christian denomination."

What is most striking in the long summary of Gramick's dealing with Rome is the complete and utter absence of anything that remotely resembles what might be called "Christian charity." The Church may profess compassion toward gay people; nowhere in this saga of inquisition is there a sentence or even a paragraph of theirs that would lend credibility to that profession. Their defense may well be that the issues here are *doctrinal*; but "doctrines" don't exist only on paper. "Doctrines" must be practiced, and only human beings *practice* "doctrines."

Gramick however is undaunted. "As terrible as the ordeal has been for me, for my religious community, and for lesbian and gay people, many of whom have found this the last straw and have left the church altogether, we have to believe in the resurrection. For some reason this is all part of the mystery of suffering and redemption. I believe that somehow it will be a catalyst for good. My faith is still very strong."

Sister Maureen Fiedler, also a Loretto, a close friend of Gramick's and the host of the Sunday afternoon radio program, Interfaith Voices, was at the Loretto motherhouse on that day in 2001, when Gramick took her vows and remembers the experience with feeling.

"Gays and lesbians came from all over," she said.[25] "Everyone wanted to express support for Jeannine, for everything she had gone through for so long. They wanted to be there for her." Of course, in the small, rural, very straight town of Nerinx, Kentucky, the location of the motherhouse, throngs of gay couples, holding hands, wandering the sidewalks, sightseeing, buying souvenirs and "making the scene," was a bit of a stretch, but the town came through "wonderfully." The chapel was crowded, Fiedler said, and with so many male voices added she thought their singing could be heard "a mile away." The very religious service opened with a Catholic hymn. The refrain of that hymn, clearly chosen for the occasion, was

"All are welcome, all are welcome, all are welcome in this place."

NOTES: PART FOUR, Chapter Four

1. www.newwaysministry.org/
2. Unless otherwise indicated, all of the following quotes are taken from several long interviews the author had with Gramick during 2013, 14 and 15.
3. *www.catholic-hierarchy.org/bishop/bmaida.html* Interestingly, there is no mention of his role in Gramick's trial in any of the websites describing his reign as bishop and later archbishop and cardinal.
4. https://www.ewtn.com/library/curia/cdfnuway.htm
5. Nugent, Gramick and Curran. *Building Bridges.* 1992.
6. https://www.ewtn.com/library/curia/cdfnuway.htm
7. Ibid.
8. Nugent, et al. Op.Cit.
9. https://www.ewtn.com/library/curia/cdfnuway.htm
10. Ibid.
11. Ibid.
12. Ibid.
13. http://natcath.org/NCR_Online/documents/gn07.htm
14. Ibid.
15. http://natcath.org/NCR_Online/documents/gn04.htm
16. http://natcath.org/NCR_Online/documents/gn07.htm
17. Ibid.
18. https://www.ewtn.com/library/curia/cdfnuway.htm
19. http://natcath.org/NCR_Online/documents/gn07.htm
20. Ibid.
21. Ibid.
22. Collins, Paul, Ed.. *From Inquisition to Freedom.* Continuum Press, New York. 2001. P.113.
23. Ibid., P.111.
24. http://www.bing.com/?scope=web&mkt=en-US&Form=
25. Personal communication to the author.

PART FIVE

Part Five: Analysis and Conclusions

How should one view the complex drama of Roman Catholicism, a centuries-long tale of men in charge of women? If, as psychologists believe, the past informs the present, what questions should be asked?

Perhaps, these: What, in the history of the Church, is relevant to the two recent confrontations between congregations of the Vatican and the nuns of the Leadership Conference of Women Religious? How have the holy men of the Church experienced women? What have they *believed* about women? How have these feelings and beliefs affected their actions? And, as a consequence, how have women fared under their aegis across the centuries? Where might one look for answers?

Possibilities are:

Legacies: In that first hundred or hundred and fifty years after the crucifixion, as the nascent religion came into being, choices were made. Certain ideas were left behind; others were kept. What was bequeathed and by whom to the future Catholic faith? To approach answers to these questions, one must examine the years prior to the ministry of Jesus.

The Bible: An examination of the books of the Bible itself, with an emphasis on Jesus' behavior towards women, as well as a close examination of their authors, and their motives.

The Gnostic Gospels: The Gnostic Gospels offer a much closer, intimate and more intense glimpse of Mary Magdalene, describing her relationships with both Peter and Jesus in greater detail.

Statistics: Facts can be inferred from numbers.

We begin then with:

Legacies:

Since Jesus was a Jew, as were the men who were his followers, one important bequest would be tenets of Judaism; these would play a significant role in providing the initial sub strata to the system of beliefs adopted by the future Roman Catholic Church. Among the ideas that were kept, two were most important. Both pertain to women. The first of these is found in the third book of the Hebrew Bible, Leviticus 15:19-30, the idea of contamination by menstrual blood. Excerpts from Leviticus are:

"When a woman has a discharge of blood, and blood flows from her body, the uncleanness of her monthly periods shall last for seven days."

"Any bed she lies on in this state will be unclean; any seat she sits on will be unclean. Anyone who touches her bed must wash his clothing and wash himself and will be unclean until evening. If there is anything on the bed or on the chair on which she sat, anyone who touches it will be unclean until evening."

"If a man sleeps with her, he will be affected by the uncleanness of her monthly periods. He shall be unclean for seven days. Any bed he lies on will be unclean."

The accusation of pollution-contamination is clear. What is equally clear is the unusual degree of *sheer power* attributed to women's menstrual blood. This assertion continues across many centuries: Rufinis, an Italian canon lawyer at the University of Bologna in the mid-12th century, wrote his Summa at an uncertain date but near 1159. In it he agrees with Gaius Solinus, a Latin grammarian, believed to have lived in the mid-third century, and to have written in De Mirabilibus Mundi as follows: menstrual blood is "so execrable and impure … that through its contacts fruits do not mature, plants wither, the grass dies, the trees lose their fruits, the air becomes dark, if dogs eat it they are afflicted with rabies."[1]

But Solinus apparently had borrowed from Pliny, a Roman author and natural philosopher, who lived from 23 CE to 79 CE and was a close friend of the Emperor, Vespasian. Jews, it should be remembered, lived within the Roman Empire and certain Roman viewpoints found their way into the main stream of Jewish thought. Pliny's much more sweeping condemnation is worth quoting at length. He wrote as follows on the subject of menstrual blood:

"But to come againe to women, hardly can there be found a thing more monstrous than is that fluxe and course of theirs. For if during the time of this their sicknesse they happen to approch or goe over a vessel of wine, bee it never so new, it will presently soure: if they touch any standing corne in the field, it will wither and come to no good. Also, let them in this estate handle any grasses, they will die upon it: the hearbes and young buds in a garden if they doe but passe by, will catch a blast, and burne away to nothing. Sit they upon or under trees whiles they are in this case, the fruit which hangeth upon them will fall. Doe they but see themselves in a looking glasse, the cleare brightnesse therof turneth into dimnesse, upon their very sight. Look they upon a sword, knife, or any edged toole, be it never so bright, it waxeth duskish, so doth also the lively hue of yvorie. The very bees in the hive die. Yron and steele presently take rust, yea, and brasse likewise, with a filthie, strong, and poysoned stinke, if they lay but hand thereupon. If dogs chance to taste of womens fleures, they runne mad therewith: and if they bite anything afterwards, they leave behind them such a venome, that the wounds are incurable."[2]

"Science," as it is understood today, did not exist when Pliny wrote those words. But, the ability to think logically if one wished to do so, did. Pliny makes genuinely absurd charges, and ones that could easily have been tested. A menstruating woman might have been asked (or told) to sit under a tree, and men could observe what transpired. Some instruments of iron or steel could have been exposed to menstrual blood and again, results readily observed. It is not as if these assertions were hard to verify. They were not.

One must ask why such absurd ideas were readily accepted, recorded and promulgated as "truths." Believing in ideas that fly in the face of everyday experience must be seen as aberrant behavior, and aberrant behavior requires explanations. Men *could* think. *They had.* Geometry and astronomy had already been mastered; mathematics had enabled the pyramids millennia before. But these same men of the ancient world could not, apparently, even *begin to think*, with even the slightest degree of clarity, to say nothing of rigor, about *women.*

Or perhaps it suited their purposes not to do so. In fairness, they were hardly alone. In "Blood Magic: The Anthropology of Menstruation," the authors contend that studies demonstrate the almost universal fear in men of menstrual blood and menstruating women, and their perception as "dangerous." They point to the widespread existence of menstrual taboos and the required seclusion of menstruous women.[3]

Psychoanalysis suggests two potentially explanatory paths. In "Civilization and its Discontents" Freud suggests that there is an "organic repression" of a sexual attraction experienced by men at the possibility of intercourse with a menstruating woman. This then would require the safety of a taboo. But that explanation seems significantly incomplete.

Other analysts, Wolfgang Lederer and Karen Horney for example, hypothesize that the sight, or imagined image, of a woman's genital area, lacking a penis as of course it would, and covered in blood, directly stimulates castration anxiety. Lederer asserts, "Castration anxiety … is a very real thing both in folklore and in the office, and "castration" as a concept a most useful metaphor. … In particular, the dangerous, devouring vagina is as prominent in myth the world over as it is in our consulting rooms."[4] John Leuba, a French psychoanalyst observes, "In therapy, impotence due to fear of the father yields rapidly [to treatment], but that due to fear of the mother is tenacious."[5]

Karen Horney, familiar with the literature of mythology and anthropology, asked in a 1932 paper entitled "The Dread of Women," "Is it not remarkable that so little recognition and attention are paid to the fact of men's secret dread of women."[6] Most dictionaries define "dread" as a mixture of fear and awe. Lederer agreed with Horney several decades later, adding "The topic of the fear of women is today, in psychoanalytic writings, as neglected as ever."[7] It was presumably this fear that prevented men from examining the reality of the "monstrous" power they attributed to menstrual blood.

This fear of women takes on an even more likely role as an explanatory concept if one considers the profound importance of the relationship of the early mother to the growing child. It is the early mother who can withhold love, who is the first to forbid, even punish various behaviors, importantly any form of self-gratification. It seems less surprising then that celibacy, which might be defined as "the absence of a woman," was exalted by the early church fathers and continues today as a priestly requirement; celibacy is one way to conquer fear, one way to solve the "woman problem." And celibacy in those centuries was exalted. And esteemed. Abstinence was the pathway to both health and safety.

The Stoics, active for several centuries before Jesus, were also in favor of celibacy. Stoicism had been at the forefront in the beliefs of the highly educated, both in the Roman Empire and the Hellenistic world. Their idealization of "dispassion" was a core concept. If "inferior emotions," of which "lust" was one, were put aside, then higher aspirations would develop. The influence of the Stoic school is apparent in the work of Paul of Tarsus.

Paul, according to Acts 17:16-18, met with Stoics on more than one occasion during visits to Athens. In his letters, he frequently used Stoic terms and clearly was well versed in Stoic philosophy. He writes in 1 Corinthians 7:38, "So then, he who marries the virgin does right, but he who does not marry her does better." It is worth noting, if difficult to understand, that at the same time those words were written, Paul was, like Jesus, behaving with a degree of freedom from the prejudices of his time; he was treating women as capable adults, giving them increasing responsibilities in the formation and governance of the early "house churches."

In conclusion, sexual activity was increasingly seen as debilitating and dangerous during the first two centuries of Christianity. The act of sexual intercourse was seen as without either merit or pleasure and divorced from any idea of love. Love was not included in Catholic thinking or related to sexual behavior in any significant way until, after a brief mention during the Council of Trent, 1545-1563, it was legitimized during the discussions of Vatican II, 1962-65. In these early centuries, men seemed to hate their sexual drives and the frustration they entailed; a natural, perhaps inevitable consequence was to blame women for arousing their desires.

Now, to the Book of Genesis. A slow and careful reading of the relevant verses is recommended; they read as follows:

[2:7] then the LORD God formed man from the dust of the ground, and breathed into his nostrils the breath of life; and the man became a living being.
[2:8] And the LORD God planted a garden in Eden, in the east; and there he put the man whom he had formed.
[2:9] Out of the ground the LORD God made to grow every tree that is pleasant to the sight and good for food, the tree of life also in the midst of the garden, and the tree of the knowledge of good and evil.

2:20] Then man gave names to all cattle, and to the birds of the air, and to every animal of the field; but for the man there was not found a helper as his partner.
[2:21] So the LORD God caused a deep sleep to fall upon the man, and he slept; then he took one of his ribs and closed up its place with flesh.
[2:22] And the rib that the LORD God had taken from the man he made into a woman and brought her to the man.
[2:23] Then the man said, "This at last is bone of my bones and flesh of my flesh; this one shall be called Woman, for out of Man this one was taken."

[2:24] Therefore a man leaves his father and his mother and clings to his wife, and they become one flesh.
[2:25] And the man and his wife were both naked, and were not ashamed.

[3:1] Now the serpent was more crafty than any other wild animal that the LORD God had made. He said to the woman, "Did God say, 'You shall not eat from any tree in the garden'?"
[3:2] The woman said to the serpent, "We may eat of the fruit of the trees in the garden;
[3:3] but God said, 'You shall not eat of the fruit of the tree that is in the middle of the garden, nor shall you touch it, or you shall die. '"
[3:4] But the serpent said to the woman, "You will not die;
[3:5] for God knows that when you eat of it your eyes will be opened, and you will be like God, knowing good and evil."
[3:6] So when the woman saw that the tree was good for food, and that it was a delight to the eyes, and that the tree was to be desired to make one wise, she took of its fruit and ate; and she also gave some to her husband, who was with her, and he ate.
[3:7] Then the eyes of both were opened, and they knew that they were naked; and they sewed fig leaves together and made loincloths for themselves.
[3:8] They heard the sound of the LORD God walking in the garden at the time of the evening breeze, and the man and his wife hid themselves from the presence of the LORD God among the trees of the garden.

[3:9] But the LORD God called to the man, and said to him, "Where are you?"
[3:10] He said, "I heard the sound of you in the garden, and I was afraid, because I was naked; and I hid myself."
[3:11] He said, "Who told you that you were naked? Have you eaten from the tree of which I commanded you not to eat?"
[3:12] The man said, "The woman whom you gave to be with me, she gave me fruit from the tree, and I ate."
[3:13] Then the LORD God said to the woman, "What is this that you have done?" The woman said, "The serpent tricked me, and I ate."
[3:14] The LORD God said to the serpent, "Because you have done this, cursed are you among all animals and among all wild creatures; upon your belly you shall go, and dust you shall eat all the days of your life.
[3:15] I will put enmity between you and the woman, and between your offspring and hers; he will strike your head, and you will strike his heel."
[3:16] To the woman he said, "I will greatly increase your pangs in childbearing; in pain you shall bring forth children, yet your desire shall be for your husband, and he shall rule over you."
[3:17] And to the man he said, "Because you have listened to the voice of your wife, and have eaten of the tree about which I commanded you, 'You shall not eat of it,' cursed is the ground because of you; in toil you shall eat of it all the days of your life;

[3:18] Thorns and thistles it shall bring forth for you; and you shall eat the plants of the field.
[3:19] By the sweat of your face you shall eat bread until you return to the ground, for out of it you were taken; you are dust, and to dust you shall return."

God asserts that it's possible to say no. *Adam didn't.* God finds him responsible. And metes out punishment: "Cursed is the ground *because of you."*(Italics the authors) God's position seems crystal clear; Adam bears responsibility. He was the one God commanded to protect and keep the Garden, not Eve, and God gave Adam his instructions before Eve had even been created. Is it not extraordinary then that, for subsequent centuries, Christian scholars blamed Eve *when God did not?*

How then could Tertullian feel empowered to say, "You are the one who opened the door to the Devil. You are the one who first plucked the fruit of the forbidden tree, you are the first who deserted the divine law; you are the one who persuaded him whom the Devil was not strong enough to attack. All too easily you destroyed the image of God, namely, man."[8]

How then could Thomas Aquinas' use these hundred words in his "Summa," to describe Eve's behavior: "First, there is a sin of pride, whereby she inordinately desired her own excellence. Second is a sin of curiosity, whereby she coveted knowledge beyond the limits fixed for her. Third is a sin of gluttony, whereby the sweetness of the fruit enticed her to eat. Fourth is a sin of infidelity, growing out of a false estimate of God, so that she believed the words of the Devil who gave the lie to God. Fifth is a sin of disobedience consisting in a transgression of God's command. The sin came to the man through the woman's blandishments."[9] Two lines then suffice for Adam: "He followed her in transgressing the divine command and ate of the fruit of the forbidden tree."[10] There is no mention of pride, curiosity, gluttony and so on.

How then could "St. Bernard of Clairvaux claim in his sermons that Eve was "the original cause of all evil, whose disgrace has come down to all other women."[11] These assertions stood fast for centuries. If there were male scholars who saw error in these assertions, and one must believe there were, they were silent. But one man, Jerome, did more than accuse. Jerome went beyond blaming; he took action. Eventually he was elevated to sainthood by the Catholic Church.

St. Jerome was a priest, confessor, theologian and protégé of Pope Damasus I. Born in an Illyrian village in 347 CE, he is most well known not for his expressed opinion, "Women with child (i.e. pregnant) present a revolting spectacle"[12] but for his commissioned work in the translation of the Bible from its original languages into Latin, the translation usually referred to as the RSV, the Revised Standard Version. This was the text in use throughout the medieval world. There is at least one critical difference between Jerome's RSV and the subsequent translation of the Bible into English; this more up-to-date version was completed in 1971 and is usually referred to as the NASB, the New American Standard Bible and is now the version most widely accepted.

"Jerome's Latin translation, the RSV, was the *first source to omit* a critical phrase, the words, **עמה**, meaning "with her," from the early versions of Genesis. The phrase was not reintroduced until centuries later when the NASB was completed."[13] In the earlier versions of Genesis, Adam is described as "with her," when the serpent presents his temptation; thus Adam hears it directly, simultaneously, at the same time Eve does. Moreover, in the Septuagint and the Samaritan traditions, the subsequent verb is in the plural, "and they ate." Since Jerome worked from both the Hebrew and Greek Old Testaments, *both of which* include the phrase "with her," his decision to make this change, to omit the phrase from the Latin translation, must be understood as intentional. His motivation for the creation of what is, in effect, a lie, seems clear.

"It is more difficult to put all the blame on the woman, and see her as innately defective, when we understand that the man was [right] there with her while the serpent was speaking and that the man ate the forbidden fruit with her."[14] If the man had been absent when the serpent made his pitch, then Eve alone would be responsible for what Adam comes to believe, ergo Eve would be to blame. Jerome, in what clearly seems a willful act of omission, rewrote the story of Eve, with just the omission of one tiny little phrase, **עמה**.

Jane Barr, writing on the subject of Jerome's translation , observed "Whenever Jerome approached a passage where women were involved his usual objectivity deserted him, and his translation became less precise, and, not infrequently, biased."[15] Both authors, Parker and Barr observe the importance of correct translations.

However it is not only feminists of the 20th century and later that have found the Bible misogynist; a woman wrote the following more than a hundred years ago: "The Bible teaches that woman brought sin and death into the world, that she precipitated the fall of the race, that she was arraigned before the judgment seat of Heaven, tried, condemned and sentenced. Marriage for her was to be a condition of bondage, maternity a period of suffering and anguish, and in silence and subjection, she was to play the role of a dependent on man's bounty for all her material wants, and for all the information she might desire on the vital questions of the hour, she was commanded to ask her husband at home."[16] That woman was Elizabeth Cady Stanton.

Can tentative conclusions be drawn from the foregoing? It would seem so. The fear-filled, irrational citations on the power of menstrual blood and the profound need for taboos, i.e. the strict controls of harmless menstruous women are compelling. Irrational fear fuels the misogynist interpretations of Scripture. That Eve is not alone in her wish for knowledge, that she and Adam share the responsibility equally, could be understood as to their credit.

No thoughtful person needs a psychoanalyst to inform them of some interrelationship between fear and hate. It is an aspect of any thinking person's everyday experience. One hates what one fears and fears what one hates. Unfortunately then, at least tentatively, hatred of women finds its way on to a list of possible explanatory concepts for obviously irrational behavior.

Now, to the Bible itself, and what additional light can be shed.

The Bible:

Addressing the works that eventually become the New Testament, the questions are:

Who were the women who followed Jesus? Where did they come from? What brought them to this new sect, to follow this new preacher?

How did Jesus behave towards these and other women and did his behavior conform to the then cultural norms? If not, in what way did it vary?

Who was Mary Magdalene, what is known of her, and what role in the crucifixion did she play? How is she portrayed in the Gnostic Gospels?

The women:

A useful point of departure would be Luke 8: 1–3, which reads as follows: "Soon afterwards he (referring to Jesus) went on through cities and villages, proclaiming and bringing the good news of the kingdom of God. The twelve were with him, as well as some women who had been cured of evil spirits and infirmities." The author then names some of the women: "Mary, called Magdalene, from whom seven demons had gone out, and Joanna, the wife of Herod's steward, Chuza, and Susanna." Posterity is then given the only sentence that explains what the women were doing there: "and many others who provided for him out of their resources."

Admittedly, reaching across centuries for understanding is a challenge; restraint is required. The task is more difficult when data is lacking, and when certain data is given little space, it must be assumed with purpose. The New Testament authors never mention the degree to which Jesus differs from the men of his time in his treatment of women; this observation is left to contemporary scholars. In fact, the authors hardly mention the women with Jesus at all, despite their consistent presence. A reluctance to do so must be inferred, especially when compared to the Gnostic Bibles. There, the women themselves are quoted directly and at length. The few passages that refer to them in the New Testament, with the exception of Luke, above, all address their role at the crucifixion: Mark 15:40–41, Matthew 27:55–56, John 19:25, and Luke 23:49, 23:55 and 24:10.

Carla Ricci points out that this "group of women followed Jesus constantly on his traveling since the beginning of his public activity in the land of Galilee … They set out with him, leaving home, family, relations, their village, their everyday life, and stayed with him, listening, speaking, traveling, offering goods and services, [in short] living with him."[17] She finds this "startling on at least two counts. First because it was revolutionary, for that time, that women should follow a master; second because this is a voice breaking through the silence on women's discipleship and appearing in the written text, if only for a moment."[18]

She asserts a conscious reluctance on the part of the bible's authors to give the women with Jesus any importance, but that the mention in Luke is "a trace that surfaces in the narrative, only to disappear again immediately, but… it is unmistakably audible and leaves behind the incontestable certainty that Jesus wanted the restricted and privileged circle that lived with him as he went from village to village to include a group of women."[19]

She further observes that the New Testament authors mention the women only when the circumstances compel them to do so. When there are no males present, there is no alternative. Their presence during the scenes of the crucifixion would attest to this. With Jesus' arrest, the apostles fled, quite rightly believing that they too could be arrested and if imprisoned, the infant movement would come to an end. The women, too unimportant to be arrested, remained with Jesus and as a consequence were the only ones who *could* bear witness to the resurrection. Ricci's point? Now that there is no alternative, the women must be heard.

In addition, although personal reasons may have influenced the authors in their decisions to include and exclude, political reasons were certainly at play; these texts were not written without purpose and their purpose was to persuade and to evangelize. The only serious competition for the nascent Christianity was the Gnostics and the Gnostics had a very different and much more inclusive view of women; a wish to differentiate themselves from this then important sect may have played a significant role in writing the women out of the story unless their presence was absolutely essential. But written out they were.

Another "unmention" of women takes place in Luke 18:15–16: "People were bringing even infants to him that he might touch them; and when the disciples saw it, they sternly ordered them not to do it." People? "But Jesus called for them and said, "Let the little children come to me." Them? Ricci notes that there are parallel passages in Matt. 19: 13–14, and Mark 10: 13–16 and "that it would have been women who brought their children to Jesus for him to touch and caress, while their presence annoyed the disciples."[20] Their presence, one infers, did not annoy Jesus. Yet the author of the passage cannot bring himself to name their gender. Awkward and indeterminate phrasing is preferred.

The women that joined Jesus on his journey would have to have been unusual. An act was required, and women in those times did not act; they followed. But these women did act, and in doing so differentiated themselves from their peers. What attracted them? What were they seeking?

Jo Ann McNamara believed that "The women of the gospel came to Jesus out of tragic and broken lives. They needed healing, for their bodies and for their souls. They needed to be relieved of whatever pressures had made them demoniacs or to be forgiven for sexual transgressions. But once restored, they did not simply go home. They joined the family of Christ. … They were a band of equals … distinctions seem to melt away."[21]

Returning to Luke, "Mary, called Magdalene, from whom seven demons had gone out," requires comment. That Mary Magdalene and others in the Bible suffered from what most modern clinicians would call conversion hysteria or other emotional illness is beyond question. Women were obliged to be without opinions, forced to remain illiterate, found their intelligence unwelcome, their sexuality discounted and most likely rarely satisfied, actually found their very *selves* unwanted and devalued. Those experiences would evoke strong emotions. With no available pathway for expression, the feelings would have to be repressed, but would find their way to the surface through the formation of physical symptoms.

Similar clinical pictures appear in Freud's earliest patients; although women's lot had improved substantially almost two millennia later, they had yet to be taken seriously. The more intelligent the woman was, in either century, the more unacceptable her experience must have been. Being taken seriously, and Jesus took women seriously, might have been sufficient to cure them of the "evil spirits and infirmities" that Luke refers to.

How Jesus behaved:

Elaine Pagels believes that the primary message of early Christianity was a message of freedom. It was "freedom in its many forms, including free will, freedom from demonic powers, freedom from social and sexual obligations, freedom from tyrannical government and from fate; and self-mastery as the source of such freedom."[22] Ideas of freedom would certainly have had resonance for women; they had so little.

Jesus can be found taking women seriously in Luke 10:38 – 42, where the following encounter is described and analyzed: "As Jesus and his disciples were on their way, he came to a village where a woman named Martha opened her home to him." This is already unusual; most men of that time would not have accepted this invitation unless other men were present. "She had a sister called Mary, who sat at the Lord's feet listening to what he said." Clearly Mary is welcome to do this, her posture that of a student. "But Martha was distracted by all the preparations that had to be made. She came to him and asked, "Lord, don't you care that my sister has left me to do the work by myself? Tell her to help me!" Jesus then defends Mary's choice.

"Martha, Martha," the Lord answered, "You are worried and upset about many things, but few things are needed — or indeed only one. Mary has chosen what is better, and it will not be taken away from her." Mary has chosen to hear, to study, to learn, to understand and independently to seek faith. Jesus does not send her back to the kitchen. Rather, he condones her active curiosity.

"Jesus counters a rigid custom that the Jews shared with the most traditional cultures, namely that a woman's fulfillment is inseparable from her homemaking role. He encourages Mary and other women to become disciples – that is students. … He admires her eagerness for learning and, in effect, her desire to be liberated from the limitations of her gender defined role."[23]

Again, in Luke 8:43–48, Jesus is seen as approachable and open to women: "Now a woman, having a flow of blood for twelve years, who had spent all her livelihood on physicians and could not be healed by any, came from behind and touched the border of His garment." A woman of faith takes independent action. "And immediately her flow of blood stopped. "And Jesus said, "Who touched Me?" When all denied it, Peter and those with him said, "Master, the multitudes throng and press You, and You say, 'Who touched Me?' " Peter is not willing to identify the woman; he almost mocks the question Jesus asks, in what seems an ancient version of "Are you kidding?" But Jesus is not deterred, as Peter apparently wished. "But Jesus said, 'Somebody touched Me, for I perceived power going out from Me.' Now when the woman saw that she was not hidden, she came trembling; and falling down before Him, she declared to Him in the presence of all the people the reason she had touched Him and how she was healed immediately. And He said to her, "Daughter, be of good cheer; your faith has made you well. Go in peace." Once again, independent, faith-based *action* , undertaken by *a woman*, is not only sanctioned but rewarded.

Turning now to Mary Magdalene as she is portrayed in the New Testament, one can note that each Book reports on the crucifixion and the resurrection, with only slight variations.

Mark 15:40–41. In the account of the passion, "There were also women looking on from a distance; among them were Mary Magdalene, and Mary the mother of James the younger and of Joses, and Salome."

Matt. 27:55–56. Again, the account of the crucifixion: "Many women were also there, looking on from a distance; they had followed Jesus from Galilee and had provided for him. Among them were Mary Magdalene and Mary the mother of James and Joseph, and the mother of the sons of Zebedee."

Luke 24:10. After the crucifixion, "Now it was Mary Magdalene, Joanna, Mary the mother of James, and the other women with them who told this to the apostles."

John 19:25. Again describing the crucifixion, "Meanwhile, standing near the cross of Jesus were his mother, and his mother's sister, the wife of Clopas, and Mary Magdalene."

What is noteworthy is the impersonal quality of the reporting. It is most unlike the image of Mary Magdalene that can be found elsewhere. Elizabeth Moltmann-Wendel[24] has commented as follows, relating "the biblical and Gnostic accounts of Magdalene to the recent Catholic treatment of women: "Testimony by witnesses both early and late indicates that Mary Magdalene, who played an important role among Jesus' followers, became one of the primary examples of this apostleship. As the Vatican today is agitated by such issues, so too Peter, as predecessor of the popes, became insecure and angry that a woman should usurp what he regarded as a masculine position," at least according to the Gnostic Gospels, to which the story must now turn.

The Gnostic Gospels:

In 1945, in Upper Egypt, a truly amazing event took place and the world of bible study as well as the thinking of biblical scholars was changed forever. Several Egyptian fellahin, two of whom were brothers, were digging for what they called "sabakh," a kind of soil that was valuable as fertilizer. The men were digging near the town of Nag Hammadi, "at the Jabal al-Tarif, a mountain honeycombed with more than 150 caves. Originally natural, some of these caves were … used as gravesites as early as the Sixth Dynasty, some 4,300 years ago."[25] Accidentally, the men hit and then uncovered a large, red earthenware jar; it was sealed. At first they were afraid to open it, since conceivably it could contain some spirit, but on further thought, it might also contain something valuable, perhaps even gold. Summoning their courage, they broke it open; for scholars of antiquity what it contained, thirteen leather bound books of papyrus, was worth much more than gold. But for the brothers, there was only disappointment.

They brought the contents home to their mother; since the papyri might make good kindling, she kept them next to the fireplace. They proved to be almost as good as straw. By chance, a local history teacher saw one of the books and thought they might have value; he forwarded one to a friend in Cairo and asked him to make inquiries. The rest, as they say, is history, and this history is complete with intrigue, black marketeering, confiscation by the Egyptian government, and the "five extraordinary texts, smuggled out of Egypt and offered for sale in America."[26] There they came to the attention of Professor Giles Quispel, of the Netherlands.

Quispel, and one can only imagine his excitement, flew to Cairo; it was now the spring of 1955. "Arriving in Cairo, he went at once to the Coptic Museum, borrowed photographs of some of the texts, and hurried back to his hotel to decipher them. Tracing out the first line, Quispel was startled, then incredulous, to read: "These are the secret words which the living Jesus spoke, and which the twin, Judas Thomas, wrote down."[27] Twin? No one thought Jesus had a twin. A *secret* gospel? What did that mean? It's hard to imagine that moment or what Quispel could have been thinking.

He "also discovered that it contained many sayings known from the New Testament; but these sayings, placed in unfamiliar contexts, suggested other dimensions of meaning. Other passages … differed entirely from any known Christian tradition: the "living Jesus," … speaks in sayings [both] cryptic and compelling: Jesus said, "If you bring forth what is within you, what you bring forth will save you. If you do not bring forth what is within you, what you do not bring forth will destroy you."[28] Quispel may have found that "cryptic;" Freud might well have murmured, "Well, yes. My point, exactly."

Where had the texts come from? Who had buried them there?" They had been translated into Coptic, "perhaps by Christian monks who treasured them as holy books in the library of one of the oldest monasteries in Egypt."[29] But when the "Archbishop of Alexandria sent out an Easter letter all over Egypt in the spring of 367, ordering believers to reject what he called "illegitimate and secret books"[30] the monks must have feared for the future of the texts. Some of them apparently defied the archbishops' order. For the sake of mankind to come, they instead "saved and protected over fifty texts from their library by sealing them in a heavy jar and burying them away from the monastery walls, under the cliff where they were found 1600 years later."[31]

Had these writing been known to the men of the earlier centuries? Apparently so. "Hippolytus, a Christian writer in Rome, [had] quoted some of the opening lines from perhaps the most famous book of the discovery, the Gospel of Thomas." This suggests that the book "had been written and widely circulated among Christian groups by the middle of the second century."[32] Some scholars came to conclude that "the Gospel of Thomas perhaps could be dated as early as the mid-first century – about 20 years after Jesus's death."[33]

Turning now to the actual texts themselves, reader instructions are required; reading them is complicated. Because the texts were badly damaged, many words, sometimes lines, sometimes whole passages were missing, had rotted away. Careful scholars did what they could to restore the original; at times, their choices can be questioned, but their integrity cannot be. In each and every instance they clarify for the reader exactly what choice they have made and why. There are instances of long passages completely intact; there are other instances when imagination has been required three times in a single sentence. As one reads, the following should be kept in mind and continually referred to:

[ ] square brackets indicate a textual lacuna (hole or omission) that has been restored.

< > Angle brackets indicate an emendation of a scribal omission or error.

{ } Braces indicate superfluous letters that ... were added by a scribe.

... Ellipsis dots indicate unrestored lacunae – portions of Coptic (or Greek) text missing in the manuscripts that cannot be restored with confidence. Three dots indicate a short break; six dots a longer one. Usually there will be an explanatory note."[34]

The reader should now be prepared to encounter new and enhanced images of Mary Magdalene. The following are excerpted from "The Gospel of Philip:"[35]

"Three women always walked with the master: Mary his mother, <his> sister, and Mary of Magdala, who is called his companion. For "Mary" is the name of his sister, his mother, and his companion."

"The companion of the [Savior] is Mary of Magdala. The [Savior loved] her more than [all] the disciples, [and he] kissed her often on the [mouth]."

"The other [disciples] … said to him, "Why do you love her more than all of us?"

"The Savior answered and said to them, "Why don't I love you like her? If a blind person and one who can see are both in darkness, they are the same. When the light comes, one who can see will see the light, and the blind person will stay in darkness."

What should be said about the above? First, the use of the word "companion" to describe Mary Magdalene requires comment. The Greek word is "koinonos," which, unfortunately, has more than one definition; it can also be defined as comrade, associate, partner, friend and even neighbor. Most biblical scholars point out that many words with more clearly sexual or marital definitions were available to translators had they been desired.

The passage "[and he] kissed her often on the [mouth]" is equally a riddle yet to be solved. Note that the word "mouth" is bracketed. Why? Because the word itself was eaten by ants. Apparently ants like parchment. Is it believable? The one word wanted, gone? And the lame explanation, ants? No, it isn't believable, but it's true. It does, however, allow the reader to entertain alternate explanations.

It should be noted that nowhere is there any information known or suggested as to Mary Magdalene's age. Consequently the word "mouth" would have to be considered an act of choice. However, alternate options are also available. If Mary were 35, mouth would be most likely. If Mary were 55, which might well explain what Jesus sees as her superior intelligence, then he might have "loved" her just as much, but kissed her on the "cheek."

Somewhere, on a scroll, a piece of parchment, buried underneath a fallen wall, waiting to be excavated, answers wait. So do we all.

Turning now to another Gnostic text, the Gospel of Mary,[37] excerpts read as follows:

"Go then, preach the good news about the kingdom. Do not lay down any rule beyond what I determined for you, nor promulgate law like the lawgiver, or else you might be dominated by it." After he said these things, he departed from them.

But they were distressed and wept greatly. "How are we going to go out to the rest of the world to announce the good news about the kingdom of the Child of Humanity?" they said. "If they didn't spare him, how will they spare us?"

Then Mary stood up. She greeted them all, addressing her brothers and sisters, "Do not weep and be distressed nor let your hearts be irresolute. For his grace will be with you all and will shelter you. Rather, we should praise his greatness, for he has prepared us and made us human beings.

When Mary said these things, she turned their heart toward the Good, and they began to debate about the words of [the Savior].

Peter said to Mary, "Sister, we know that the Savior loved you more than all other women. Tell us the words of the Savior that you remember, the things you know that we don't because we haven't heard them."

Mary responded, "I will teach you about what is hidden from you." And she began to speak these words to them. …

"Andrew responded, addressing the brothers and sisters, "Say what you will about the things she has said, but I do not believe that the Savior said these things, for indeed these teachings are strange ideas."

Peter responded, bringing up similar concerns. He questioned them about the Savior, "Did he, then, speak with a woman in private without our knowing about it? Are we to turn around and listen to her? Did he choose her over us?"

Then Mary wept and said to Peter, "My brother Peter, what are you imagining? Do you think that I have thought up these things by myself in my heart or that I am telling lies about the Savior?"

Levi answered, speaking to Peter, "Peter, you have always been a wrathful person. Now I see you contending against the woman like the adversaries. For if the Savior made her worthy, who are you then for your part to reject her? Assuredly the Savior's knowledge of her is completely reliable. That is why he loved her more than us."

"Rather, we should be ashamed. We should clothe ourselves with the perfect human, acquire it for ourselves as he commanded us, and announce the good news, not laying down any other rule or law that differs from what the Savior said." After [he said these] things, they started going out [to] teach and to preach."[38]

These citations are all that the world knew of Mary Magdalene in the first five centuries of the Church. In the accepted orthodox texts, she is all but sexless; in even those texts deemed heretical, she is in an undefined but loving relationship with Jesus. Is she a prostitute? Certainly not. How does it come about, then, that around the globe, for hundreds of years, the Catholic Church ran homes for unwed mothers, called "Magdalene Houses"? The explanation follows.

Gregorius Anicius (Pope Gregory I) in the sixth century, made a mistake. He conflated several of the women in the Bible, one of whom was not even named Mary. She was the "sinner," who washed the feet of Jesus with her tears, and dried them with her hair (admittedly an arresting image even for non-celibates) and begged forgiveness for her sins, which Jesus willingly granted. That passage was Luke 7:36-38 and had nothing to do with Mary Magdalene. Anicius, (Gregory I) then, apparently still thinking about Mary Magdalene, remembered the clause describing her, "from whom seven demons had gone out." (Luke 8:2) He concluded then that the "seven demons" were the seven deadly sins.

Sins, sinners, women – confusion clearly reigned. But for whatever reason, Mary Magdalene, the independent woman whose "means" provided for Jesus, the woman chosen to announce the Resurrection, has been transformed by a confused pope; she is now a whore, albeit repentant. Houses for unwed pregnant women, her supposed companions in degradation, are built around the world. Her name takes on a whole, new meaning, which no one corrects. No one is outraged.

Perhaps Anicius, (Gregory I) had poor eyesight or inept advisors. But by a combined path of papal error and impulse-ridden imagination, the intelligent, thoughtful "companion" of Jesus became a sorrowful prostitute. And the error went unquestioned and uncorrected *for centuries.* The question "why" must be asked.

There were biblical exegetes throughout the many subsequent years; was no one concerned with the misrepresentation, the obvious, undeserved disrespect of this woman? Why did the error remain, enshrined in certitude, until the decade after the close of Vatican II, a period when liberal clergy had not yet been overtaken by conservatives? In 1967, with neither comment nor apology, and after all what actually could they have said, the error was corrected. *But the question remains.*

The answer can only be inferred; *because it satisfied some deep need among these men*. What might the origin of that need have been? The previous discussion of the interrelationship of fear and hatred seems germane here. The woman was diminished and remained so for centuries. Whether it was fear or hatred that prevented fairness or redress, as with all "chicken/eggs" issues, it is impossible to say. Nor does it matter. What matters is whether or not and to what degree the driving force behind this centuries-long accusation is still operative. Recent events would suggest that it is.

Are the citations of the previous pages in any way relevant for contemporary women? For the nuns of America? The case can be made that they are more than relevant, and that they are in fact both basic and instructive. It should be emphasized that they were not cherry-picked; they were not selected little nuggets discovered amid lines of neutral prose. In many instances, blind, literally blind choices could have been made, in that books could have been opened at random and a finger lowered with eyes closed, and similar insults found. Women are routinely blamed and castigated, with little or no regard for truth.

Before continuing, the following statistics are offered without comment.

****

Catholic population changes in America, 1965-2014:

Nuns: 179,954 to 49,883.	Declined 72%
Priests: 58,632 to 38,275.	Declined 35%
Parochial schools, elementary: 10,667 to 5,368.	Declined 49%

Parochial schools, secondary: 1,527 to 1,200. Declined 27%

Students: 689,264 to 579,605. Declined 16%

Number of parishes: 17,637 to 17,483. Declined .01%

Parishes with no resident priest: 549 to 3,496. Increased 79%

(Center for Applied Research in the Apostolate, Washington DC)

Catholic Population Changes in America, 1975-2014:

Total Catholic population percentages:

22.5% to 21%. Declined 1.5%

Foreign-born Catholic population percentages:

4,700,000 to 21,500,000 Increased 450%

(S&P US Population by Year)

Global Catholic Population Changes, 1910 to 2010:

Asia-Pacific Region: 13.8m to 130,5m, 5% to 12% Increased 7%

Sub-Saharan Africa: 1.2m to 171.5m, -1% to 16% Increased 17%

Latin America: 70.6m to 425m, 24% to 39% Increased 15%

North America: 15,150m to 88,550m, 5% to 8% Increased 3%

Europe: 188,060m to 257,160m, 65% to 24% Declined 41%

(Pew Research Center, 2/13/13)

Worldwide Catholic Population, 1965, 70 to 2014:

1965 to 2014: 46,300 to 66,600. Increased 44%

Percentage, world population: 1970 to 2014:

653.6m, 18% to 1.229b, 17% Declined 1%

(Center for Applied Research in the Apostolate, Washington, D.C.)

Bergoglio (Francis) has reiterated that the door to women priests is closed. As recently as 2015, women continue to clamor for it to be unlocked. One must ask why. What do these women imagine, were they to be admitted, their treatment would be? Do they imagine that, if they were to remain true to themselves, they would actually ever be accepted? Or welcomed? Let the Vatican remain "the last womanless space."[39]

But just for a moment, imagine that women had not been initially marginalized and finally completely excluded from the Catholic power structure but welcomed. Could anyone doubt that the Church would have evolved very differently? That the Church of Jesus would have held its' own with the Church of Constantine? If women had been welcomed rather than excluded? If their skills had been acknowledged and utilized and given a place? Just imagine. What a church Roman Catholicism could have been.

But they were not welcomed. Despite the fact that "the women of Galilee were the first Christians [who] came up to Jerusalem with Jesus and stayed with him in the bitter hours of his death. They buried him and later announced to the other disciples who were hiding from the Romans that the tomb was empty."[40] Despite the fact that "there has never been a Christianity that did not rely on the prayers and services of dedicated women [who] were with Jesus before there was a church and devoted lives to prayer and service before men wrote rules and prelates enforced them." Despite the fact that "for two millennia, they successfully responded to the challenges of history without losing fidelity to the ancient Gospel."[41]

Were we now to encounter the 900 plus women of the LCWR, standing together, perhaps on a stage, perhaps in a crowded room, what would we see? Almost all are over 70, gray-haired, dressed perhaps plainly, a little jewelry here and there. They are aging, yet their posture is resolute. They are no longer swathed in medieval costumes, drowned in the black robes that hid their bodies and the white wimples, pinching off their faces, successfully hiding each and every lock of hair.

Rather they stand before us as modern women, religious to their core, needing no uniform; admittedly they are no longer willing soldiers in a Catholic army, to be deployed without question by the nearest cleric in need. They no longer accept as their purpose the staffing of Church institutions, about which they have no say. They are not on their knees. Although they pray.

They have answered for themselves the question as to where their value lies and they have answered it clearly – they see their value in their apostolate, the work they do in God's name and, they believe, as God wishes them to do. They maintain that their apostolate *is* prayer – *prayer in action.* This may seem to the hierarchy to be rebellion; in fact, these women have simply returned to their roots, each order to its' own individual charism. It may be a source of inconvenience for the church, but inconvenience is not disobedience. Inconvenience is not heresy. Claiming the authority of their own religious experience does place them in conflict with the hierarchy. They are "prepared to obey God speaking through their consciences, but they are less willing to admit that the Pope and the rest of the male hierarchy speak for God."[42]

As a consequence, they were more than ready, as one sister put it, to "step sideways" out of the chain of command, to redefine their sense of mission and themselves. They have taken as their behavioral model the path that Jesus traveled. As he did, they eschew power or force as solutions. They point out that Jesus never coerced, never accepted a position of authority; he never resorted to intimidation; he did not ask for "loyalty oaths."

They are committed to "prophetic obedience." This is a process in which the one who seeks tries to discern what God would want from him or her and then *to live that understanding*. It is not blind obedience to some external system of rules; it is rather obedience to an internal vision, of what God wishes for that person at that time and in that place. This is their answer to the question, what is the source of religious authority? It follows then that obedience to God might sometimes override obedience to Roman mandates. Obedience now is no longer automatic.

In 2015, these sisters won an unqualified victory in their most recent struggle; wisely, they stand quietly. Their triumph is of necessity fleeting, since there has been no change in the substructure; yet it would be well to note that nuns around the world have been watching. And watching closely. These grey haired women will not live to see the changes they so dearly want, but they have shown the way; they may have cleared a path. Sisters unaccustomed to democratic governance, raised neither in the United States or western Europe, may need time to integrate the necessary knowledge and the necessary courage to take the next steps. But can anyone doubt that they will? In future decades? Or centuries?

The sisters of the Leadership Conference of Women Religious have lived a lesson for women everywhere, a lesson about living in truth and living in courage. They never were "a source of scandal to the faithful" as the Vatican alleged. They were accused of being "lacking in religious submission of will and mind"[43] and that accusation holds; indeed they were and are. They steadfastly refuse the blunt sledge hammer of absolutism upon which the Vatican is so adamant. They are not willing to submit, indeed they insisted and continue to insist on using those minds in question.

They have never been either the "rebel nuns" of the Catholic left or the "nuns gone wild" of the Catholic right. They have led no salt marches to the sea nor have they exhorted anyone to join them. They have simply been themselves: profoundly intelligent, deeply religious women, seeking that place where they could stand freely, and, of the utmost importance to them, "in good conscience." Irreplaceable, they will leave us soon. May they go in peace and with the gratitude of thoughtful men and women everywhere.

NOTES: PART FIVE

1. Rufinus, *Die "Summa Decretorum" des Magister Rufinus*, ed. H. Singer, Paderborn 1902, p. LXVII, P. 9.
2. C. Plinius Secundus, *The Historie of the World,* Book VII, P.152-191. Holland, Philemon, translator, (1601).
3. Buckley, Thomas and Gottlieb, Alma, *Blood Magic: The Anthropology of Menstruation,* University of California Press, Berkeley, California, 1988. P. 25.
4. Lederer, Wolfgang, *The Fear of Women*, Grune and Stratton, New York 1968, P. 217.
5. *Ibid.,* P. 218.
6. Horney, Karen, *"The Dread of Women,"* International Journal of Psychoanalysis, Vol 13, 1932, Pp. 348-360.
7. Lederer, op. cit., P.220.
8. Parker, Julie Faith, *"Blaming Eve Alone: Translation, Omission, and Implications of* עמה *in Genesis 3:6b."* P.729-747,| DOI: 10.1353/jbl.2013.0050.
9. Aquinas, St. Thomas, *"Aquinas's Shorter Summa,"* Sophia Institute Press, Manchester, New Hampshire, 2002. P. 221.
10. Ibid., P.222.
11. Witcombe, Christopher L. C. E., *"Eve and the Identity of Women," witcombe.sbc.edu/eve-women/evebibliography.html.*
12. Parker, op. cit., P. 729-747.
13. Ibid.
14. Ibid., Pp. 729-747.
15. Barr, Jane, "The Vulgate Genesis and St. Jerome's Attitude to Women," in *Papers Presented to the Eighth International Conference on Patristic Studies Held at Oxford,* 1979, ed. Elizabeth A. Livingstone; StPatr 17; Oxford: Pergamon, 1982, P. 269.
16. Stanton, Elizabeth Cady and the Revising Committee, *The Woman's Bible.*
17. Ricci, Carla. *Mary Magdalene and Many Others.* Fortress Press, Minneapolis, Minnesota, 1994. P.53.
18. Ibid., P.53.
19. Ibid., P.54.
20. Ibid., P.68.
21. McNamara, Jo Ann. *Sisters in Arms; Catholic Nuns Through Two Millenia.* Harvard University Press, Cambridge, Massachusetts, 1996, P.12.

22. Pagels, *Gnostic Gospels.* Random House, New York. 1979. P. Xxv.
23. Ibid., P. 61.
24. Phipps, William E. *Assertive Biblical Women*, Greenwood Press, Westport, Connecticut. 1992. P.113.
25. Pagels, op. cit., P. xiii.
26. Ibid., P. xiv.
27. Ibid., P. xv.
28. Ibid., P. xv.
29. Meyer, Marvin, Ed. *The Nag Hammadi Scripture,* Harper One, NY, 2007. P.6.
30. Ibid., P. 6.
31. Ibid., P. 7.
32. Ibid., P. 6.
33. Ibid., P. 9.
34. Ibid., P. 12.
35. The Gospel of Philip, http://gnosis.org/naghamm/gop.html.
36. The Gospel of Mary Magdalen, http://www.maryofmagdala.com/GMary_Text/gmary_text.html.
37. Meyer, op. cit., P. 742-74.
38. McNamara, op. cit., P. 630.
39. Ibid., P.9.
40. Ibid., P. 644.
41. Ibid., P. 643-44.

BIBLIOGRAPHY

Allen, Charlotte. 1998. *The Human Christ; the Search for the Historical Jesus*, The Free Press, New York.

Allen, Jr., John L. 2004. *All the Pope's Men.* Doubleday, New York.

2000. *Cardinal Ratzinger.* Continuum, New York.

Ampleforth Abbey Trustees, Ed. 2003. *The Rule of Saint Benedict.* Liturgical Press, Collegeville, Minnesota.

Aquinas, St. Thomas. 2002 *Aquinas's Shorter Summa.* Sophia Institute Press, Manchester, New Hampshire.

Beane, PhD, Marjorie Noterman. 1993. *From Framework to Freedom.* University Press of America, Lanham, Maryland.

Briggs, Kenneth. 2006. *Doublecrossed; Uncovering the Catholic Church's Betrayal of American Nuns.* Doubleday, New York.

Conference of Major Religious Superiors of Women's Institutes of the United States of America. 1970. CMSW Proceedings. M & S Printing, Washington DC.

Buckley, Thomas and Gottlieb, Alma, Eds. 1988. *Blood Magic: the Anthropology of Menstruation.* University of California Press, Berkeley, California.

Carey, Ann. 1997. *Sisters in Crisis.* Our Sunday Visitor, Inc., Huntington, Indiana.

Caspary, Anita Marie. 2001. *Witness to Integrity: The Crisis of the Immaculate Heart Community.* Liturgical Press, Collegeville, Minnesota.

Collins, Paul, Ed. 2001. *From Inquisition to Freedom.* Continuum Press, New York.

Crossan, John Dominic. 1992. *The Historical Jesus.* Harper, San Francisco.

Daigler, Mary Jeremy. 2012. *Incompatible with God's Design.* Scarecrow Press, Toronto, Canada.

de Boer, Esther. 1997. *Mary Magdalene; Beyond the Myth.* Trinity Press International, Harrisburg, Pennsylvania.

Delaney, Janice, Lupton, Mary Jane and Toth, Emily, Eds. 1998. *The Curse: a Cultural History of Menstruation.* University of Illinois Press, Urbana, Chicago, Illinois.

de Troyer, Kristin et al, Eds. 2003. *Wholly Woman, Holy Blood.* Trinity Press International, New York.

Douglas, Mary. 2002. *Purity and Danger.* Routledge Classics, NY.

Ebaugh, Helen R. 1993. *Women in the Vanishing Cloister: Organizational Decline in Catholic Religious Orders.* Rutgers University Press, Rutgers, New Jersey.

Eisen, Ute E. 2000. *Women Office Holders in Early Christianity.* Liturgical Press, Collegeville, Minnesota.

Fausto-Sterling, Anne. 1985. *Myths of Gender.* Basic Books, NY.

Ferraro, Barbara and Hussey, Patricia. 1990. *No Turning Back: Two Nuns Battle with the Vatican over Women's Right to Choose.* Poseidon Press, New York.

Fialka, John J. 2003. *Sisters; Catholic Nuns and the Making of America.* St. Martins, New York.

Fiedler, SL, Sr. Maureen. 2010. *Breaking Through the Stained Glass Ceiling: Women Religious in Their Own Words.* Church Publishing, Inc., New York.

Fiedler, Maureen and Rabben, Linda, Eds. 1998. *Rome Has Spoken.* Crossroad Publishing, New York.

Foley, OP, Nadine, Ed. 1988. *Claiming Our Truth.* Leadership Conference of Women Religious, Washington, D.C.

Ford, George Barry. 1969. *A Degree of Difference: Memoirs of George Barry Ford.* Farrar, Strauss and Giroux, New York.

Fry, OSB, Timothy, Ed. 1981. *The Rule of Saint Benedict.* Vintage Books, New York.

Gardiner, SSND, Anne Marie, Ed. 1976. *Women and Catholic Priesthood: An Expanded Vision.* Paulist Press, New York.

Gibson, Margaret Dunlop. 2013. *The Didascalia Apostolorum in English.* Isha Books, New Delhi, India.

Gonzalez, Justo L. 2010. *The Story of Christianity, Volume I.* Harper One, Revised Edition, New York.

Gramick, Jeannine. 1983. *Homosexuality and the Catholic Church.* The Thomas More Press, Chicago, Illinois.

Gray, Francine du Plessix. 1970. *Divine Disobedience: Profiles in Catholic Radicalism.* Knopf, New York.

Greeley, Andrew. 2004. *The Catholic Revolution; New Wine, Old Wineskins and the Second Vatican Council.* University of California Press, Berkeley, California.

Gryson, Roger. 1980. *The Ministry of Women in the Early Church.* Liturgical Press, Collegeville, Minnesota.

Halter, Deborah. 2004. *The Papal "No."* Crossroad Press, New York.

Helman, Ivy A. 2012. *Women and the Vatican.* Orbis Books, NY.

Henold, Mary J. 2008. *Catholic and Feminist.* University of North Carolina Press, Chapel Hill.

Johnson, Sister Elizabeth. 2007. *Quest for the Living God.* Continuum International, New York.

1992. *She Who Is.* Crossroads Press, NY.

Kennedy, Phillip. 2010. *Twentieth Century Theologians.* I. B. Tauris, NY.

King, Margot, Ed. 1993. *A Leaf from the Great Tree of God; Essays in Honor of Ritamary M. Bradley.* Peregrine Press, Toronto, Canada.

Kittel, Phyllis M. 2009. *Staying in the Fire.* Woven Word Press, Boulder, Colorado.

Koehlinger, Amy. 2007. *The New Nuns: Racial Justice and Religious*

Reform in the 1960s. Harvard University Press, Cambridge, MA.

Kung, Hans and Swidler, Leonard, Eds. 1986. *The Church in Anguish.* Harper and Row, San Francisco, California.

Lederer, MD, Wolfgang. 1968. *The Fear of Women.* Grune and Stratton, New York.

Lerner, Gerda. 1986. *The Creation of Patriarchy.* Oxford University Press, New York.

Macy, Gary. 2008. *The Hidden History of Women's Ordination.* Oxford University Press, New York.

Madges, William and Daley, Michael J., Eds. 2012. *Vatican II; 50 Personal Stories.* Orbis Books, New York.

Massa, SJ, Mark J. 2010. *The American Catholic Revolution.* Oxford University Press, New York.

McEnroy, Carmel. 1996. *Guests in Their Own House; the Women of Vatican II.* Crossroad, New York.

McNamara, Jo Ann. 1996. *Sisters in Arms; Catholic Nuns Through Two Millenia.* Harvard University Press, Cambridge, Massachusetts.

Meyer, Marvin. Ed. 2007. *The Nag Hammadi Scriptures,*" Harper One, New York.

Neal, SNDDeN," Sr. Marie Augusta. 1990. *From Nuns to Sisters: An Expanding Vocation.* 23rd Publications, Mystic, Connecticut.

O'Donovan, Patrick. 1980. *Benedict of Nursia.* Collins, London.

O'Malley, John W. 2013. *Trent; What Happened at the Council.* Harvard University Press, Cambridge, Massachusetts.

2008. *What Happened at Vatican II.* Harvard University Press, Cambridge, Massachusetts.

Pagels, Elaine. 2003. *Beyond Belief.*" Random House, New York.

1988. *Adam, Eve and the Serpent.* Random House, New York.

1979. *Gnostic Gospels*. Random House, New York.

Parker, Julie Faith. 2013. "Blaming Eve Alone: Translation, Omission, and Implications of עמה in Genesis 3:6b." Journal of Biblical Literature, Volume 132, Number 4.

Patrick, Anne. 1998. *Conscience and Calling: Ethical Reflections on Catholic Women's Church Vocations*. Bloomsbury, New York.

Phipps, William E. 1992. *Assertive Biblical Women*. Greenwood Press, Westport, Connecticut.

Quinonez, CDP, Sr. Laura Ann. 1980, *Starting Points: Six Essays Based on the Experience of U. S. Women Religious*. LCWR, Washington DC.

Quinonez, Laura Ann and Turner, Mary Daniel. 1991. *The Transformation of American Sisters*. Temple University Press, Philadelphia, Pennsylvania.

Reese, Thomas J. 1996. *Inside the Vatican*. Harvard University Press, Cambridge, Massachusetts.

Ricci, Carla. 1994. *Mary Magdalene and Many Others*. Fortress Press, Minneapolis, Minnesota.

Robinson, James M. Ed. 1990. *The Nag Hammadi Library*. Revised Edition, Harper, San Francisco.

Rynne, Xavier. 1964. *Vatican Council II*. Farrar, Strauss and Giroux, New York.

Schneiders, Sr. Sandra. 1991. *Beyond Patching; Faith and Feminism in the Catholic Church*. Paulist Press, Mahwah, New Jersey.

1986 *New Wineskins*. Paulist Press, Mahwah, NJ.

Segal, Alan F., 1986. *Rebecca's Children*. Harvard University Press, Cambridge, Massachusetts.

Shuttle, Penelope and Redgrove, Peter. 1986. *The Wise Womb; the Myths, Realities, and Meanings of Menstruation*. Grove Press, New York.

Stanton, Elizabeth Cady. 2010. *The Woman's Bible.* Pacific Publishing Studio, Seattle, Washington.

Steichen, Donna. 1992. *Ungodly Rage; the Hidden Face of Catholic Feminism.* Ignatius Press, San Francisco.

Suenens, Leon Joseph Cardinal. 1962. *The Nun in the World.* The Newman Press, Westminster, Maryland.

Tobin, Mary Luke, SL. 1981. *Hope is an Open Door.* Abingdon Press, Nashville, Tennessee.

Turner, John D. and McGuire, Anne, Eds. 1997. *The Nag Hammadi Library After Fifty Years.* Brill, New York.

Ware, Ann Patrick, Ed. 1985. *Midwives of the Future: American Sisters Tell Their Stories.* Leaven Press, Kansas City, Kansas.

Weaver, Mary Jo. 1985. *New Catholic Women; A Contemporary Challenge to Traditional Religious Authority.* Harper and Row, New York.

Weber, Francis J. 1999. *Magnificat: Timothy Cardinal Manning.* Kimberly Press, Santa Barbara, California.

1997. *His Eminence of Los Angeles: James Francis Cardinal McIntyre,* 2 Volumes. Kimberly Press, Santa Barbara, California.

White, L. Michael. 2004. *From Jesus to Christianity.* Harper, San Francisco, California.

Witham, Larry. 1991. *Curran Vs. Catholic University.* Edington-Rand, Inc., Riverdale, Maryland.

INDEX OF NUNS NAMED

APPENDICES

Appendix A

www.bbc.com/news/uk-11294877

The following is a glossary of Roman Catholic terms, edited by the author from the website listed above with additional terms added.

Archbishop: A senior bishop, heading an archdiocese.

Apostolate: The activity or work which fulfills the apostolic nature of the Church.

Apostolic Visitations: When the Holy See delegates an *Apostolic* visitor (or visitors) to evaluate an ecclesiastical institute such as a seminary, diocese, or religious institute to assist the institute in question to improve the way in which it carries out its function in the life of the Church.

Apostle: One of the 12 original followers of Jesus Christ as named in the New Testament.

Bishop: A bishop is the third tier of ministerial ordination (after deacon and priest). of, according to, or ordered by church canon

Canonical standing: Having been accepted as authoritative.

Canon Law: The rules, *canons or laws*, which provide the norms for good order in the society of the Church. Those canon laws that apply universally are contained in the Codes of Canon Law.

Cardinal: Cleric (normally archbishop) appointed by the Pope to join the College of Cardinals - the Pope's principal advisers.

CDF: The Congregation for the Doctrine of the Faith (Latin:

Congregatio pro Doctrina Fidei; CDF) is the oldest among the nine congregations of the Roman Curia. It was founded to defend the church from heresy; today, it is the body responsible for promulgating and defending Catholic doctrine.

CICLSAL: The Congregation for Institutes of Consecrated Life and Societies of Apostolate Life. This Congregation is responsible for everything which concerns institutes of consecrated life (orders and religious congregations, both of men and of women, secular institutes) and societies of apostolic life regarding their government, discipline, studies, goods, rights, and privileges.

Clergy: The body of people ordained for religious service, (deacons, priests, bishops) as opposed to laity. NB religious (monks, nuns, friars) are not clergy, unless (in the case of male religious) they are also ordained.

CMSWR: The Council of Major Superiors of Women Religious is a Roman Catholic association of major superiors (superiors general or provincial superiors) of religious institutes for women in the United States of America. The council's purpose is to promote collaboration and inter-communication among its members, participation, dialogue and education about the teaching of the Catholic Church on the religious life, unity with the Pope and cooperation with the United States Conference of Catholic Bishops.

Consecration: The consecration at Mass is that part of the Eucharistic Prayer during which the Lord's words of institution of the Eucharist at the Last Supper are recited by the priestly minister.

Convent: An enclosed religious house where nuns (female religious) live under a rule and dedicate themselves to prayer.

Council (Vatican): A meeting of bishops/Church elders to discuss doctrinal and pastoral needs of Church. The most recent example was the Second Vatican Council (or Vatican II) held in Rome (1962-1965).

Curia: Administrative structure of the Vatican; a collection of "government" departments.

Decree: The *word* is used to denote certain specified collections of church law.

Diocese: The territory, or churches, under the authority and leadership of a bishop.

Disciple: Those who accepted Jesus' message to follow him, as opposed to the apostles.

Dissent: An act of will to deny, refute or knowingly disobey the teachings of the Church.

Dogma/Doctrine: The revealed teachings of Christ as defined by the Church's magisterium, or teaching authority. Doctrine is what the Church believes.

Encyclical: A pastoral letter written by the Pope and published to outline Church teaching on an issue.

Evangelist: One of the four authors credited with writing the Gospels (Matthew, Mark, Luke and John). More generally, someone who works actively to spread and promote the Christian faith.

Excommunication: The formal process of expulsion from the Church which excludes an individual from receiving the sacraments and from the exercise of any Church office, ministry, or function.

Declared by Church authorities for defiance of the Church's teaching authority, or magisterium.

Habit: The distinctive form of dress worn by members of religious communities.

Heresy: The denial (by someone who is baptised) of accepted Church teaching (dogma).

Hierarchy:

The Apostles and their successors, the college of bishops, to whom Christ gave the authority to teach, sanctify, and rule the Church in his name.

Holy See: The seat of the central administration of the worldwide Catholic Church

Infallibility (papal): Belief that a pope cannot err when he speaks in a formal capacity as head of the Church on matters of faith and morals. Infallibility was formally introduced at the First Vatican Council in 1870, and is rarely invoked.

Inquisitions: Official investigations by the Church of suspected heresies.

LCWR: The *Leadership Conference of Women Religious* is an association of the leaders of congregations of Catholic women religious in the United States.

Laity: Collective term for lay people - ordinary members of the Church who have not received holy orders (ie, are not clergy).

Liturgy: General term for a religious service or ceremony performed by a group of believers.

Magisterium: The teaching office of the universal Church, articulated by a pope. Papal statements which teach on a matter of faith and morals are called magisterial pronouncements and are binding on Catholics.

Mandate: A command or authorization to act in a particular way on a public issue, an order issued by the pope.

Nuncio: Pope's ambassador/representative in a country, with diplomatic status. The nunciature is the nuncio's residence.

Nuns' names: The initials following the names of nuns designates the order to which they belong. For example, IHM stands for the Immaculate Heart of Mary.

Ordination: The service by which individuals are made deacons, priests or bishops

Papacy: The office and jurisdiction of a pope; or the tenure or period of office of a pope. See also: Pontificate.

Parish: The principal unit of Christian community headed by a parish priest selected by the bishop. A number of parishes make up a diocese.

Pastoral letter: A letter sent from a bishop to the parishes of his diocese, often read out to people at Mass.

Prelate: An ecclesiastic of a high order, as an archbishop, bishop, etc.; a church dignitary.

Pontificate: The office and jurisdiction of a pope; or the tenure or period of office of a pope. See also: Papacy.

Pope: The successor of St Peter as bishop of Rome and head of the Catholic Church.

Prefect: The term for the head of a Vatican congregation.

Priest: Someone who is ordained to the second level of ministry within the Church.

Sacraments: The seven ceremonies that mark Catholics' religious development through life. They are Baptism, Eucharist (Communion), Reconciliation (often called Confession), Confirmation, Marriage, Holy Orders and the Anointing of the Sick.

Scripture: The writings of the Old and New Testaments.

Synod: A meeting of bishops to discuss doctrinal and pastoral needs of Church.

Vatican: The official residence of the Pope in Rome. It also refers to the central government of the Church.

Vigil: The eve of a religious festival observed by special prayer services and devotional exercises.

Vocation: A religious calling.

Appendix B

Timeline of interactions between LCWR and doctrinal congregations.

NCR Staff | *May. 8, 2014* NCR Today

LCWR-CDF 2014

Global Sisters Report, NCR

Edited, emended by author.

The following is a timeline of the investigations of the Leadership Conference of Women Religious.

2008: The Congregation for Institutes of Consecrated Life and Societies of Apostolic Life ordered an investigation, known as an Apostolic Visitation, of U.S. orders of women religious. The results of that study were submitted to Rome at the end of 2011. The reasons given for the examination were possible "irregularities and/or omissions in American religious life," "a certain 'feminist' spirit," and "a certain secularist mentality."

February 2009: Cardinal William Levada, head of the Vatican's Congregation for the Doctrine of the Faith, sent a letter to LCWR leadership, informing them that his office has begun a doctrinal assessment of the group. Levada stated that Toledo, Ohio, Bishop Leonard Blair, a member of the U.S. bishops' Committee on Doctrine, will conduct the assessment. The nuns were accused of "corporate dissent" on issues of abortion, women's ordination, the promotion of "certain radical feminist themes," ministry to the "homosexual community," and an "over-involvement in issues of social justice."

March 2009: LCWR received Levada's letter.

April 2009: LCWR informed its members of the doctrinal assessment and met with members of the doctrinal congregation in Rome for their annual April meeting.

May 2009: LCWR leaders met with Blair for the first time.

August 2009: LCWR held its annual assembly in New Orleans. Afterward, LCWR leaders released a statement asking the Vatican congregation for more details on the causes of the investigation. LCWR leaders also pledged to cooperate in the assessment, saying they are committed to "serving at and speaking from the margins of the Catholic church."

October 2009: The Asia-Oceania Meeting of Religious, which represents 113 women religious leaders from 17 Asian and Oceania nations, released a statement in support of U.S. women religious, saying, "We offer you our solidarity and prayers." California's bishops also issued a statement of support for U.S. sisters, saying they "join our people in thanking Women Religious ... for their witness to the richness and varied gifts of the Spirit."

December 2009: The Continental Assembly of Europe, a gathering of women religious across Europe, issued a statement of support for U.S. sisters, saying they want to express "our most fervent solidarity."

April 2010: LCWR leaders attended their yearly April meeting with members of the Vatican congregation in Rome. Reporting to LCWR membership, the leaders stated that much of the meeting concerned the sisters' support of the U.S. Affordable Care Act. In the meeting, Cardinal Levada said that the sisters' support for the legislation, which the U.S. bishops opposed, was "a public display of disunity within the church."

July 2010: Blair submitted an eight-page report on his investigation to the Vatican. The results of that report were not made public.

January 2011: João Braz de Aviz was appointed the prefect of the Congregation for Institutes of Consecrated Life and Societies of Apostolic Life (SICLSAL) by Pope Benedict XVI.

April 2012: LCWR leaders met with members of the Vatican congregation for the yearly April meeting in Rome. At that meeting, they were informed of the order to revise their group. In a press release, the U.S. bishops' conference announced appointment of Seattle Archbishop J. Peter Sartain to the role of "Archbishop Delegate" of the group, with wide-ranging authority over its revision.

July 2, 2012: Cardinal Levada's resignation as prefect of the CDF was accepted on Monday, July 2, 2012 for reasons of age, (having reached 75 years of age in 2011, the canonical age at which all Catholic bishops must submit an offer of resignation to the Pope). He was succeeded that same day by Bishop Gerhard Ludwig Müller of the Roman Catholic Diocese of Regensburg in Regensburg, Germany, who was named an archbishop.

August 2012: LCWR responded to the Vatican's findings. After gaining consensus from its body, it committed itself to an "open and honest" dialogue with Sartain, but only as long as it could maintain its integrity.

March 13, 2013: Pope Francis was elected.

April 15, 2013: In the yearly April meeting with LCWR

leadership, Müller informed the group that he had met with Pope Francis who "reaffirmed the findings of the assessment and the program of reform for this Conference of Major Superiors."

May 2013: Cardinal João Bráz de Aviz attended an international women's religious meeting in Rome and told the sisters that their leadership as consecrated persons in the church was "co-essential" to that of the hierarchy. He said the lack of CDF discussion over whether to criticize LCWR caused him "much pain."

August 2013: Sartain attended LCWR's assembly, addressed the group, and met with leadership for the first time. Further meetings were planned for later in the fall.

April 2014: Müller met with LCWR leadership for the annual April meeting in Rome, and in his opening remarks, said the organization must show "more substantive signs of collaboration" for implementing the mandate the doctrinal congregation ordered in 2012.

December 2014: The Vatican released the final report of the investigation of U.S. communities of women religious by CICLSAL at a press conference with the prefect of the religious congregation, Cardinal João Bráz de Aviz, and its secretary, Archbishop José Rodríguez Carballo. The visitation was carried out between 2009 and 2012. The report praised the work of women religious in living out the charisms of their founders. "Sisters today generously and creatively place their charism at the service of the needs of the Church and the world."

April 2015: The Vatican's Congregation for the Doctrine of the Faith unexpectedly issued a Joint Final Report regarding the implementation of the LCWR Doctrinal Assessment and Mandate of April 2012 by the CDF. The Report outlined the manner in which the implementation of the Mandate had been accomplished and "marked the conclusion" of the oversight two years before its scheduled conclusion.

Following the meeting, Cardinal Müller stated: "The Congregation is confident that LCWR has made clear its mission to support its member Institutes by fostering a vision of religious life that is centered on the Person of Jesus Christ and is rooted in the Tradition of the Church."

Sr. Sharon Holland, IHM, President of LCWR, expressed pleasure at the conclusion of the Mandate.

Archbishop Sartain stated, "Such substantive dialogue between bishops and religious women has been mutually beneficial and a blessing from the Lord."

Appendix C: Perfectae Caritatus

DECREE ON

THE ADAPTATION AND RENEWAL OF RELIGIOUS LIFE

PERFECTAE CARITATIS

PROCLAIMED BY HIS HOLINESS

POPE PAUL VI

ON OCTOBER 28, 1965

1. The sacred synod has already shown in the constitution on the Church that the pursuit of perfect charity through the evangelical counsels draws its origin from the doctrine and example of the Divine Master and reveals itself as a splendid sign of the heavenly kingdom. Now it intends to treat of the life and discipline of those institutes whose members make profession of chastity, poverty and obedience and to provide for their needs in our time.

Indeed from the very beginning of the Church men and women have set about following Christ with greater freedom and imitating Him more closely through the practice of the evangelical counsels, each in his own way leading a life dedicated to God. Many of them, under the inspiration of the Holy Spirit, lived as hermits or founded religious families, which the Church gladly welcomed and approved by her authority. So it is that in accordance with the Divine Plan a wonderful variety of religious communities has grown up which has made it easier for the Church not only to be equipped for every good work (cf. 2 Tim 3:17) and ready for the work of the ministry-the building up of the Body of Christ (cf. Eph. 4:12)-but also to appear adorned with the various gifts of her children like a spouse adorned for her husband (cf. Apoc. 21:2) and for the manifold Wisdom of God to be revealed through her (cf. Eph. 3:10).

Despite such a great variety of gifts, all those called by God to the practice of the evangelical counsels and who, faithfully responding to the call, undertake to observe the same, bind themselves to the Lord in a special way, following Christ, who chaste and poor (cf. Matt. 8:20; Luke 9:58) redeemed and sanctified men through obedience even to the death of the Cross (cf. Phil. 2:8). Driven by love with which the Holy Spirit floods their hearts (cf. Rom. 5:5) they live more and more for Christ and for His body which is the Church (cf. Col. 1:24). The more fervently, then, they are joined to Christ by this total life-long gift of themselves, the richer the life of the Church becomes and the more lively and successful its apostolate.

In order that the great valuc of a life consecrated by the profession of the counsels and its necessary mission today may yield greater good to the Church, the sacred synod lays down the following prescriptions. They are meant to state only the general principles of the adaptation and renewal of the life and discipline of Religious orders and also, without prejudice to their special characteristics, of societies of common life without vows and secular institutes. Particular norms for the proper explanation and application of these principles are to be determined after the council by the authority in question.

2. The adaptation and renewal of the religious life includes both the constant return to the sources of all Christian life and to the original spirit of the institutes and their adaptation to the changed conditions of our time. This renewal, under the inspiration of the Holy Spirit and the guidance of the Church, must be advanced according to the following principles:

a) Since the ultimate norm of the religious life is the following of Christ set forth in the Gospels, let this be held by all institutes as the highest rule.

b) It redounds to the good of the Church that institutes have their own particular characteristics and work. Therefore let their founders' spirit and special aims they set before them as well as their sound traditions-all of which make up the patrimony of each institute-be faithfully held in honor.

c) All institutes should share in the life of the Church, adapting as their own and implementing in accordance with their own characteristics the Church's undertakings and aims in matters biblical, liturgical, dogmatic, pastoral, ecumenical, missionary and social.

d) Institutes should promote among their members an adequate knowledge of the social conditions of the times they live in and of the needs of the Church. In such a way, judging current events wisely in the light of faith and burning with apostolic zeal, they may be able to assist men more effectively.

e) The purpose of the religious life is to help the members follow Christ and be united to God through the profession of the evangelical counsels. It should be constantly kept in mind, therefore, that even the best adjustments made in accordance with the needs of our age will be ineffectual unless they are animated by a renewal of spirit. This must take precedence over even the active ministry.

3. The manner of living, praying and working should be suitably adapted everywhere, but especially in mission territories, to the modern physical and psychological circumstances of the members and also, as required by the nature of each institute, to the necessities of the apostolate, the demands of culture, and social and economic circumstances.

According to the same criteria let the manner of governing the institutes also be examined.

Therefore let constitutions, directories, custom books, books of prayers and ceremonies and such like be suitably re-edited and, obsolete laws being suppressed, be adapted to the decrees of this sacred synod.

4. An effective renewal and adaptation demands the cooperation of all the members of the institute.

However, to establish the norms of adaptation and renewal, to embody it in legislation as well as to make allowance for adequate and prudent experimentation belongs only to the competent authorities, especially to general chapters. The approbation of the Holy See or of the local Ordinary must be obtained where necessary according to law. But superiors should take counsel in an appropriate way and hear the members of the order in those things which concern the future well-being of the whole institute.

For the adaptation and renewal of convents of nuns suggestions and advice may be obtained also from the meetings of federations or from other assemblies lawfully convoked.

Nevertheless everyone should keep in mind that the hope of renewal lies more in the faithful observance of the rules and constitutions than in multiplying laws.

5. Members of each institute should recall first of all that by professing the evangelical counsels they responded to a divine call so that by being not only dead to sin (cf. Rom. 6:11) but also renouncing the world they may live for God alone. They have dedicated their entire lives to His service. This constitutes a special consecration, which is deeply rooted in that of baptism and expresses it more fully.

Since the Church has accepted their surrender of self they should realize they are also dedicated to its service.

This service of God ought to inspire and foster in them the exercise of the virtues, especially humility, obedience, fortitude and chastity. In such a way they share in Christ's emptying of Himself (cf. Phil. 2:7) and His life in the spirit (cf. Rom. 8:1-13).

Faithful to their profession then, and leaving all things for the sake of Christ (cf. Mark 10:28), religious are to follow Him (cf. Matt. 19:21) as the one thing necessary (cf. Luke 10:42) listening to His words (cf. Luke 10:39) and solicitous for the things that are His (cf. 1 Cor. 7:32).

It is necessary therefore that the members of every community, seeking God solely and before everything else, should join contemplation, by which they fix their minds and hearts on Him, with apostolic love, by which they strive to be associated with the work of redemption and to spread the kingdom of God.

6. Let those who make profession of the evangelical counsels seek and love above all else God who has first loved us (cf. 1 John 4:10) and let them strive to foster in all circumstances a life hidden with Christ in God (cf. Col. 3:3). This love of God both excites and energizes that love of one's neighbor which contributes to the salvation of the world and the building up of the Church. This love, in addition, quickens and directs the actual practice of the evangelical counsels.

Drawing therefore upon the authentic sources of Christian spirituality, members of religious communities should resolutely cultivate both the spirit and practice of prayer. In the first place they should have recourse daily to the Holy Scriptures in order that, by reading and meditating on Holy Writ, they may learn "the surpassing worth of knowing Jesus Christ" (Phil. 3:8). They should celebrate the sacred liturgy, especially the holy sacrifice of the Mass, with both lips and heart as the Church desires and so nourish their spiritual life from this richest of sources.

So refreshed at the table of divine law and the sacred altar of God, they will love Christ's members as brothers, honor and love their pastors as sons should do, and living and thinking ever more in union with the Church, dedicate themselves wholly to its mission.

7. Communities which are entirely dedicated to contemplation, so that their members in solitude and silence, with constant prayer and penance willingly undertaken, occupy themselves with God alone, retain at all times, no matter how pressing the needs of the active apostolate may be, an honorable place in the Mystical Body of Christ, whose "members do not all have the same function" (Rom. 12:4). For these offer to God a sacrifice of praise which is outstanding. Moreover the manifold results of their holiness lends luster to the people of God which is inspired by their example and which gains new members by their apostolate which is as effective as it is hidden. Thus they are revealed to be a glory of the Church and a well-spring of heavenly graces. Nevertheless their manner of living should be revised according to the principles and criteria of adaptation and renewal mentioned above. However their withdrawal from the world and the exercises proper to the contemplative life should be preserved with the utmost care.

8. There are in the Church very many communities, both clerical and lay, which devote themselves to various apostolic tasks. The gifts

which these communities possess differ according to the grace which is allotted to them. Administrators have the gift of administration, teachers that of teaching, the gift of stirring speech is given to preachers, liberality to those who exercise charity and cheerfulness to those who help others in distress (cf. Rom. 12:5-8). "The gifts are varied, but the Spirit is the same" (1 Cor. 12:4).

In these communities apostolic and charitable activity belongs to the very nature of the religious life, seeing that it is a holy service and a work characteristic of love, entrusted to them by the Church to be carried out in its name. Therefore, the whole religious life of their members should be inspired by an apostolic spirit and all their apostolic activity formed by the spirit of religion. Therefore in order that their members may first correspond to their vocation to follow Christ and serve Him in His members, their apostolic activity must spring from intimate union with Him. Thus love itself towards God and the neighbor is fostered.

These communities, then, should adjust their rules and customs to fit the demands of the apostolate to which they are dedicated. The fact however that apostolic religious life takes on many forms requires that its adaptation and renewal take account of this diversity and provide that the lives of religious dedicated to the service of Christ in these various communities be sustained by special provisions appropriate to each.

9. The monastic life, that venerable institution which in the course of a long history has won for itself notable renown in the Church and in human society, should be preserved with care and its authentic spirit permitted to shine forth ever more splendidly both in the East and the West. The principal duty of monks is to offer a service to the divine majesty at once humble and noble within the walls of the monastery, whether they dedicate themselves entirely to divine worship in the contemplative life or have legitimately undertaken some apostolate or work of Christian charity. Retaining, therefore, the characteristics of the way of life proper to them, they should revive their ancient traditions of service and so adapt them to the needs of today that monasteries will become institutions dedicated to the edification of the Christian people.

Some religious communities according to their rule or constitutions closely join the apostolic life to choir duty and monastic observances. These should so adapt their manner of life to the demands of the apostolate appropriate to them that they observe faithfully their way of life, since it has been of great service to the Church.

10. The religious life, undertaken by lay people, either men or women, is a state for the profession of the evangelical counsels which is complete in itself. While holding in high esteem therefore this way of life so useful to the pastoral mission of the Church in educating youth, caring for the sick and carrying out its other ministries, the sacred synod confirms these religious in their vocation and urges them to adjust their way of life to modern needs.

The sacred synod declares that there is nothing to prevent some members of religious communities of brothers being admitted to holy orders by provision of their general chapter in order to meet the need for priestly ministrations in their own houses, provided that the lay character of the community remains unchanged.

11. Secular Institutes, although not Religious institutes involve a true and full profession of the evangelical counsels in the world. This profession is recognized by the Church and consecrates to God men and women, lay and clerical, who live in the world. Hence they should make a total dedication of themselves to God in perfect charity their chief aim, and the institutes themselves should preserve their own proper, i.e., secular character, so that they may be able to carry out effectively everywhere in and, as it were, from the world the apostolate for which they were founded.

It may be taken for granted, however, that so great a task cannot be discharged unless the members be thoroughly trained in matters divine and human so that they are truly a leaven in the world for the strengthening and growth of the body of Christ. Superiors, therefore, should give serious attention especially to the spiritual training to be given members as well as encourage their further formation.

12. The chastity "for the sake of the kingdom of heaven" (Matt. 19:12) which religious profess should be counted an outstanding gift of grace. It frees the heart of man in a unique fashion (cf. 1 Cor. 7:32-35) so that it may be more inflamed with love for God and for all

men. Thus it not only symbolizes in a singular way the heavenly goods but also the most suitable means by which religious dedicate themselves with undivided heart to the service of God and the works of the apostolate. In this way they recall to the minds of all the faithful that wondrous marriage decreed by God and which is to be fully revealed in the future age in which the Church takes Christ as its only spouse.

Religious, therefore, who are striving faithfully to observe the chastity they have professed must have faith in the words of the Lord, and trusting in God's help not overestimate their own strength but practice mortification and custody of the senses. Neither should they neglect the natural means which promote health of mind and body. As a result they will not be influenced by those false doctrines which scorn perfect continence as being impossible or harmful to human development and they will repudiate by a certain spiritual instinct everything which endangers chastity. In addition let all, especially superiors, remember that chastity is guarded more securely when true brotherly love flourishes in the common life of the community.

Since the observance of perfect continence touches intimately the deepest instincts of human nature, candidates should neither present themselves for nor be admitted to the vow of chastity, unless they have been previously tested sufficiently and have been shown to possess the required psychological and emotional maturity. They should not only be warned about the dangers to chastity which they may meet but they should be so instructed as to be able to undertake the celibacy which binds them to God in a way which will benefit their entire personality.

13. Religious should diligently practice and if need be express also in new forms that voluntary poverty which is recognized and highly esteemed especially today as an expression of the following of Christ. By it they share in the poverty of Christ who for our sakes became poor, even though He was rich, so that by His poverty we might become rich (cf. 2 Cor. 8:9; Matt. 8:20).

With regard to religious poverty it is not enough to use goods in a way subject to the superior's will, but members must be poor both in fact and in spirit, their treasures being in heaven (cf. Matt. 6:20).

Religious should consider themselves in their own assignments to be bound by the common law of labor, and while they procure what is required for their sustenance and works, they should banish all undue solicitude and trust themselves to the provident care of their Father in heaven (cf. Matt. 6:25).

Religious congregations by their constitutions can permit their members to renounce inheritances, both those which have been acquired or may be acquired.

Due regard being had for local conditions, religious communities should readily offer a quasi-collective witness to poverty and gladly use their own goods for other needs of the Church and the support of the poor whom all religious should love after the example of

Christ (cf. Matt. 19:21, 25:34-46 James 2:15-16; 1 John 3:17). The several provinces and houses of each community should share their temporal goods with one another, so that those who have more help the others who are in need.

Religious communities have the right to possess whatever is required for their temporal life and work, unless this is forbidden by their rules and constitutions. Nevertheless, they should avoid every appearance of luxury, excessive wealth and the accumulation of goods.

14. In professing obedience, religious offer the full surrender of their own will as a sacrifice of themselves to God and so are united permanently and securely to God's salvific will.

After the example of Jesus Christ who came to do the will of the Father (cf. John 4:34; 5:30; Heb. 10:7; Ps. 39:9) and "assuming the nature of a slave" (Phil. 2:7) learned obedience in the school of suffering (cf. Heb. 5:8), religious under the motion of the Holy Spirit, subject themselves in faith to their superiors who hold the place of God. Under their guidance they are led to serve all their brothers in Christ, just as Christ himself in obedience to the Father served His brethren and laid down His life as a ransom for many (cf. Matt. 20:28; John 10:14-18). So they are closely bound to the service of the Church and strive to attain the measure of the full manhood of Christ (Eph. 4:13).

Religious, therefore, in the spirit of faith and love for the divine will should humbly obey their superiors according to their rules and constitutions. Realizing that they are contributing to building up the body of Christ according to God's plan, they should use both the forces of their intellect and will and the gifts of nature and grace to execute the commands and fulfill the duties entrusted to them. In this way religious obedience, far from lessening the dignity of the human person, by extending the freedom of the sons of God, leads it to maturity.

Superiors, as those who are to give an account of the souls entrusted to them (Heb. 13:17), should fulfill their office in a way responsive to God's will. They should exercise their authority out of a spirit of service to the brethren, expressing in this way the love with which God loves their subjects. They should govern these as sons of God, respecting their human dignity. In this way they make it easier for them to subordinate their wills. They should be particularly careful to respect their subjects' liberty in the matters of sacramental confession and the direction of conscience. Subjects should be brought to the point where they will cooperate with an active and responsible obedience in undertaking new tasks and in carrying those already undertaken. And so superiors should gladly listen to their subjects and foster harmony among them for the good of the community and the Church, provided that thereby their own authority to decide and command what has to be done is not harmed.

Chapters and deliberative bodies should faithfully discharge the part in ruling entrusted to them and each should in its own way express that concern for the good of the entire community which all its members share.

15. Common life, fashioned on the model of the early Church where the body of believers was united in heart and soul (cf. Acts 4:32), and given new force by the teaching of the Gospel, the sacred liturgy and especially the Eucharist, should continue to be lived in prayer and the communion of the same spirit. As members of Christ living together as brothers, religious should give pride of place in esteem to each other (cf. Rom. 12:10) and bear each other's burdens (cf. Gal. 6:2). For the community, a true family gathered together in the name of the Lord by God's love which has flooded the hearts of its members through the Holy Spirit (cf.Rom. 5:5), rejoices because He is present among them (cf. Matt. 18:20). Moreover love sums up the whole law (cf. Rom. 13:10), binds all together in perfect unity (cf. Col. 3:14) and by it we know that we have crossed over from death to life (cf. 1 John 3:14). Furthermore, the unity of the brethren is a visible pledge that Christ will return (cf. John 13:35; 17:21) and a source of great apostolic energy.

That all the members be more closely knit by the bond of brotherly love, those who are called lay-brothers, assistants, or some similar name should be drawn closely in to the life and work of the community. Unless conditions really suggest something else, care should be taken that there be only one class of Sisters in communities of women. Only that distinction of persons should be retained which corresponds to-the diversity of works for which the Sisters are destined, either by special vocation from God or by reason of special aptitude.

However, monasteries of men and communities which are not exclusively lay can, according to their nature and constitutions, admit clerics and lay persons on an equal footing and with equal rights and obligations, excepting those which flow from sacred orders.

16. Papal cloister should be maintained in the case of nuns engaged exclusively in the contemplative life. However, it must be adjusted to conditions of time and place and obsolete practices suppressed. This should be done after due consultation with the monasteries in question. But other nuns applied by rule to apostolic work outside the convent should be exempted from papal cloister in order to enable them better to fulfill the apostolic duties entrusted to them. Nevertheless, cloister is to be maintained according to the prescriptions of their constitutions.

17. The religious habit, an outward mark of consecration to God, should be simple and modest, poor and at the same becoming. In addition it must meet the requirements of health and be suited to the circumstances of time and place and to the needs of the ministry involved. The habits of both men and women religious which do not conform to these norms must be changed.

18. Adaptation and renewal depend greatly on the education of religious. Consequently neither non-clerical religious nor religious women should be assigned to apostolic works immediately after the

novitiate. Rather, their religious and apostolic formation, joined with instruction in arts and science directed toward obtaining appropriate degrees, must be continued as needs require in houses established for those purposes.

In order that the adaptation of religious life to the needs of our time may not be merely external and that those employed by rule in the active apostolate may be equal to their task, religious must be given suitable instruction, depending on their intellectual capacity and personal talent, in the currents and attitudes of sentiment and thought prevalent in social life today. This education must blend its elements together harmoniously so that an integrated life on the part of the religious concerned results.

Religious should strive during the whole course of their lives to perfect the culture they have received in matters spiritual and in arts and sciences. Likewise, superiors must, as far as this is possible, obtain for them the opportunity, equipment and time to do this.

Superiors are also obliged to see to it that directors, spiritual fathers, and professors are carefully chosen and thoroughly trained.

19. When the question of founding new religious communities arises, their necessity or at least the many useful services they promise must be seriously weighed. Otherwise communities may be needlessly brought into being which are useless or which lack sufficient resources. Particularly in those areas where churches have recently established, those forms of religious life should be promoted and

developed which take into account the genius and way of life of the inhabitants and the customs and conditions of the regions.

20. Religious communities should continue to maintain and fulfill the ministries proper to them. In addition, after considering the needs of the Universal Church and individual dioceses, they should adapt them to the requirements of time and place, employing appropriate and even new programs and abandoning those works which today are less relevant to the spirit and authentic nature of the community.

The missionary spirit must under all circumstances be preserved in religious communities. It should be adapted, accordingly, as the nature of each community permits, to modern conditions so that the preaching of the Gospel may be carried out more effectively in every nation.

21. There may be communities and monasteries which the Holy See, after consulting the interested local Ordinaries, will judge not to possess reasonable hope for further development. These should be forbidden to receive novices in the future. If it is possible, these should be combined with other more flourishing communities and monasteries whose scope and spirit is similar.

22. Independent institutes and monasteries should, when opportune and the Holy See permits, form federations if they can be considered as belonging to the same religious family. Others who have practically identical constitutions and rules and a common spirit should unite, particularly when they have too few members. Finally, those who

share the same or a very similar active apostolate should become associated, one to the other.

23. This synod favors conferences or councils of major superiors, established by the Holy See. These can contribute very much to achieve the purpose of each institute; to encourage more effective cooperation for the welfare of the Church; to ensure a more just distribution of ministers of the Gospel in a given area; and finally to conduct affairs of interest to all religious. Suitable coordination and cooperation with episcopal conferences should be established with regard to the exercise of the apostolate.

Similar conferences should also be established for secular institutes.

24. Priests and Christian educators should make serious efforts to foster religious vocations, thereby increasing the strength of the Church, corresponding to its needs. These candidates should be suitably and carefully chosen. In ordinary preaching, the life of the evangelical counsels and the religious state should be treated more frequently. Parents, too, should nurture and protect religious vocations in their children by instilling Christian virtue in their hearts.

Religious communities have the right to make themselves known in order to foster vocations and seek candidates. In doing this, however, they should observe the norms laid down by the Holy See and the local Ordinary.

Religious should remember there is no better way than their own example to commend their institutes and gain candidates for the religious life.

25. Religious institutes, for whom these norms of adaptation and renewal have been laid down, should respond generously to the specific vocation God gave them as well as their work in the Church today. The sacred synod highly esteems their way of life in poverty, chastity and obedience, of which Christ the Lord is Himself the exemplar. Moreover, their apostolate, most effective, whether obscure or well known, offers this synod great hope for the future. Let all religious, therefore, rooted in faith and filled with love for God and neighbor, love of the cross and the hope of future glory, spread the good news of Christ throughout the whole world so that their witness may be seen by all and our Father in heaven may be glorified (Matt. 5:16). Therefore, let them beseech the Virgin Mary, the gentle Mother of God, "whose life is a model for all," that their number may daily increase and their salutary work be more effective.

Acknowledgements

Both my children, Jessica Galligan Goldsmith and Zachary Galligan, have always been staunch supporters and honest critics; I rely on one for encouragement, the other for caution. And offer sincerest thanks to my son-in-law, James Goldsmith, not only for his consideration and generosity, but for the addition of a new and wonderful wing (his) to the family (ours). And to my three grandchildren, Connor, Brian and Katherine, whose company I always enjoy.

My thanks to Donna Laspia Kilb for introducing me to Janet Roach, already then well known for "Prizzi's Honor," who became not only a fast friend but a valued critic. It was with her help, that I found an agent.

Barbara Hogenson has been my agent now for several decades. We've never had a contract. We never even shook hands, since our first agreement was on the phone. And it always shocks me that she describes my work better than I do. I appreciate her confidence in me more than she'll ever know.

Laurie Goodstein, one of the religion writers for the New York Times, a fellow Shelter Islander and the daughter-in-law of colleagues, Drs. Carole and Stanley Grand, was the first person I turned to for advice when the thought of doing this book crossed my consciousness. She was full of encouragement, excellent advice, and always there when I needed help.

And now to the nuns.

First and foremost I must thank Sr. Theresa Kane, the first nun I interviewed. It was not just that she was helpful, but at the end of our first series of meetings, she told me if I had difficulty reaching anyone, to put her name in the subject box of the email, and then continued, "Use it whenever you like, and you don't need to get back to me, I trust your judgment entirely." It was an "Open Sesame!"

I want to state for the record, since I know the sisters are reading this, how completely I misunderstood their situation for at least the first year, perhaps even longer. I saw their struggle in political terms and I thought they were making a mistake in not fighting back "politically." It was a long time before I finally saw Jesus's footsteps and began to understand what was at stake for them. But they were relentlessly encouraging and that was more meaningful for me than I can say. I'm so glad to have met them. It was a wonderful adventure. They leave me with much to think about.

I hope they feel I've documented their struggle fairly and accurately. I know they won't agree with many (most?) of my conclusions in Part Five. Nuns don't think a great deal about hatred; psychologists do. And I've been in clinical practice for more decades than I like to remember.

So thank you, Sisters. So very much.

And now to friends. Thank you. You all know who you are, and how steadfast you've been, how encouraging over the years. But I must acknowledge one in particular, met in our first year at Barnard,

Elizabeth O'Leary Dreier, who, when my older brother died, "raised the fallen banner," and has, since, as he did, read every single one of my words. And thought about them. And then was willing to talk about them. A lot.

And my community; Shelter Island is a very special place. And the Shelter Island Library in particular, has been there for me, without fail. And the local newspaper, the Shelter Island Reporter, a club I am proud to be a member of, lets me come and go and write as I choose, for which I am endlessly grateful; I'm on my third editor now, Ambrose Clancy, and he has yet to let me down.

Made in the USA
Columbia, SC
27 September 2021